Barbados

A History from the Amerindians to Independence

Sir Alexander Hoyos
Former Member of the Privy Council for Barbados

CARIBBEAN

First published 1978 by
MACMILLAN EDUCATION LTD
London and Basingstoke
Companies and representatives throughout the world

ISBN 0–333–23819–2

22	21	20	19	18	17	16	15	14	13
07	06	05	04	03	02	01	00	99	98

This book is printed on paper suitable for recycling and
made from fully managed and sustained forest sources.

Printed in Hong Kong

Contents

Especially for Gladys
whose love, encouragement
and assistance made this
book possible.

Preface

Readers are no doubt familiar with the three 'ancient' histories of Barbados.

The first was written by Richard Ligon in 1657 and was entitled *A true and exact history of the island of Barbados*. It is an invaluable source for any study of social and economic conditions in Barbados during its earliest years as an English settlement.

The second was *The history of Barbados, from the discovery of the island, in the year 1605, till the accession of Lord Seaforth, 1801*, and was written by John Poyer (1808). In spite of its bias and the wrong date the author gives for the discovery of Barbados by the English, it is a useful contribution to the extent that it relies on the records of the House of Assembly.

The third was written in 1848 by Sir Robert Schomburgk. His *History of Barbados* is a scholarly study and has been described as "a classic in West Indian history". It is an indispensable guide to the history of the island up to and just after the time of emancipation. The author based his book on material gained from official publications and local newspapers. His research made full use of such sources as the library of the Literary Society of Barbados and the collections in the British Museum.

Since then there have been quite a number of publications on one aspect or another of Barbadian history. They take the form of learned theses, journal articles, monographs and popular works on various periods of the island's history. Altogether, they present a mass of material which is invaluable to the scholar and the general reader alike. No-one, however, has attempted a single comprehensive work on the history of Barbados since Schomburgk's publication in 1848. I hope I am not guilty of undue immodesty when I say that it is the aim of my book to fill this gap in the historical literature of the island.

Barbados has a distinct history of its own. Yet inevitably the course of local events in many respects follows the wider pattern of West Indian history. I have, therefore, sought to integrate the history of this island with the general history of the West Indies and to indicate, wherever necessary, the impact of events from the world beyond the Caribbean. It was the natural and logical way to tell the story of the island, not as an isolated narrative, but in relation to events and developments in the world beyond its shores.

The object of this book is to satisfy some of the requirements of students and teachers who will soon be involved in the new syllabus proposed by the Caribbean History Panel. That syllabus places less emphasis on traditional methods and recommends new directions in the teaching-learning process. The significant trend is to train the young not so much to memorise and recall factual information as to acquire the skills that will enable them to carry out independent research and correlate historical data. The aim will be not so much to acquire a facility for writing essays but to respond to stimulus material such as pictures, maps, statistical tables and the like. It is proposed to teach Caribbean history by themes but these will be selected from the entire period of our history and due regard will be paid to the chronological framework which provide the background of the themes. Not the least important feature of the new syllabus is the Project method which will call for a great deal of work in the selecting and extracting of suitable material.

It is expected that local history will get a place in the syllabus, which the Caribbean History Panel desires, when the necessary material becomes more readily available. It is hoped that this book will give Barbadian history the attention it deserves in the new plan proposed by the Panel. For it aims at providing material and indicating other sources of information that will be required for the new directions in the teaching of West Indian History.

I may add that this book is also aimed at the general reader who wants to know as much as he can about his island home. Students, teachers and the general public will all be able to pursue their investigations as far as they like by looking up the sources I have mentioned and thus acquire a greater understanding and appreciation of our cultural heritage.

My history of Barbados covers the period from the time of the Amerindians to the attainment of independence in 1966. Here I have to acknowledge the invaluable help I received from my friend and former student, Dr. Keith Hunte, Head of the History

Department at the Cave Hill Campus of the University of the West Indies. He read the draft manuscript with great care and offered many suggestions for its improvement. To all of these I gave due attention and, if the book can claim any substance and depth in significant areas of Barbadian history, it is largely due to Dr. Hunte's scholarly suggestions and criticisms.

I also have to thank Trevor Marshall, another friend and former student, whose association with the History Department at Cave Hill, U.W.I., helped to keep me in touch with the steadily increasing output of research-based studies. And there is Monica Skeete, Senior History Mistress of Queen's College, Barbados, who made me more vividly aware of the many skills required for the teaching-learning process in history. She gave valuable assistance in preparing the questions and exercises at the end of each chapter.

There are many others who have given me the benefit of their counsel in the preparation of this book, but I am afraid they are too many to mention. I must, however, express my thanks to my wife who, with undaunted spirit, typed and re-typed my manuscript until it arrived at its final shape.

F. A. H.
August, 1976.

Areas of Carib and Arawak settlement in the West Indies

CHAPTER ONE

Our Amerindian Ancestors

The First Barbadians

To begin the story of the people of Barbados, one has to go back some 35,000 years to the time when the first men came to the New World. They came from the East through the Bering Strait to the North-West of the American continent and roamed through the plains of that area. We know them today as the Red Indians who lived and hunted in the prairies and centuries later fought a fierce but unsuccessful battle to stem the advance of the white man and his civilisation.

Other men of the same kind came across the wider expanses of the Pacific Ocean to the southern part of the continent. Unlike their fellow men in the North, they did not have far-reaching plains through which they could wander at will. They had to face thick and almost impenetrable forests and they made their way along the great rivers and waterways of the region. Their skill in navigating these waters enabled them to travel across vast areas and eventually they reached Brazil, Venezuela and the Guianas.

It was mainly from this area that these people, our Amerindian ancestors, began to enter the southern shores of the Caribbean Sea and to spread throughout the West Indies.

Other Amerindians, who were later to be known as the Ciboney, came from Florida and sailed southward from island to island in the Caribbean. It is believed by some that they may have occupied Barbados for a time. It is tempting to assume this, since, for one thing, there are many caves in Barbados and the Ciboney were cave-dwellers. But there is little evidence to prove that they ever made Barbados their home.

It is certain, however, that the first Amerindians who came to this island and made a permanent settlement were the Barrancoid people. We know this because of a significant discovery that was made by Ronald Taylor of the Barbados Museum as recently as April 22nd, 1966. On that day a site of archaeological remains was found by him near the South Point Lighthouse in the parish of Christ Church. An expert in the field,

1

Professor R. P. Bullen of the Florida State Museum, was invited to inspect the find and succeeded in identifying the remains as those of the Barrancoid people, a branch of the Amerindian family.[1] Radio carbon dates were obtained by exposing the charcoal remains to radium - a process which establishes the dates of remains thousands of years old, through noting the decrease of radioactivity at a rate that can be calculated within five hundred years.

Taylor and Bullen continued their investigations at a site in Chancery Lane. Digging on this site disclosed first a layer of Carib remains, followed by a layer of Arawak remains, then grey sand and, finally, a layer of Barrancoid relics. Taylor proceeded to dig on sites at Boscobelle in St. Peter and Golders Green in St. Lucy. On both of these sites he discovered archaeological remains of the Barrancoid people.

It would appear from the evidence available that the Barrancoid people lived in the Orinoco Valley about the year 800 B.C. Some six to seven hundred years later they moved to the north-eastern portion of Venezuela and then to Trinidad. Before long they began island-hopping through the Caribbean and arrived in Barbados at about the time of Christ. The pottery they

Time Line Indicating Pre-history of Barbados

B.C.1000	
B.C. 800	Barrancoid Indians lived in Orinoco Valley
B.C. 200	They moved to Venezuela and Trinidad
B.C. 500	
A.D.	They arrived in Barbados
A.D. 500	
A.D. 600	Barrancoid Indians left Barbados
A.D. 800	Arawaks came to Barbados
A.D.1000	
A.D.1200	Arawaks conquered by Caribs
A.D.1500	Caribs disappeared from Barbados
A.D.1627	Settlement of Barbados by English

made was richly decorated and perhaps the best to be found in the Antilles.[2] They were the first to introduce not only pottery-making but also the skills and techniques of agriculture. It was their pottery that was discovered and identified on the new site at South Point.

Because of the progress of research in recent years, the dates formerly given to the earliest settlements in Barbados have to be reconsidered. From the evidence that had been unearthed, it would seem that the Barrancoid people lived in Barbados from the beginning of the Christian era to about 600 A.D. They were followed by the Arawaks, after an interval of about two hundred years; these later settled in the island until approximately 1200 A.D. when they were conquered by the Caribs. But it is impossible at this stage to get a clear picture of the three settlements or to arrive at anything like firm dates. A great deal more research has to be done and more radio carbon dates have to be established to give us a final picture.[3]

The Arawaks

The Arawaks came from South America and, with their knowledge of navigation, swept northwards among the islands of the West Indies. They occupied both the Lesser and the Greater Antilles and spread their language through all the territories of the area. It is interesting to note that this was the only time in our history that one language was spoken throughout the whole of the Caribbean.

When they reached Barbados, the Arawaks decided to settle on the island. They had travelled in long, narrow, flat-bottomed canoes, which could travel at great speed, and they found in Barbados the sort of place in which they could establish a permanent abode. There were many reasons why the Arawaks found this island to be an almost ideal place in which to settle.[4]

First, there were no dense rain forests, such as they had known in South America, to impede their movements from one part of the island to another. This meant that there were no forests inhabited by wild animals which they could track and hunt for food, but the Arawaks did not depend on hunting for their living.

What they found particularly attractive were the coral reefs around the island. From the shores of the northern areas, down the west coast and along the south, they fished almost daily, and caught enough fish to satisfy their needs. To equip themselves for this major occupation they made all the things they required, such as harpoons, hooks and nets. Not surprisingly, however, they avoided the east coast since in their frail canoes, which had no keels, they could not cope with the rough seas that beat unceasingly against that part of the island.

While Barbados had no dense tropical forests, it possessed the sort of soil that suited their agricultural pursuits. The Arawaks were not a wandering or nomadic people and they wanted to settle in a land where they could grow their crops. [5]

Perhaps their most important crop was cassava. They knew how to take the poison out of the cassava juice and they made this into a kind of vinegar, now known as casareep, which they used to spice their food.

They made graters, juice squeezers and ovens of clay on which they baked the cassava cakes that formed a main item of their diet. They also grew maize and found some relief from the hardships of their primitive life by drinking the strong liquor they made from cassava.

In addition to cassava and maize, the Arawaks grew peanuts, squash and certain kinds of fruit such as guavas, papaws, pineapples and berries of various kinds. They also cultivated tobacco to which, for good or for ill, they later introduced the Europeans. They enjoyed their tobacco either by chewing it or by making it into cigars which they smoked in their leisure moments. They also grew cotton, from which they made hammocks; indeed, their use of these hammocks for sleeping was one of their main contributions to European civilisation.

One handicap the Arawaks had to face was that there was no hard stone in the island from which they could make the tools they needed. But they found a large number of conch shells and from these they made sharp-edged tools such as axes and hoes, pointed tools such as picks and awls, blunt tools such as hammers and wedges and utensils such as spoons and cups. [6]

Certainly what appealed to the Arawaks was the plentiful supply of clay in the island of Barbados. From this clay they made pottery and the remains of this, which can be seen today, tell us a great deal about the culture of our Amerindian ancestors. They made vessels of various sizes and shapes and we can deduce the purposes for which they were manufactured. And the way these vessels were decorated gives us information about the animals, fish and birds they found in the island.

Arawak Artifacts

Ashanti Stool

Thus we see why the Arawaks settled in Barbados. The coral reefs, the absence of rain forests, the nature of the soil which suited the crops they grew, the abundance of conch shells and the supply of clay – these are some of the factors that attracted them to the island. In addition, there was the shape of the island, rising gently by terraces from the sea to the central uplands. This not only enabled them to grow their crops but made their system of communications easier both to establish and to maintain.

The Arawaks were olive-skinned, of medium height and wore few or no clothes. Such scanty clothes as they sometimes wore were made from the cotton they grew. They had slightly pointed heads, wore their hair long and were active and energetic. They were blessed with a gay and happy disposition and were fond of dancing and singing.

They lived in houses that were round or square, with cone-shaped roofs. The posts, which supported the thatched roofs, were planted at short intervals and were held together by "lashings of woody vines". In the high roofs there was ample room for essential commodities and here too was included a place where the remains of their ancestors were preserved. A pottery vessel, serving as a kind of a chimney, protected the tip of the roof.[7] The houses they built in this fashion were so sturdy that they could stand up to strong gales.

Thousands of Arawaks lived in the island during the centuries they occupied it. The island as a whole was governed by a head-chief, who wielded great power; he was advised by a council of nobles as to how he should use that power. Under the head-chief were a number of headmen who ruled over the villages established in various parts of the island. Some of these larger villages were built in such districts as Pie Corner in St. Lucy, Silver Sands and Chancery Lane in Christ Church and Indian River in St. Michael.[8] There were other settlements, it is believed, in places now known as Indian Castle, Indian Mound, Indian Pond, Indian Ground and Indian Garden.

In those far-off days, water availability was a grave problem for the Arawaks.[9] That is why they settled either on the coast in the north, west and south of the island or in areas where they found ponds and fresh water springs. They occupied districts that were situated on river beds leading from the uplands, in the central parts of the island, down to the sea coast, and they took other precautions. To protect themselves against the storms and hurricanes that sometimes visited the island, they settled in gulleys and caves that sheltered them from such natural disasters.

The early inhabitants of the island reached a fairly high level of culture. They were a kindly and peaceful people who readily accepted the rules of a society that made them law-abiding citizens. They did not sacrifice human beings in the practice of their religion, as a more primitive and barbaric people might have done, and they placed their women on a high plane by their practice of monogamy - no man, except the leaders, was permitted to have more than one wife.

Thus did the Arawaks live in Barbados for some four to five hundred years. For several reasons they lived in almost complete isolation from the rest of the Caribbean. The island lay outside the main chain of the neighbouring territories and was seldom visited by outsiders. Moreover, in order to get to it, visitors would have to make their way against contrary winds and against the prevailing current. Cut off from the outside world, they lived in peace and tranquillity and were able to develop a culture that was peculiarly their own. But there came a time when that peace and tranquillity was to be rudely shattered.

The story we have told of the Arawaks has been reconstructed mainly from the work of such men as E. M. Shilstone, G. T. Barton and C. N. C. Roach.[10] Since then the work of excavation has gone steadily ahead. A great deal still needs to be done, however, to gather complete information about those who lived in this island before the beginning of our recorded history. Digging among the ancient remains over a period of years has taught us much about our Amerindian ancestors, but further efforts in this field are certain to reveal yet more of the manifold and mysterious messages from the past. We must continue to dig in certain sites of the island for the relics of our prehistoric times and by a careful study of the findings we shall surely increase our knowledge of the earliest inhabitants of Barbados.

Significant Discoveries

Until recently it had been stoutly maintained that the only Amerindians who ever occupied Barbados were Arawaks. The archaeological remains that had been excavated up to that time showed that there had been Carib contacts with the island but nothing more. Artifacts of Carib manufacture, as identified by experts, were discovered from time to time in the island but, it was suggested, they were too few to justify the conclusion that the

Caribs ever settled in Barbados. They may have been lost by the Caribs during their raiding forays in Barbados or they may have been dropped by them on their hunting expeditions after the Arawaks abandoned the island. This version of the story of the early inhabitants of Barbados was supported by Shilstone and relayed to Barton. The former took the view that the Caribs would have had little interest in the island, that Carib hunters would have looked for hunting grounds such as were to be found in other islands but not in Barbados and that the nature of the Barbadian land, the thinness of its soil and its coral reefs, would be admirably suited to the farming and fishing habits of the Arawaks.[11]

Since the time of the three learned men we have mentioned above, excavation on various sites has established that the Caribs lived in Barbados and not only in the rest of the Lesser Antilles, as had previously been believed. In earliest times, it seems, the Arawaks lived in Venezuela and later came to Trinidad and then to Barbados. Pottery of undoubted Arawak manufacture, of a fine quality and handsomely decorated, had long been found in the West Indies from Barbados and Grenada to Jamaica.

Carib pottery, which was easily recognised, being of a cruder type than that of the Arawaks, was found mainly in the Lesser Antilles. Such Carib pottery as previously existed in Barbados was found in Brandons in St. Michael, Beachmount in St. Joseph and Greenland in St. Andrew. In recent years, however, "a vast quantity of Carib potsherds" has been found in Barbados and this has satisfied the experts that the Caribs were once settlers and not merely temporary visitors to the island. Indeed, the work of excavation at various sites has shown that Arawak remains lie under Carib remains and this has convincingly demonstrated to the archaeologists that the settlement of the Arawaks in Barbados was followed by a period during which the island was occupied by the Caribs.[12]

The Caribs

The Caribs were settled in Barbados from 1200 A.D. until the time of the arrival of the Spaniards in the New World. They were like the Arawaks in their physical appearance but were of great stature. They were "all tall and lusty people",[13] handsome, well-shaped and "well-proportioned in all parts of their bodies". Like the Arawaks they were olive-skinned and their foreheads and noses were flat. The reason for this was that both Arawaks and Caribs flattened the heads of their children, considering that this was "a kind of beauty and perfection". They were both proud of their long, straight hair and the Caribs were reputed to have "some handsome Maids and Women" in their midst. [14]

The Caribs had clean, healthy habits and their span of life was quite extraordinary. They were usually naked, though on rare occasions they would wear a short cotton garment. As a rule, the only covering the women wore was "a kind of buskin" on their legs and sometimes a string of pearls around their necks. The men decorated themselves with a head-dress of bird's feathers, rings in their noses, bodkins through their lips and necklaces consisting of either coral or human bones. [15]

The Caribs differed from the Arawaks to a marked degree in several respects. They were a fierce and warlike people, while the Arawaks were peaceful and amiable. They indulged in human sacrifice in their religion. They were a nomadic people and did not engage in agriculture at the same level of competence as the Arawaks. But they were unsurpassed as seamen and fishermen.

It is not surprising that they excelled in boat-building. They made their canoes "out of one piece from a tree, which is hollowed out like a trough". Some of these were large enough to carry two or three tons of goods. Other canoes were quite different, being "a small kind of craft with one mast" capable of making voyages of "a hundred and fifty leagues at sea". [16] Their arms were arrows "in place of iron weapons". These arrows, for lack of iron, were pointed with tortoise shells. Sometimes their arrow heads were made of fish spines which were "naturally barbed like coarse saws". These were capable of inflicting "severe injury" on "a naked people" like the Arawaks. [17]

As happened with other peoples at other times in the history of the world, the conquerors were in some respects taken captive by the conquered. The culture of the Caribs was considerably influenced by that of the Arawaks. Though they never acquired the skilled craftsmanship of the Arawaks, they tried to imitate them in the type of their houses and the nature of their utensils. And like the Arawaks they were particularly fond of dancing and other innocent forms of amusement. They drank no alcoholic beverages and, contrary to some accounts, there is no evidence that they indulged in drunken festivals. [18]

Their food was similar to that of their predecessors in the island, but they held a number of curious beliefs. They refrained from eating pigs because that would cause their eyes to grow small. They did not eat turtle because that would make them heavy and stupid. They did not flavour their food with salt. They ate their meals in common in the village hall, but the women were required to eat by themselves after the men had finished eating. [19]

The Caribs resembled the Arawaks in their system of government, but there was one important difference. While the Arawak chiefs (*caciques*) were aristocratic, holding office by right of birth, the Carib chiefs (*ubutu*) were frequently democratically selected because of their strength and skill. Those who held office among the Caribs were of three classes: there were those who held office for life; there were those who were chosen as leaders for certain expeditions only; and there were others again whose appointment was limited to the office of captains of canoe crews.

Their meetings for managing their affairs were held in the village halls which were known as the Carbets. Here the chief met the men of the village and held council with them. The Carbet, which was regarded as an important symbol, was kept clean by the Carib men and boys, while the lesser jobs of cleaning the houses of the village was assigned to the women and girls.

The Arawaks were so called because they were cassava-eaters. The Caribs derived their name from the Spanish word, '*caribal*', which means cannibal. When they attacked the Arawaks in Barbados, as in other parts of the West Indies, they ate those whom they killed in battle. Those whom they captured as prisoners they kept for a later meal. The boys who fell into their hands were castrated and fattened. They were then killed and eaten as a more delectable dish. But the Arawak women were kept as concubines; they were skilled craftswomen and continued to make pottery for the benefit of their conquerors. The Carib women did not have the same skill but they, too, continued to make pottery, which was of a more primitive type. The fact that Arawak and Carib pottery was made at the same time explains why a mixture of the artifacts of both peoples have been found in lower levels in certain sites in Barbados. [20]

Conquest and Destruction

It has been estimated that there may be five times as much Carib pottery in this island as in other islands and from this it has been deduced that Barbados may well have been the headquarters of the Caribs in the years before Columbus discovered the New World.[21]

Indeed, it is not difficult to re-create in our imagination the activities of the Caribs some one thousand years ago, when they occupied Barbados as their stronghold in the West Indies. From early boyhood the Carib was trained to be a hardy warrior. He was subjected to ordeals which were designed to test his courage. A bird of considerable size was beaten to death against his body. He had to endure scratches from an agouti's tooth and the wounds thus inflicted were rubbed with pepper. He then had to eat a piece of the dead bird's heart. All this, and more, he was required to endure to show he was a brave warrior and could undergo pain and agony without showing any sign of cowardice.

When a campaign was to be launched against one of the neighbouring islands the General, or Supreme Captain, would send a stick to each of the villages with as many notches on it "as there were days remaining before they are to come to the place of meeting".[22] In the meantime, while their womenfolk provided a supply of food for the expedition, the warriors busied themselves with the last-minute preparation of their weapons. To terrify their enemies, they inflicted deep gashes on their faces with the teeth of agoutis and painted white rings around their eyes. Then on the eve of the campaign, they gathered for a bout of drinking and revelry and listened to a recital of the imaginary wrongs the Arawaks had done them.

At the appointed time, they set out to do battle against the enemy. Their weapons were "bows with poisoned arrows and short staves of speckled wood". Some carried bucklers and shields which were "handsomely made and cut with figures". They seemed to keep no order in fighting and usually attacked at night unless they saw "a marked advantage" to do so in day time. Those whom they captured they put to death "with the greatest cruelty that bloodthirsty people can think of towards their enemies".[23] Sometimes they took their women with them to protect their canoes and look after their food, but more often they left them behind to protect their headquarters in Barbados for they were as skilled as the men in the use of bow and arrow.

The Arawaks were mortally afraid of the Caribs because of their fierce methods of waging war. They were even more afraid of them because they were cannibals. The Caribs were regarded as "bloody and inhuman man-eaters" and for this reason "were

11

dreaded by the inhabitants of the great islands of Cuba, Hispaniola and Jamaica, who were harmless people, and on whom they preyed".[24] When they killed the more famous of their enemies, they cured them, by drying and smoking on a wooden tripod, and then handed them around to be eaten during their celebrations of victory. Nor were they squeamish about their cannibalism. For they hung up the heads of men and had baskets filled with human bones in their houses.[25]

Père Labat has submitted that the Caribs of Dominica, while eating those they killed in battle, were not usually cannibals.[26] It is true the Caribs may have improved on their customs in historic times. Yet the evidence of cannibalism is overwhelmingly against them. It is recorded that in 1564 a Spanish ship was wrecked off the coast of Dominica and the Caribs of that island killed and ate the entire crew.[27] Forty-two years later, the same fate befell a French ship which was wrecked off the coast of St. Vincent. The Caribs there killed and devoured the "whole companie".[28] It was no wonder that they were able to say from experience that, while the Spaniards were the hardest to digest, the Frenchman made the most delicate dish.[29]

Early in the sixteenth century, the Spaniards found the Caribs still living in Barbados. But when the Portuguese, led by Pedro a Campos, came to the island in 1536, they were all gone.

It is not difficult to ascertain the fate that must have overtaken the Caribs. One reason for their disappearance from Barbados may well have been that they were infected by the Spaniards with strange diseases such as smallpox and tuberculosis. If this is so, as it was in other parts of the New World, such diseases would have worked havoc among a people who had had no chance to build up immunity against them.

It is now known, however, that the main reason for the disappearance of the Caribs from Barbados was that the Spaniards transported them to work as slaves in Espânola. The fact that they were so transported clearly indicates that the inhabitants of Barbados at that time were Caribs and not Arawaks. The Spanish Cedula of 1511 permitted the Spanish conquistadores to enslave the Caribs and transport them from their islands in the Lesser Antilles. When the Arawaks of Trinidad were subjected to a similar fate, however, the Spaniards were instructed to return them immediately to their island. If it had been the Arawaks who were taken from Barbados and transported to slavery in Espânola, orders would at once have been issued for their return to the island. The new Spanish policy was due to the labours of Bartolomé de las Casas, the Apostle of the Indians, who had secured from Spain the right of the Arawaks to live as free men and not as slaves.

Thus history and archaeology seem to have combined to confirm the new version of the earliest settlements in Barbados. All the available evidence appears to give substance to the theory that the Arawaks lived in Barbados for about four hundred years and were then displaced by the Caribs. It was the latter who met the impact of Spanish influence in Barbados and fought in vain to preserve their freedom against the strangers from the western world. It is one of the ironies of our history that those who conquered and destroyed the Arawaks were themselves conquered and destroyed by a stronger and more warlike people.

Questions and Exercises to Consider

1. Why is it now believed that Caribs as well as Arawaks once lived in Barbados? What evidence can you find to justify the new interpretation?
2. Pay a visit to the Barbados Museum and look at the artifacts of the Amerindians. What can you deduce from these artifacts about the art forms and the manner of living of the Amerindians?
3. Imagine you are a young Carib and have just returned from your first raid against the Arawaks. Write an account of the preparations you would have made and of how the raid went.
4. Go on a field trip to one of our archaeological sites and find out how those involved in the digging obtain information about the Amerindian way of life from the various layers in the excavations.
5. What features of Barbados might have qualified it to be the headquarters of the Caribs in the area?

CHAPTER TWO

The English Settlers

The First Visit

Columbus did not discover Barbados during any of his four voyages to the New World. But the Spaniards, following in his wake, came to the island early in the sixteenth century, as we have seen in the first chapter of this book, and so did the Portuguese, who came a few years later, led by Pedro a Campos. The Spaniards and the Portuguese paid only temporary visits and neither settled in the island.

The first English ship that came here touched at the island on May 14th, 1625, and was probably called the "Olive". It seems that the English visit was the result of an accident. Their ship was on its way from Pernambuco, in Brazil, to England and it was due to a mistake by its sailing master, Richard Chambers, that it was taken off its regular course and came to Barbados.

On arrival at the island, John Powell landed some men at Holetown, which was called St. James's town, and on a nearby tree they wrote the words "James K. of E. and this Island". After this, they proceeded southward along the coast until they came upon a river, later known as Indian River, and again formally took possession of the island in the name of King James I of England. [1]

After satisfying himself that the island was uninhabited, Powell returned to England and reported his discovery to his employer, Sir William Courteen. On receiving this report, without delay Courteen sent an expedition under Powell to occupy Barbados and to establish a settlement. On his way, however, Powell captured a Spanish ship and decided to return to England, thus abandoning his expedition.

Before long another expedition was fitted out and financed by a company consisting mainly of Courteen and the brothers John and Henry Powell. Their ship was called the "William and John" and was under the command of Captain Henry Powell. On the way, the "William and John" captured a prize from which it took ten Negro slaves, but this time the expedition did not turn back. It arrived at Barbados on February 17th, 1627, and on this day,

Holetown Monument

15

which marks the beginning of the English settlement, it landed eighty settlers to occupy and settle the island.

The settlers from the "William and John" landed at the same place on the west coast of the island as the men of the "Olive" had done less than two years before. They changed the name of the place from St. James's town to Jamestown and unfurled the royal standard to show that Barbados was an English possession. [2]

Overcoming Difficulties

The English settlers thus came to the island about one hundred years after the Caribs disappeared. Barbados had returned to its primitive condition and the English must have found it in much the same state as the Caribs had on their arrival several hundred years previously.

The island was covered with woods and brush and all traces of the Caribs and their villages seem to have disappeared from the surface of the earth. The east coast was barren, with rocky cliffs and rab lands which were covered only with wild grass and brushwood. That part of the island must have seemed as uninviting to them as it had been to the Caribs many years before.

The English settlers experienced as much difficulty as the Caribs in obtaining an adequate supply of water. The island still had a large number of ponds but the rivers, such as they were, and the springs did not yield the volume of water they needed. Accordingly, they had to depend for their supply on catching rain water and keeping it in cisterns.

But the new settlers found that there were other things, such as the coral reefs and the nature of the land, that compensated for the hardships of their new environment. They therefore set to work with zeal and energy, cutting down trees and building simple, rude houses for their shelter.

At first they confined themselves to the west coast, clearing the land around them, without venturing inland. To keep body and soul together they hunted the wild hogs which the Portuguese had left behind them during their visit to the island. These wild hogs they found in the surrounding woods but within a few years they had killed them off completely. [3]

Thereupon Captain Henry Powell went to Guyana to visit a friend, who was Governor of the Dutch settlement there, and to procure seeds for crops that could best grow in a tropical climate.

With the agreement of the Dutch Governor, Powell brought forty Amerindians back to Barbados with him and, with their special knowledge and skill, they helped the English settlers to produce such crops as yams, cassava and Indian corn, plantains, cotton and tobacco. These Amerindians were brought to Barbados as free men but were later enslaved mainly as a result of the quarrel that arose between those who, as we shall see, made rival claims to the island.[4]

In the meantime, John Powell had arrived in Barbados with a cargo of supplies and another group of ninety settlers. With such an increase in their number and with the help of the Amerindians, the settlement began to prosper and by 1629 the population grew to nearly eighteen hundred persons.[5]

The Great Barbados Robbery

The growth and prosperity of the colony was due to the management of Sir William Courteen and his band of associates. The enterprise was undoubtedly successful and the entire expense was borne by Courteen and his company.[6] The settlers owned neither the land nor the stock; they were mainly Courteen's "tenants at will" and all the profits had to be returned to the merchant prince.

Yet Courteen knew what he was about and looked after the needs of the settlement. He paid the colonists regular wages and supplied them with all their vital requirements. It is doubtful whether Barbados could have been colonized without the financial backing of a man like Courteen. A group of settlers, without the resources that were placed at their disposal, could scarcely have survived the hazards that were inevitable in such a venture: slow communications between the Mother Country and themselves, slow returns on the large sums of money invested in the venture, strange diseases and possible attacks by hostile Indians or by the Spaniards, who resented the intrusion of anyone on their monopoly of the New World.

Some have argued that it was bad for the island to be owned and administered by a merchant like Courteen. But at least Courteen knew a great deal about the business of colonization and attended to the welfare of the colonists. Barbados was soon to learn that it was infinitely worse to come under the ownership of a man like the Earl of Carlisle, who knew and cared nothing about the needs of a settlement.[7]

The Earl of Carlisle, whose memory is perpetuated in the name we have given to the island's most important bay, was a Scotsman who enjoyed great influence in the court of James I. He had followed the King from Scotland when James came over to accept the English Crown and his first reward was to be created an Earl.

Carlisle was a notorious spendthrift and was always heavily in debt. To solve his financial difficulties he began to sell his influence at Court to the merchants of London. The latter had heard that the business of colonization in the Leeward Islands was a profitable one and they resolved to make use of Carlisle's influence to gain a footing in this area.

Beset by his creditors, Carlisle began the necessary negotiations and in due course was granted the proprietorship of the Caribbee Islands, including Barbados. Carlisle's first step was to pay off his debts to Sir Marmaduke Royden and his syndicate of London merchants, by leasing them 10,000 acres in Barbados, with full authority and power to raise revenue by taxation. [8]

How, one may well ask, did this happen?

There are several answers to this question. First, Courteen was kept in the dark while the negotiations were proceeding for the grant to the Earl of Carlisle. Secondly, Carlisle deceived his rivals by making them believe that his claims to the ownership of the Caribbee Islands would not include Barbados. Thirdly, Courteen did not have a powerful friend at Court who would protect his interests.

When the Carlisle grant was announced, Courteen enlisted the support of the Earl of Pembroke who persuaded the King, Charles I, to restore Courteen his rights. But this happened only because Carlisle was absent from England at the time. When he returned, he easily induced the King, who was "criminally careless and indifferent"[9] in the matter, to confirm him in the ownership of the Caribbee Islands. And on this occasion it was clear beyond the shadow of a doubt that Barbados was included in the Carlisle grant.

It was in these circumstances that the "Great Barbados Robbery" was committed. Although the leading lawyers of the day were of the opinion that Sir William Courteen had the better case because he had made an earlier claim and was "first in occupancie",[10] they were over-ruled; the pioneer in the settlement of Barbados suffered a great injustice and lost his right completely.

Open Conflicts

The change of proprietorship from Courteen to Carlisle was to launch Barbados on a sea of troubles.

Barbados was now set up as a colony under a "tenant-in-chief" who had the power to enforce obedience by corporal punishment or sentence of death. Under this feudal system the Earl of Carlisle was granted all subsidies, customs and impositions for a period of ten years and his profits were greatly increased at the expense of the colonists. Indeed, the latter were exploited by more than one syndicate of merchants in London and within a short period of time they were forced to ask the King to save them from the authority of their over-lord, the Earl of Carlisle, and from a "slavery worse than villanay", to use their own words. [11]

Equally distressing were the confusion and strife that followed the Carlisle grant. The Governor of the Courteen men, who were settled on the west coast of Barbados, was John Powell. But in June 1628 Charles Wolverston was sent to the island with sixty-four men. He was appointed Governor for three years and he landed at a place which was later to become Bridgetown.

At first there was no trouble. But when it was announced that Wolverston was to take the place of Powell as Governor and that he claimed jurisdiction over the Courteen settlers, the latter at once prepared to offer resistance. After establishing himself, Wolverston summoned the Courteen men to acknowledge his authority. Only one man, William Deane, Powell's second-in-command, obeyed his summons, but all the other settlers stood solidly behind their own Governor.

Things reached such a pitch that open conflict between the Courteen men and the Carlisle men seemed inevitable, but this was averted at the last moment by the intervention of a clergyman by the name of Kentlane. It took Wolverston nearly three months to establish his authority in the island, for the Courteen men did not surrender until September 14th, 1628.

But this was not to be the end of the island's troubles. For when Sir William Courteen heard what had happened in Barbados, he at once prepared to deliver his counter-stroke. He sent Henry Powell to Barbados with a hundred new settlers and a supply of arms. When Henry Powell reached the island he invited Wolverston and his new ally, William Deane, to a conference on board his ship and when they came he seized them, put them in chains and took them to England as prisoners. That was in

February 1629. Thus in two days Henry Powell did what it had taken Wolverston nearly three months to accomplish.[12]

Before long, however, the Carlisle forces struck back.

On learning that his Governor, Charles Wolverston, was a prisoner, the Earl of Carlisle sent out Henry Hawley to redress the situation. When Hawley arrived in Barbados in a ship, appropriately named the "Carlisle", Governor John Powell refused to give him permission to land. It is very strange, however, that Powell accepted an invitation to a function on board the "Carlisle" and thereupon Hawley, following the example of Henry Powell, seized him and made him a prisoner.[13]

Within a week of his arrival Hawley had thus totally changed the situation. The conquest of the island was completed and the "Great Barbados Robbery" was finally achieved. Both in the English Court and in the Colony of Barbados the Earl of Carlisle had won an undeserved and shameful victory.

Questions and Exercises to Consider

1. What kind of houses did the first settlers build? How do these compare with the more substantial residences constructed after sugar brought the island wealth. A field trip to Nicholas Abbey and/or Drax Hall would be helpful.
2. Visit the Archives and look for any evidence you can find to explain how Courteen lost the island to the Earl of Carlisle.
3. Arrange an imaginary interview with early settlers such as the owner of a tobacco plantation and a white indentured servant. (Refer, if necessary, to Chapter 4 of this book).
4. Write an eye witness account of life among the early settlers. Study Ligon's map (pp. 36 and 37) and see what information you can obtain from it.
5. Imagine you are an English boy or girl and write a paragraph explaining why your family emigrated to Barbados in the seventeenth century.

CHAPTER THREE

A Bid for Independence

Assembly Established

The end of the duel between Sir William Courteen and the Earl of Carlisle did not bring peace to the unhappy inhabitants of the island. Nor did they regain the prosperity they had enjoyed in the early days of the settlement. Drought and the shortage of supplies brought on a period that came to be known as "The Starving Time"[1] and, to make matters worse, a lawless spirit seemed to be abroad in the land.

Henry Hawley, who was appointed as Carlisle's Governor of the island, was to become known as one of the most notorious figures in Barbadian history. Before long (in September 1629) he was replaced as Governor by Sir William Tufton who tried, among other things, to relieve the harsh treatment to which the white indentured servants had been subjected. (For more information about these indentured servants, see the following chapter.)

Tufton's régime was marked by a number of good works. He divided the island into six parishes, set up vestries to run the affairs of these parishes and built several churches. Yet his humane policy in regard to the white bond servants soon caused him trouble. With discontent in the island among the employers of these servants and with Hawley's intrigues in the Mother Country, he was quickly deposed from the office of Governor. Tufton handed over peacefully to his successor, none other than Hawley himself, yet the latter soon had him tried on a trumped-up charge and executed for treason.[2]

Hawley was a restless and scheming soul. Twice in 1633 and 1634, he was out of the island, leaving Richard Peers to perform the duties of Deputy Governor. When the Earl of Carlisle died in 1636, Hawley returned to the island as Governor. He showed no enthusiasm for his patron's son, the second Earl of Carlisle, and refused to acknowledge the authority of Sir Thomas Warner as Lieutenant-General of all the colonies of the Caribbees. He had previously subdued the Courteen settlers and he now set about quelling the Carlisle men. He governed the island as he thought fit but his harsh rule soon united all men against him.

When the tide began to turn against him and the second Earl of Carlisle decided to recall him, Hawley changed his policy suddenly and completely. He now sought to win the goodwill and support of the settlers and, with this object in view, he established the House of Assembly in 1639.[3]

A word of explanation is perhaps needed at this stage. For, with the establishment of the House of Assembly, a representative element was introduced in the island's system of government which was to continue right up to the present time. After the death of the first Earl of Carlisle, the ownership of the island passed to the trustees whom the Earl had appointed to look after the duties of the proprietorship and to attend to the just claims of his creditors. The government of the island was continued by Hawley, with the permission of the trustees. Hawley had been appointed Governor by the Earl for a number of years and this appointment was confirmed by the trustees. The second Earl of Carlisle now engaged in a struggle with the trustees for the control of Barbados. He appointed Henry Huncks to take Hawley's place as Governor and Hawley was dismissed by the trustees. Yet, determined not to give up without a struggle, Hawley returned to England where he secured a Commission from the King. That Commission was intended merely to enable Hawley to go around to the plantations and enquire why tobacco had been produced in excessive quantities, to the neglect of other staple crops. It did, however, give him the title of Lieutenant-General and Governor of Barbados.

Hawley had already lost the confidence of both the trustees and the second Earl of Carlisle. Yet the schemer was not to be so easily defeated. He managed to return to Barbados before Huncks arrived in the island and succeeded in persuading the planters to accept him as Governor. For he had one great advantage: his Commission bore the signature of the King of England, Charles I. Thereupon he assumed the office of Governor and proceeded to act with characteristic ruthlessness. First, he called in all Commissions and filled all the offices with his own supporters. Secondly, he released from prison all those who had committed offences against the proprietary government run by the Carlisle men. And thirdly, he established or "settled a parliament" which consisted of the Council and a number of burgesses or citizens.[4]

Why It Succeeded

Why, one may well ask, did this experiment succeed? Why was an arrangement, that was conceived in such peculiar circumstances, destined to become an effective and permanent part of the island's constitution?

When Huncks arrived in Barbados, he found Hawley fully in control of the Government of the island and enjoying the support of a formidable party. Huncks was not allowed to read his Commission, presumably on the ground that a Commission from the proprietors of the island could not be as important as a Commission from the King of England. To make his position more secure, Hawley drove Huncks out of the island, threatening he would use violence against him if he did not leave peacefully.

It is certain that the House of Burgesses, which was summoned by Hawley in 1639, was the first assembly of elected representatives in Barbados. And early in 1640 it was recognized in England when the Privy Council referred to the "Council and Burgesses of Barbados, their representative body".[5] But Hawley could not continue indefinitely to flourish like the green bay tree. Later in 1640 he was forced to yield to the Commissioners who were sent out by the King to settle the matter. He had to submit to the second Earl of Carlisle and Huncks succeeded him as Governor.

To appreciate the new spirit that was abroad in the land, one has to understand that Barbados was an English settlement and England was her Mother Country. The great issues that were being fought out in England at this time were bound to have an impact on the inhabitants of Barbados. Since 1629 the English people had been governed by the arbitrary rule of the King and this period of personal government was to last for eleven years. This was the era that saw John Hampden, the squire from Buckinghamshire, protesting against the payment of ship money on the grounds that it was an arbitrary form of taxation. It witnessed the struggle of the English people for the revival of the parliamentary system. When Parliament was recalled in 1640, the Commons House of England heard the impassioned speech of Pym in which he proclaimed that the "powers of Parliament are to the body politic as the rational faculties of the soul to man". And the Long Parliament, at the outset of its career, announced that ship money and all such forms of taxation were illegal unless they had Parliamentary sanction.

The spirit that animated the hearts of Englishmen living in England was certain to strike a responsive chord in the Englishmen living in Barbados. Thus it was that, when Huncks was re-instated as Governor, the planters of Barbados joined battle with him to secure the liberties that had been granted to them by Henry Hawley. They wanted those liberties confirmed and their Assembly accepted in the same way that Englishmen had wanted Charles I to end his term of despotism and re-instate the Parliament of England.

Huncks did not last long as Governor; the following year he was succeeded by Philip Bell. By this time the settlement in Barbados had been in existence for fourteen years and its total population had increased to more than 10,000. In these circumstances, and with the spirit prevailing at the time, it was too much to expect that so considerable a body of Englishmen, many of whom had left their native land to seek after liberty and freedom, would be content to be governed by a nominee chamber such as the Council of the island undoubtedly was. [6]

Fortunately, Bell was a "wise, honest and just man". He restored a great measure of stability to the island by organising the machinery of government in such a way as to meet the demand for popular representation. Whereas Tufton had divided the island into six parishes, Bell introduced a new system under which the number of parishes was increased to eleven, which system has remained in force up to the present time. Moreover, he arranged for each parish to send two representatives to the Assembly and raised the latter's status by investing it with the power of passing laws. [7] It was no longer merely an advisory body but a part of the legislative machinery, with definite powers and rules of procedure.

Dutch Assistance

It is strange to relate that, in spite of the turbulence of this period, the island was soon prospering again. The settlers began to produce large crops of tobacco, indigo and cotton. Tobacco led the way almost from the beginning, but cotton made rapid strides and increased at such a rate that before long it became as important an export crop as tobacco. It is interesting to note that the settlers were taught the art of cotton cultivation and spinning by the Amerindians of whom mention was made in the previous chapter.

The prosperity the colony thus enjoyed was mainly due to the Dutch, who provided it with the provisions and equipment that were necessary. The Mother Country did not approve of this. England believed that since so much money was required to establish a colony, that colony should trade entirely with her and not with foreigners. Accordingly, England tried to follow a policy that would exclude all foreigners from trade with her colonies. But Barbados resisted this policy with a stubborn and unyielding spirit because of the great advantage it gained by trading with the Dutch, who sold their goods at lower prices than the English merchants did. [8]

The difficulties that faced the Barbadians can be easily imagined. Having only recently surmounted the chaos and confusion of the early years, they now had to cope with other problems. The market the Mother Country supplied for its products was limited and now its profitable trade with the Dutch and other foreigners was forbidden.

But fortune was soon to prove to be on the side of the Barbadians. The English Civil War, which began in 1642, distracted the attention of the Mother Country from her colonies. Indeed, England soon ceased to exist as a market for colonial goods and Barbados took the opportunity to continue her trade with the Dutch. We shall see in the next chapter of what great help and support the Dutch traders were in the development of Barbados.

At the same time, the course of the Civil War brought misfortune both to the Cavaliers who supported King Charles I and the Roundheads who supported the English Parliament. Thus refugees from both sides began to come to Barbados. Their object was to escape from the strife of the old country and to seek to rebuild their fortunes in the new colony of Barbados.

The new settlers now attracted to the island were of a different character from those who originally established the settlement in Barbados. Regarded as "gentlemen" of England, they enhanced the prestige of the island in the eyes of the Mother Country and soon gave it an importance, both in the political and economic sense, that it had not previously enjoyed.

It is from this time that Barbados began to call itself "Little England". The new settlers were determined to re-create in the island the fortunes they had lost in England and this brought Barbados increased activity and prosperity. But it was perhaps inevitable that they would bring with them the dissensions and difficulties they thought they had left behind them in the Mother Country.[9]

The English Civil War, sometimes known as the English Revolution, was concerned with political and religious ideas that divided almost every rank of English society. In the main the old aristocratic families favoured the King, while the new business class, which had arisen since the time of the Protestant Reformation, sided with Parliament. The former, though there were exceptions, supported the Monarchy and the Established Church of England; the latter opted for the rule of Parliament and a Presbyterian form of church government and doctrine.

Cavaliers and Roundheads

At first, all went well in Barbados. The Cavaliers and Roundheads agreed to abide by a "Treaty of Turkey and Roast Pork". According to this, anyone who mentioned the words "Cavalier" or "Roundhead" was required to provide a young hog and a turkey which were to be eaten at the offender's house by all those who had heard him utter the forbidden words.[10] Sometimes the treaty was deliberately broken to give the gentlemen of both sides an excuse to enjoy one another's company.

Life in Barbados continued happily for a number of years and during this period the island enjoyed a measure of independence, pledging its loyalty neither to the King nor to the Parliament of England. But by 1650 the situation was completely changed. More and more Cavaliers had been coming to the island and they were connected with families that had played an important part in the politics of the Mother Country. These men were resolved to establish their ideas in Barbados and to gain ascendancy over all their political opponents.

The leaders of this group were Colonel Humphrey Walrond and his brother, Edward. The Walronds found ready support among the men who swarmed the island, mourning the execution of King Charles I and deploring the loss of their property in England. They regarded Charles as a martyr and pledged support for the Church of England which, they loudly asserted, was being desecrated. The situation was not eased by those rash young men who openly drank to the health of the King and threatened to seize the property of the Roundheads in the island.

26

All the efforts of Governor Bell to maintain a policy of neutrality were gradually undermined and Cavaliers and Roundheads were now bitterly at odds with one another. The Walronds made themselves masters of the island and on May 3rd, 1650, issued a proclamation affirming their loyalty to the Royalist cause. The son of the late King was solemnly proclaimed as the lawful sovereign of Barbados and it was commanded that the Book of Common Prayer be read in every Parish church as "the only Pattern of true worship".

Such was the answer of the Cavaliers in Barbados to those who had replaced the Monarchy in England by the Commonwealth and had swept away the Church of England, establishing the Presbyterian religion in its stead. [11]

It was in these circumstances that Francis Lord Willoughby arrived in Barbados to take over the governorship of Barbados from Captain Philip Bell, who had administered the island's affairs for nearly ten years. Once on the side of Parliament, Willoughby had turned against the extremists of this group and joined the Royalist forces. He came to Barbados as Governor, and as a representative of the King, and he also brought with him a Commission from the second Earl of Carlisle appointing him Lieutenant-General of the Caribbee Islands.

The arrival of Lord Willoughby soon brought to an end the rule of the Walronds and their plans to destroy the Roundheads in the island. For Willoughby's policy was to reconcile both parties, to save the island from the bitter strife and dissensions that threatened its welfare and to settle the issue that separated Barbados from the Mother Country.

Barbadian Defiance

After being installed as Governor, Lord Willoughby set about trying to win the confidence of the Moderates who were led by Colonel James Modiford. [12] He made it clear that he intended to follow a course of moderation since he considered that such a policy was in the best interest of the island. He sent a special agent to England to confer with the Mother Country on her differences with Barbados and he took steps to relieve the bitterness between the Royalist and Parliamentary parties in the island. [13]

Chief among these steps was the repeal of the Act which confiscated the estates of the Roundheads. It is not surprising that Willoughby won the co-operation both of the Roundheads and of the Cavaliers of moderate views. It was with such support that he was able to challenge the authority of Colonel Walrond and his brother and deprive them of the power they wielded in the island.

Unfortunately, Willoughby's policy of conciliation did not meet with the success it deserved. In the first place, the English Parliament was greatly annoyed by the stubborn defiance Barbados had shown in the past. They were by no means pleased by a number of things the Cavaliers had done: the proclamation of Prince Charles as the lawful sovereign of the island, the banishment of Roundheads and the seizure of their property and, perhaps most important of all, the continuing trade between the Dutch and the merchants and planters of Barbados. All this was emphasised by the Roundheads who went to England to present their case to the English Parliament. They urged that their estates should be restored to them and that the Cavaliers in Barbados should be reduced to submission by force of arms.

This was the sort of action that the English Parliament was only too ready to take against the Royalist party in Barbados. No time was lost in branding the Barbadians as rebels and traitors to the commonwealth under Oliver Cromwell, which had taken the place of the Monarchy in England, and a fleet, consisting of two warships and five merchantmen, with 820 men on board, was despatched to subdue the rebellious spirits in Barbados.[14]

That was in February 1651. Lord Willoughby seemed to have no alternative but to resist the armed force that was now to be employed against the island. On February 18th a Declaration against the British Parliament was issued by Willoughby and the Legislature of Barbados. The Declaration pointed out that the inhabitants of the island were English people who, with great danger to their persons and with great charge and trouble, had settled and inhabited the colony of Barbados.

Then Willoughby and the Legislature proceeded to question whether the Barbadians should be subjected to the will and command of those who had stayed at home in England. "Shall we be bound," they defiantly asked, "to the government and lordship of a Parliament in which we have no representatives, or persons chosen by us, as also to oppose and dispute all what should tend to our disadvantage and harm? In truth, this would be a slavery far exceeding all that the English nation hath yet suffered."[15]

In these words the Barbadians set out the sort of protest that other colonial peoples were in the future to make against domination by imperialist powers. Then they proceeded to the climax of their Declaration which they expressed in ringing terms. "We cannot think that there are any amongst us, who are so simple and so unworthily minded, that they would not rather choose a noble death than forsake their old liberties and privileges".[16]

To meet the impending threat, the Barbadians mustered a force of cavalry and infantry and repaired their defences along the coast. Special attention was paid to the forts at strategic points which we now know as Carlisle Bay, Holetown and Speightstown. And the Dutch, willing as ever to help the inhabitants of the island, again came to their aid by providing urgently needed supplies of arms and ammunition.

After considerable delay, the Commonwealth squadron, known as the "Barbados Fleet", arrived at the island under the command of Sir George Ayscue.[17] That was as late as October 1651. The squadron found fifteen Dutch merchants ships in Carlisle Bay and captured twelve of them. But by this time the Dutch ships had already discharged their valuable cargoes.

In the meantime, the forces under Lord Willoughby's command had risen to 6,000 infantry and 400 cavalry. Realising that he was too weak to invade and occupy Barbados, Ayscue called on Willoughby to surrender the island to the English Parliament. The Governor replied, saying that he acknowledged no authority but the King's and that he would defend the island against any attack. Ayscue thereupon decided to seize all ships that approached the island and to starve the inhabitants into surrender. In addition, he launched a successful raid at the "Hole" where the defences were breached and a number of prisoners were captured. To make things worse for the Barbadians, Ayscue's squadron was re-inforced by a fleet that was on its way to Virginia, which had also declared itself a Royalist colony and was now to be reduced to submission.

Again Ayscue called on the islanders to surrender and on receiving an unsatisfactory reply he resolved to use force, with the combined "Barbados Fleet" and the "Virginia Fleet" at his disposal. One night in December he landed a force of four hundred men and in the engagement that followed the Barbadians suffered heavy losses. But again Ayscue found that he was not strong enough to hold the island.[18]

The Articles of Agreement

With the departure of the "Virginia Fleet", which in due course had to proceed on its way to its appointed destination, Ayscue had to fall back on a policy of negotiation rather than on the use of armed force. His plan was now to divide the Barbadians among themselves, to separate the Cavaliers from the Roundheads.

All did not go smoothly at first, though the new plan eventually succeeded. The support of Colonel Modiford and the Moderate Cavaliers was secured by Ayscue. After much discussion and disagreement, Modiford decided to abandon his fellow Barbadians and take direct action. He marched his regiment to the coast near Oistin's (then called Austin's Bay), and there, by agreement, he linked up with forces that had been landed by Ayscue.

When informed of this development Willoughby still held out and the combined forces of Modiford and Ayscue marched forth to meet his troops. But at the last moment, a trumpeter sent by Willoughby delivered a letter which earnestly asked for peace and stopped the imminent engagement. Negotiations for the peaceful surrender of the island were conducted at the Mermaid Tavern in Austin's Bay.[19] The terms that were agreed upon provided that all the Roundheads who had lost their estates in Barbados should have their property restored to them. In the same spirit, all the Cavaliers in Barbados who had lost their possessions in England, Scotland, and Ireland, were to have their lands and goods returned to them.

The Articles of Agreement, sometimes known as the Charter of Barbados, contained twenty-three clauses and perhaps the most important of these were as follows.[20]

1. That liberty of conscience in matters of religion was to be allowed to all.
2. That no taxes, customs, imposts, loans and excise should be levied on the inhabitants of Barbados without their consent in a General Assembly.
3. That all port-towns and cities under the English Parliament's power should be open to the people of the island and that trade should be free with all nations that traded amicably with England.
4. That the government of the island should be by a Governor, Council and Assembly, the Governor to be appointed by the

States of England, the Council to be chosen by him and the Assembly to be elected by the freeholders of the island in the several parishes.

The Articles of Agreement were generous and for that reason Sir George Ayscue feared that the English Parliament would not accept them. But the leaders of the English Commonwealth were persuaded to take a liberal view and Parliament duly ratified the Articles on August 18th, 1652.[21]

Questions and Exercises to Consider

1. How does the bid for independence in 1651 compare with attainment of independence in 1966? Was the notion of independence similar in both cases or were there important differences?

2. Why were those who came to Barbados during the English Civil War unable to escape the dissensions and difficulties they had left behind in England?

3. Arrange a debate about the principles that separated Cavaliers from Roundheads both in England and in Barbados.

4. Look at the map on p. 53 and explain why the forts are all on the western side.

5. Examine the clauses from the Charter of Barbados (p. 30). What do you deduce from it were the most important parts of the Charter? What was of particular interest to Barbadians at the time and what was of more lasting value to all who came afterwards?

6. Why did the colonists dislike the Carlisle proprietorship?

CHAPTER FOUR

The Sugar Revolution

The White Servants

After the early years of hardship and privation, the fortunes of the island began to change for the better.

The Civil War between the Cavaliers, supporters of the English King, and the Roundheads, supporters of the English Parliament, brought an era of free trade which was of great benefit to the island. When the dispute over the proprietorship was settled, immigrants came to Barbados in large numbers because they wanted to get away from the political controversies that were raging in England. With the island's population steadily increasing, there was a boom in the price of land and this boom rose higher still with the introduction and development of the sugar industry.

At first, the Barbadian economy was based on tobacco and white indentured servants. The latter came or were brought to Barbados through a variety of ways. Men or women who wanted to emigrate overseas, and were too poor to do so on their own, would sign an agreement to serve a planter in Barbados and other territories for a period of five or seven years. In return for this, the contract guaranteed that their passages would be paid, that they would be maintained at the expense of the planters and, when their term of indenture was ended, they would be given a sum of money or a piece of land.[1]

Another source for the supply of indentured servants was the transportation of convicted criminals. In those days the penal system was extremely severe in England. If a man was convicted of minor crimes, such as theft, he was condemned to be hanged at the gallows. But if he wanted to avoid such a fate he could ask to be transported to the colonies and in many cases he was allowed this minor form of punishment.[2]

These were two methods of bringing indentured servants to Barbados. It was a voluntary system and, though it was open to abuse from time to time, it served to attract many immigrants to the island. But the labour requirements of the planters could not be completely satisfied by these methods and before long the Mother Country resorted to the system of compulsory transportation.

Kidnapping became a lucrative source of supplying white labour to planters in Barbados and other colonies. Children were stolen and put on board ship; men and women were shanghaied and, when they regained consciousness, would find themselves well on their way to some plantation overseas where they were to spend a period of servitude of up to ten years.[3]

There was another form of transportation that brought many servants to the island. Oliver Cromwell was probably the first person in British history to use this as a method of getting rid of his opponents. After his victorious battles, Cavaliers who were captured as prisoners of war were sent out to the Caribbee islands where they were sold to the planters. This method was no respecter of persons and sometimes officers of high rank were compulsorily transported to the West Indies.[4]

Indeed, Cromwell was only continuing a practice he had started at the time of the Irish Rebellion of 1649. This rebellion was ruthlessly suppressed and those who survived the suppression were transported to Barbados. After this, transportation became a regular form of punishment for those who rose in rebellion against the government of the day. Those who were involved in the Penruddock rising in 1655, the Monmouth Rebellion of 1685 and, later still, the Jacobite uprisings of 1715 and 1745, were transported to the colonies and Barbados received its quota of these convicted persons.

The indentured system by which all this labour was supplied seemed at first sight to be fair and reasonable, but there was a basic defect in the system. The indentured servants became chattels of their masters who could dispose of them as they wished. They were set to work at the mills, "attending the furnaces, or digging in this scorching land, having nothing to feed on (notwithstanding their hard labour) but potato roots". They were bought and sold from one planter to another or "attached as horses and beasts for the debts of their masters". They were whipped at the whipping posts as rogues for their "masters' pleasure" and slept "in styes worse than hogs in England".[5]

While there were instances of kind treatment, especially after the earlier years of the settlement, there is no doubt about the cruelty experienced by many of the indentured servants. Murder and torture were not unknown and much violence and oppression were exercised upon them. It is true that the law of the land gave the servant the right to appeal against ill-treatment. But this law was not always faithfully observed and, if the servant's complaint was deemed frivolous, he was soundly whipped for being a nuisance.

Indeed, it has been truly said that the conditions under which white labour was obtained and employed in Barbados were "persistently severe, occasionally dishonourable, and generally a disgrace to the English name".[6]

It is small wonder that on two occasions the white servants conspired to rise in protest against their condition. The first was in 1634 when the ring leaders planned to massacre their masters and then put to sea in the first ship that came to the island. It took 800 armed men to crush the conspiracy.[7]

In 1649 the white servants planned to kill their masters and then assume control of the island. Its secret was kept until the day before the uprising was due to begin, when it was betrayed to Judge Hothersall by one of his servants. The ringleaders were promptly arrested, eighteen of them were executed and the planned insurrection was thus completely frustrated.[8]

Richard Ligon has given a grim picture of the conditions under which the white servants lived.[9] In later years, however, their circumstances improved, as may be deduced from the annual supply of clothing they received from their masters. The following list of articles of clothing, as recorded by our earliest historian, was issued to each domestic servant:

Six Smocks, at four shillings apiece £1 4s. 0d.
Three petticoats, at six shillings apiece £0 18s. 0d.
Three Waistcoats, at three shillings apiece £0 9s. 0.
Six Coifs or caps, at eighteen pence apiece £0 9s. 0d.
Twelve pairs of shoes, at three shillings each £1 16s. 0d.

Those working in the field did not fare quite as well. A female labourer was given annually four smocks, three petticoats, four coifs and twelve pairs of shoes, while a male labourer received as his annual supply, six shirts, six pairs of drawers, twelve pairs of shoes and three caps.[10]

In spite of all this, however, the island of Barbados continued to make progress. Those who survived the rigours of servitude were given a sum of money or three to five acres of land as guaranteed by their contracts. They set themselves up as yeomen farmers and played a valuable part in the social and economic activity of the island. By 1645 there were 11,200 smallholders in Barbados out of a population of 36,600 whites and the stability of the island rested on this wide distribution of land.[11] Moreover, Barbados enjoyed representative institutions and there was a healthy political environment in which the yeomen farmers played a not insignificant role.

From Tobacco to Sugar

But the island's economy, based as it was on white indentured servants and tobacco as a peasant crop, could not last forever.

As the realities of servitude became known to them, the flow of white immigrants to Barbados gradually slowed down to a trickle. Moreover, the settlers were now forced to look for an alternative to tobacco as a staple crop. Cotton did not grow well in the interior of the island and another crop was clearly needed to supplement it. The settlers were faced with other problems. They had to produce more food. They were required by their economic situation to give some attention to such crops as cotton, indigo and ginger. And they were compelled to face the melancholy truth that their tobacco was inferior to the tobacco grown in Virginia. Moreover, Barbadian tobacco suffered a setback when the English tariff was raised to a higher level than that imposed on Virginia tobacco. The reason for raising the tariff on the island's tobacco was the determination of the English Government to discourage the cultivation of such crops on plantations like Barbados. It was the considered opinion of the Mother Country that, unless such crops were strongly discouraged, the settlers in colonies like Barbados would become dependent on the Dutch and other foreigners for their foodstuffs.[12]

Tobacco Imports to London

From:	1628	1638	1639
Barbados	⎰ 102,700	204,000	28,000
St. Kitts	⎱ (pounds)	407,000	107,000

Another heavy blow was sustained by the Barbadians when, with the increasing output from Virginia, the price of their

A Scale of five Miles

From *A True and Exact History of Barbados*, Richard Ligon, 1673

36

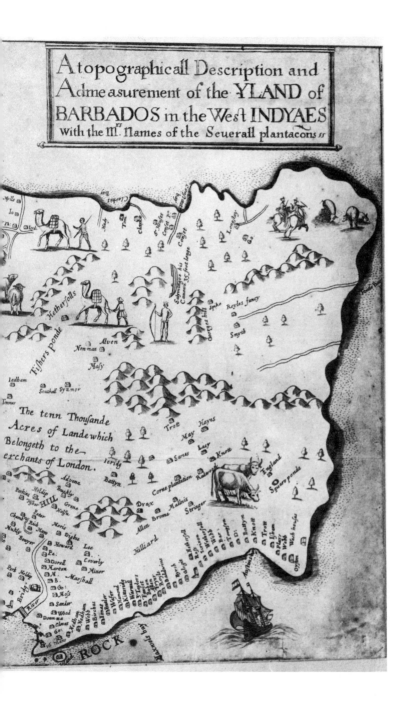

tobacco fell to three farthings a pound. The writing was clearly on the wall and it was at this stage that the Dutch came to the rescue of the Barbadians. They provided the islanders with such sorely needed commodities as salted provisions and clothing at lower rates than the English traders. They supplied cheap loans, inexpensive equipment and insurance at modest rates. They sent the Barbadians on what may be regarded as guided tours to Brazil where they acquired the skills and expertise that were essential for the development of the sugar industry.

Pieter Blower in 1637 was the first man to bring canes to Barbados from Brazil.[13] In the earlier years these canes were used only to produce rum but from 1642 the Barbadian planters began to manufacture sugar. They found this a difficult art at the beginning but Brazil gave them the knowledge to achieve success. And, when they wanted a work force for the new industry, the Dutch again came to their aid by introducing them to the vast reservoir of labour in West Africa. Many enterprising planters were involved but undoubtedly the outstanding figure in Barbados was Sir James Drax.

Barbados had thus found the answer to its immediate problem. An acre of land in Barbados now produced three times as much sugar as tobacco and the price of land skyrocketed to such an extent that a plantation of five hundred acres, owned by Major William Hilliard, a Councillor and eminent planter, rose to thirty-five times the value at which it had been assessed before the introduction of sugar. This was typical of the trend. Barbados was now established on a path that led to a period of unprecedented prosperity.[14]

Drax Hall and Kendal

Richard Ligon, who lived in Barbados from 1647 to 1650, included a map in his history of the island which was published in 1657. From that map we get a fairly clear picture of conditions in Barbados at that time. We see the ten thousand acres that were granted the Merchants of London of the Royden Syndicate, the wooded areas that still remained in the island, the plantations that were established in the clearings made by the early settlers, the wild hogs that were left behind them by the Portuguese, the Indian who used his bow and arrow to catch fish, runaway slaves hotly pursued by their owner and camels that transported all manner of produce and merchandise.

Among the earliest plantations, as shown in Ligon's map, were Drax Hall and Hilliard. The former owes its origin to Sir James Drax, whom we have already mentioned. To Colonel Holdip must be given the credit of establishing one of the earliest sugar works in the New World. This was at the plantation named after him (see Ligon's map) and now known as Locust Hall. Drax improved the process of manufacturing sugar by bringing a Dutch model of a sugar mill to Barbados and conducting important experiments. Under his directing genius, Drax Hall, which is in the parish of St. George, became one of the most prosperous plantations in the island — a distinction it shared with Kendal in the parish of St. John.

Thomas Modiford, who was later to become Governor of Jamaica, set himself up as a planter in Barbados in the 1640's. He bought a half share of Hilliard, now known as Kendal, for £7,000, whereas the whole plantation was valued at £400 before sugar was established as a successful crop. Of its five hundred acres, two hundred were allotted to cane, eighty to pasture land, one hundred and twenty to wood, twenty to tobacco, five to ginger, five to cotton wool and seventy to ground provisions. It had ninety-six African slaves, twenty-eight white servants and three Indian women with their children.[15]

Like other parts of the island, Kendal depended entirely on its ponds for its drinking water in the early years of the Barbadian settlement. But, with the passing of the years, as other sources of water became available, these ponds were drained for the purpose of providing more land for cultivation of sugar cane. Today only two of these ponds remain, one of them being known as Yarico's Pond. A Barbadian folk song relates the story of a beautiful Amerindian who fell in love with a British sailor whom she rescued from hostile Indians somewhere on the Spanish Main. They were saved by a rescue party which took them to Barbados where Inkle, the girl's lover, sold her as a slave. Yarico joined the other Amerindians who were then enslaved in Barbados. Later she became pregnant by a white servant and, when her time was come, she walked to the edge of a pond where she was delivered of "a lusty boy, frolick and lively".[16] That pond still bears her name, while Inkle died of yellow fever soon after his return to England.

Today Kendal, to which Hallet has been added, is one of the largest plantations in the island. It covers a total area of 718 acres of which 534 are arable. 85 per cent of the arable acres is planted with cane and the rest with foodcrops such as potatoes, yams, eddoes, peas and vegetables. Of the 184 acres of non-arable land, 50 acres are occupied by a tenantry and the rest taken up by pasture land and gullies. The closing of the factory in 1970 has reduced its labour force. Yet 125 people are employed in the crop season and 55 to 60 out of crop.[17] It is interesting to compare Kendal as it is now with its predecessor in the seventeenth century.

African Slaves

Perhaps the most important single factor in the development of the sugar industry was a skilled and disciplined labour force. This could not be supplied by the indentured system and once again the Dutch came to the aid of the Barbadian planters. They had recently taken over the slave barracoons in West Africa from the Portuguese and from this almost inexhaustible reservoir of human beings they were to supply Barbados and other territories in the West Indies with their requirements of forced labour.

The slaves who were brought from West Africa to the West Indies belonged to that vast territory which now forms such modern states as Sierra Leone and Guinea, Ghana and the Ivory Coast, Nigeria and the Cameroons. They originated from such tribes as the Eboes, the Pawpaws and the Ashanti, the Whydahs, the Mocoes and the Nagoes, the Angolas, the Congoes and the Mandingoes. They came from the Fanti-Ashanti peoples of the Gold Coast, the natives of Dahomey, the Yoruba of Western Nigeria and the Bini of the southern part of that country.

Inevitably, though they shared many characteristics, they spoke many languages and showed numerous differences of culture and custom. They came from a populous region where slavery had long been in existence by purchase, by kidnapping or by the fortunes of war. They were owned in considerable numbers by the rulers of West Africa where they were accounted of great value as items for export, as victims for sacrifice or as workers who were employed as serfs in parts of that vast and intractable region.[18]

But it is important to bear in mind that the slavery they experienced in Africa bore little or no resemblance to the chattel slavery they were to endure in the Caribbean. It was not slavery in the European sense of the term. It did not strip a man of all his rights and property. The slaves in Africa were more like the

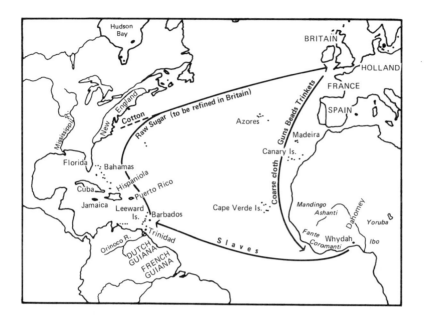

The Triangular Trade

'vassals' of medieval Europe under a feudal system that imposed the notions of servility and obligation which varied from time to time and place to place. Under the "domestic slavery" they experienced, they were serfs and vassals under a feudal system, but not slaves deprived of all human dignity.[19]

The slaves came to Barbados in thousands and tens of thousands. Many failed to survive the horrors of the Middle Passage but many still reached their destination. In 1645 there were 5,680 blacks in Barbados and by 1684 that number had grown to 60,000. The slaves at this time outnumbered the whites by four to one and this accounted for the cruel repression with which they were controlled and the attempts they made to overthrow and massacre their masters. The leadership of their insurrections was provided by the members of the more spirited tribes who were captured as prisoners of war in Africa and sent out as slaves to be auctioned in Barbados.

In these circumstances, it is not surprising that the first slave uprising took place in Barbados in 1675. Here they were probably treated worse than in any other sugar colony and the insurrection was organised by the warlike Coromantees who resented their enslavement more than any other tribe.

41

The Ashanti planned to set up one of their own people, a slave by the name of Cuffy, as king of the island. At the appointed time they were to sound conch shells as trumpets and light the canes, thus giving the signal for the uprising. They were to kill all their masters and to take possession of the most beautiful of the white women.

But the conspiracy was betrayed by a slave woman to her master, Judge Hall, who promptly informed the Governor, Sir Jonathan Atkins, of the impending outbreak. While the woman was later given her freedom, immediate action was taken against the ring-leaders of the planned uprising. Seventeen of them were executed, six of them being burnt alive and eleven beheaded. Their bodies were dragged through the streets as a warning to other conspirators, more of whom were later executed.[20]

Mass Emigration

In the meantime, the character of Barbadian society was undergoing a far-reaching transformation. Thousands of whites who saw no future for themselves in the island began to emigrate to other parts of the world where they sought to rebuild their fortunes.

There were several categories of people who left Barbados at this time. Among these were some of the bigger planters who were not successful in the new enterprise of growing sugar. They set out from the island, some with white indentured servants, others with black slaves among their possessions. If their labour force was white they headed for a place like Carolina in North America; if it was black, they emigrated to countries like Surinam. In both Jamaica and Surinam there was a great deal of fertile land. The landless freedmen headed for Jamaica, the more substantial farmers for Surinam.[21]

But the overwhelming majority of the emigrants were landless freedmen and small farmers. These saw no hope of procuring or retaining property in Barbados now that the indentured system was not being actively operated and land was no longer available for those who had completed their term of servitude.

The exodus of white Barbadians was not so much a continuous movement as a series of waves or cycles that occurred from time to time within a definite period. This lasted for about thirty years, from 1650 to 1680, and during that period some thirty thousand whites left Barbados to seek their fortunes overseas.

The first large wave of emigration carried the Barbadians to the neighbouring Dutch and French islands, to territories in the British Caribbean and to the English colonies on the North American mainland. Other waves were to follow, taking the emigrants in greater numbers to various parts of the New World where their experience as colonisers and their agricultural skills helped them to plant new settlements or to strengthen those already established.[22]

Barbadian whites joined the forces of Penn and Venables on their expedition to capture Hispaniola and, when this failed, they proceeded to Jamaica and helped to take possession of that island for the British. In St. Lucia they established a settlement, but this never flourished and after a time it was exterminated by the Indians of that island. In the Leeward Islands, such as Antigua and St. Kitts, they helped to rebuild the economy which had been severely damaged, if not wrecked, by the ravages of the war between the English and the Dutch.

The emigrants went in larger numbers to Surinam where they assisted in establishing a new colony in that territory. From Surinam, which they used as an advanced training station, they sent out experienced colonists who played an invaluable part in the first settlement of Carolina. In other continental colonies such as New York, Virginia and New England, the Barbadians sought to escape from the gloomy future which their own country seemed to offer them. Among those settling in New York was Richard Morris who bought a property that later was known as the manor of Morrisania. His son became Chief Justice of New York, his grandson Governor of Pennsylvania, while his two great grandsons attained eminence during the American and French Revolutions.[23]

Not the least celebrated of the indentured servants who came to Barbados was Henry Morgan, who was later knighted and appointed Lieutenant Governor of Jamaica. After experiencing the asperities of the indentured system, Morgan escaped from Barbados and began his career as a buccaneer. There is reason to believe that a number of the Barbadians who emigrated from the island joined Morgan at Port Royal and followed him in his bloodthirsty enterprises in the Caribbean and on the Spanish Main.

The year 1682 saw the last great wave of emigration from the island and the redundant section of the white population had by then disappeared. Two years later a census revealed that the total white population of Barbados numbered 19,861 and of these only 2,381 were indentured servants. The black slaves now outnumbered the white servants by thirty to one.[24]

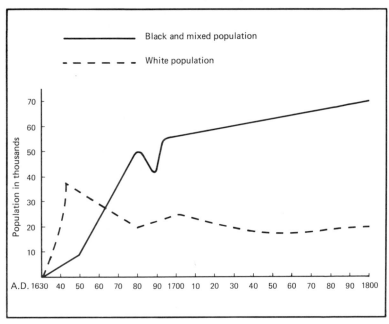

Population of Barbados, 1630-1800

A Changed Society

The early settlers in Barbados had established a society of a distinct pattern. Its main characteristic was provided by the small farmer, cultivating tobacco and a number of other crops, with the help of a few indentured servants who looked forward to the time when they themselves would become owners of land. But this condition of things now belonged to a vanished era.

A peasant economy had been changed to a plantation system. The thousands of small farmers, who once owned a substantial portion of the island's arable acreage, were now replaced by a few hundred planters who could afford to purchase the machinery and equipment necessary for the development of the sugar industry.

A diversified economy, resting on the growth of several crops, was changed to a system of monoculture which gave its attention exclusively, or almost exclusively, to the cultivation of sugar. The many small holdings, which guaranteed the social stability of the island, were swallowed up by wealthy capitalists who transformed them into virtually one sugar plantation. [25]

Along with the yeomen farmers had gone the white indentured servants. The latter could not be attracted to an island where land was no longer available for distribution under the indentured system. In any case, they were far less efficient than the African slaves, many of whom were more accustomed than the white servants to working in the plantation under a hot tropical sun. Moreover, the money needed to purchase a white servant for ten years could buy an African for life.

Formerly a virile community, where land was widely distributed, it was now controlled by a plantocracy under which wealth accumulated and men decayed. Once a politically healthy island, which enjoyed a measure of representative government, it was now an Oligarthy which dominated the life of the country. A seemingly homogeneous society, consisting of English, Scots and Irishmen, was changed into a colony in which a small number of Europeans tried to hold down a mass of discontented African slaves. It is not surprising that the uprising of 1675 was followed by others in 1696 and 1702, which were frustrated by measures of stern repression.

Clearly, sugar had effected a revolution in the Barbadian society, transforming it beyond recognition from what the pioneers had established in the early years of the settlement.

Questions and Exercises to Consider

1. In what ways was the Barbadian society affected by the sugar revolution?
2. Arrange a class discussion on significant characters. Is the planter kind or cruel, are the slaves docile or rebellious, how do they communicate since they come from different parts of Africa?
3. Arrange a project on one or more aspects of the sugar revolution. The following ideas are suggested for the writing of short reports.
   (a) Virginia tobacco.
   (b) The labourers who worked on the tobacco farms.
   (c) The help given by the Dutch in the change from tobacco to sugar.
   (d) The labourers on the sugar plantations.

(e) Who owned the tobacco farms?

(f) Who owned the sugar plantations?

4. Draw a map showing Virginia and the West Indies, indicating clearly where Barbados is.

5. Is sugar as vital to Barbados today as it was then?

6. The children of the English settlers born in Barbados were creoles. So were the children of the slaves born in the island. What do we mean by the process of creolisation? How far has this helped to produce the 'Bajan' of modern times? What progress are we making towards a homogeneous society?

7. What can you deduce from the population chart (p.44)? Give a list of reasons why there was a rapid growth of the white population in the early years, then a steady decline with a rapid increase in the black population.

8. Draw a larger population chart, bringing it as far as possible up-to-date, showing the proportion of the whites to the black and coloured sections of the population. Look up the latest census for your material.

9. Visit Kendal plantation and make a rough plan of the buildings and the lay-out of the land. Using Ligon's description as a source, compare it with the original plantation in the seventeenth century.

CHAPTER FIVE

The Island Fortress

International Rivalry

From the time Christopher Columbus made his first landfall in the New World on October 12th, 1492, he brought the Caribbean lands into the field of international rivalry. These lands entered on the stage of world affairs and became for a long period of time the centre of the struggle for global power. Columbus claimed to have succeeded in the long quest for the riches of the Indies and this threatened to rekindle the dangerous rivalry that had existed until recently between Spain and Portugal. A perilous situation was averted in 1494 when the Treaty of Tordesillas settled the rival claims of the Spaniards and the Portuguese in that age of discovery. By this Treaty, a line of demarcation was set, running north and south 370 leagues to the West of the Cape Verde Island, and Spain and Portugal accepted it as the boundary between their respective claims. [1]

The agreement, based on the decrees of Pope Alexander VI, brought peace and stability to the Caribbean for many years. The Spaniards failed in their dream of finding untold riches in the gold mines of Española and soon left for the mainland where they eventually built their vast empire. But neither the decrees of the Pope nor the provisions of the Treaty of Tordesillas could tie the hands of other European peoples like the Dutch, the English and the French, who soon began to challenge Spain's monopoly of the New World. It was the Dutch who offered the most serious challenge to that monopoly. They aimed at subjecting the Spanish colonies to "a sustained attack in force upon a scale such as they had never suffered before". [2] Their capture of Bahia in Brazil in May 1624 was to have far-reaching consequences. Among other things it gave the English and the French the opportunity to plant permanent settlements in the islands.

While the English and French proceeded to establish colonies in the Eastern Caribbean, the Dutch continued to aim at the virtual monopoly of the maritime trade of the world. For a time all went well, but as the new colonies grew prosperous, it became obvious that they owed their flourishing condition to the trading and financial conditions they enjoyed with the Dutch. And in no colony was this more the case than in Barbados. In these circumstances the English Government decided to demand the trade over which the Dutch enjoyed almost exclusive control. The Navigation Act was passed in 1651 and the Dutch were prohibited from trading with the English islands. This led to the first of a series of bitterly contested wars between the English and the Dutch, during which attacks were launched on almost every settlement in the Caribbean.

The pattern of trading that developed after the Navigation Act came to be known as the mercantile system. On paper, it appeared fair enough. It was a monopoly system which was designed to confer benefits both on the Mother Country and her colonies. But the Barbadians strongly resented it for two reasons. First, it was imposed by an Imperial Parliament over which they had no direct control. And secondly, it banned their trade with the Dutch which had brought them a great deal of their prosperity right up to the year in which the Navigation Act was passed. These and other reasons, which have been mentioned in an earlier chapter, explain why the island came out in open defiance of Cromwell's regime.

By the end of the seventeenth century, the Dutch lost the power and influence they had once enjoyed and their old enterprises in the Caribbean were checked or stifled. With their virtual eclipse, the centre of the stage was occupied during the eighteenth century by the English and the French who were locked in a struggle for supremacy in such far-flung areas as India, North America and the Caribbean. The latter became involved in the contest for a number of reasons. The Dutch Admiral De Ruyter, the finest seaman of his day, had devised the tactic that an attack on the Caribbean colonies was an important naval diversion when the Great Powers were engaged in other theatres of war. Secondly, the islands enjoyed a prosperous trade which attracted the dominant nations of Europe. And thirdly, when the islands were captured they were useful as bargaining counters when treaties were being negotiated.

The Militia

In all the vicissitudes that affected the other colonies, Barbados was proud of the fact that it never changed hands during the many struggles for supremacy in the Caribbean. This was largely due to the position it gradually assumed as an island fortress. Yet it always reserved the right to be critical when imperial interests seemed to be regarded as more important than the interests of the island. For this reason there arose frequent occasions of conflict between the Governor and his Council on the one hand and the Assembly on the other.

Almost from the beginning of its history, Barbados provided itself with a militia both for internal security and to protect itself from the dangers of foreign attack. At that time it was from the yeoman farmers that the members of this force were mainly recruited. But when this class of Barbadians virtually disappeared from the scene, it became more difficult to keep the militia up to strength at the very time when it was most needed to preserve the tranquility of the island.

Late in 1652 it was decided to establish a regiment of cavalry and every planter who owned a hundred acres of land or more was required to provide one member for the militia and a well-equipped horse. This action was taken by the island's parliament on the ground that such a force was necessary and would function on terrain that was "open and Champaigne" owing to the manner in which the land had been cultivated. [3]

The maintenance of a militia as a real and effective force was a matter that was commended to the attention of the House of Assembly by one Governor after another. Every male inhabitant between the age of eighteen and fifty-five years was required to serve on the militia. But the proviso was added that such male inhabitants should possess five or more acres of land, should have an income of twenty pounds per annum or occupy a house at a rent of twenty pounds a year. Those who served on the militia were required to provide themselves with the necessary equipment. In due course, free coloured men, along with whites, who had the required qualifications, were obliged to serve on the militia and the age range was increased from sixteen to sixty years. [4]

The militia was made up of eleven regiments and at times numbered more than a thousand men. Its senior officers consisted of a number of colonels and lieutenant-colonels as well as majors, captains and lieutenants. When an enemy fleet was reported in or around Barbadian waters, martial law could be declared and the militia mobilised for the defence of the island. The importance of this force was constantly stressed by the

British Government, yet this did not obviate spirited and protracted debates in the Assembly whenever amendments to the Militia Act were proposed. [5]

The Imperial Forces

The militia was not the only defence force at the disposal of Barbados. In addition, there were the Imperial forces that were sent out from Britain and quartered in the island from time to time.

If we omit Ayscue's troops, which came to Barbados as enemies, the first Imperial forces that came as friends arrived in 1655. Sixty ships, carrying four thousand soldiers, visited the island and were billeted on the Barbadians for a short period of time. They were commanded by Penn and Venables, who used Barbados as a port of call and a recruiting ground for the expedition first against Hispaniola, which was a fiasco, and then against Jamaica, where it was successful.

Twelve years later, a regiment of British soldiers under the command of Sir Tobias Bridges came to Barbados and were quartered on the inhabitants. During its time here, it set out to Nevis to defend it against the French, returning after six months for another short stay in Barbados. The Governor of the time, William Lord Willoughby, expressed the view to the British Government that the troops "set an example of good conduct" to the planters and advised that a permanent garrison be established in Barbados. The regiment was kept in Barbados, the cost of its maintenance being met from part of the 4½ per cent duty, but it was disbanded in 1671. [6]

Twenty-one years were to pass before Barbados was again used as a base for the operation of British troops in the neighbouring islands. In 1692, when British soldiers were in action in the Leeward Islands, some two to three hundred men, who were sent out from England to strengthen the forces in the area, were billeted on the Barbadians in the manner to which they were now growing accustomed. And the following year, when the British launched an attack on the French island of Martinique, a number of troops who took part in the expedition were stationed in Barbados for about a month.

In these circumstances, the Legislature of Barbados was moved to petition the British Government for a permanent garrison to be established in the island. As a result, during the administration of Colonel Francis Russel as Governor, the soldiers under his command were established as a garrison, though this only lasted until 1696 when, after his death, it was disbanded.

Barbados continued to be used as an advance station for the operations of the British in their military ventures against the French. For two months during the end of 1702 and the beginning of 1703, four regiments were billeted on the Barbadians and from this base they were able to launch their attacks on the French at various points throughout the West Indies.

This does not represent all the occasions when British troops were quartered on the inhabitants of the island. For some time in the eighteenth century Barbados continued to provide temporary accommodation for British troops until it was finally decided in 1780 to station a permanent garrison in the island. Indeed, throughout that century Britain was almost constantly at war with the French. During thirty-eight years of intermittent warfare, expedition after expedition was sent against the French in the West Indies and the commanders of those expeditions never failed to make Barbados their chief port of call and rendezvous.[7]

Accommodation in the island, on the plantations and elsewhere, was not the only form of assistance given by the Barbadians. Volunteers enlisted for service with some of the expeditions, food supplies were provided and slaves were made available for the removal of artillery and for fatigue work in general. Clearly the patriotic exertions of the island were of quite substantial assistance to the British in their wars against the French.

One of the outstanding services rendered by Barbados during this long and troubled period was the part it played in the capture of Martinique by the celebrated Admiral Rodney in 1762. The Barbadians provided 588 men for active service and 583 slaves who served as a labour battalion. This contingent, which formed part of Rodney's expeditionary force, was commanded by a Barbadian, Sir John Yeamans. The cost of raising and equipping the contingent was £24,000 and this was met by the island, though £10,000 was subsequently repaid by the British Government. For this contribution to his victory, Barbados was suitably thanked by Rodney in a letter which is preserved in the minutes of the House of Assembly.[8]

De Ruyter Defeated

From the earliest days, Barbados was recognised as strategically the most important of the Leeward and Windward Islands. Occupying the most easterly position of the archipelago, it was considered as the most prominent base whether for defence or attack. The legislature of Barbados was frequently addressed by the Governors of the day on this subject and steps were taken from time to time to make Barbados an island fortress.

By 1650 Barbados was already furnished with considerable defences. These consisted of trenches and ramparts which were established along the sea coast, while further inland there were three forts, one of which was used for storing ammunition and the other two provided an inner means of defence to which the island's defenders could retreat if they were hard pressed by an invading enemy. [9]

Further measures were taken at the insistence of the Governor, Francis Lord Willoughby, to strengthen the defences of the island. The value of these measures was demonstrated when England, under Charles II, declared war against Holland. Soon after the declaration, the redoubtable Dutch Admiral De Ruyter set out on a naval rampage. The tactic, as mentioned above, was to weaken and spread out England's defences by attacking her far-flung possessions.

The expedition led by De Ruyter consisted of twelve ships of the line, a number of smaller vessels and 2,500 troops. First, it destroyed the English settlements on the African coast and then proceeded on its way to the West Indies. When De Ruyter approached Barbados, he encountered some thirty merchant ships and wrought havoc by running most of them on to the shore.

On April 30th, 1665, the expeditionary force entered Carlisle Bay, resolved to do all the damage it could with its destructive power. But the island's defenders were prepared to give it a hot reception. The merchant ships in the harbour were brought close to land and, when De Ruyter drew near to attack them, he was fired on by the shore batteries protecting the bay. His flagship, the Mirror, was hit with a direct shot and he was unable to effect the landing he had planned. Recognising the futility of his attempt at invasion, he withdrew his expeditionary force from Carlisle Bay. [10] The Barbadians had reason to be satisfied with their performance on this occasion.

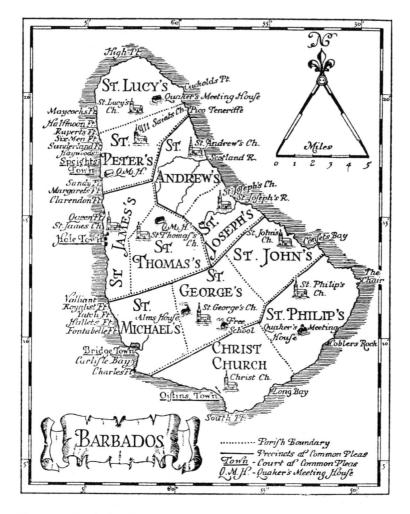

The Forts of Barbados (from *A History of Barbados, 1625-85*, V. T. Harlow)

After this encounter with De Ruyter, Barbados lost little time in further strengthening its defences. Bridgetown was made almost impregnable with the forts and batteries set up along the road facing the sea. There was Charles' Fort with as many as forty guns, while on the other side of Carlisle Bay was James' Fort with twenty guns. In addition, there was Willoughby's Fort with a formidable armament of forty guns and nearby was another fort with ten guns. On an eminence overlooking the town was Britton's Fort with twenty-five guns. The west coast of the island

St. Anne's Fort today

was defended by a battery of thirteen guns at Holetown, a battery of thirteen guns at Reid's Bay and another of twenty-five guns at Speightstown. Stone breastworks were erected in the open spaces between these batteries to prevent an enemy from using them as landing places.[11]

The wars against the Dutch were followed by the wars with France and steps were taken to further strengthen the fortifications of the island. These soon amounted to a total of twenty-two forts and batteries equipped with two hundred and eighty guns. The intervening spaces between these strong points were linked with parapets, lines and ditches. Even such homely weapons as prickly thorns and irritating pimploes were used to render the ditches more unwelcome to the intruder.

The construction of St.Anne's Fort was commenced about two years after the outbreak of war in 1702 and this was mainly due to the initiative of the Governor, Sir Bevil Granville. Some thirty years later, Barbados was reported to have twenty-two castles and forts, twenty-six batteries of 463 guns and a militia of over four thousand, consisting of cavalry and infantry.[12]

It is not surprising that, with such armaments, Barbados was never invaded and occupied by an enemy. Sir George Ayscue's forces, it is true, succeeded in reducing the island to submission in 1652 but this was after a seige of three months and after the Barbadians had negotiated the Articles of Agreement.

The Military Establishment

After the installation of British troops as a permanent garrison, Barbados assumed more and more the character of a military establishment.

St. Anne's Castle was never completed, yet it was to prove the nucleus of an impressive military encampment. The first barrack was built of massive walls and was situated near the Castle. It was designed to withstand not only military assault but the ravages of any hurricane. The cost was borne by the Government of Barbados, which was later re-imbursed by the British Government. Within a few decades, the latter purchased a considerable acreage of land nearby. Thereon they established a parade ground, now known as the Garrison Savannah, and constructed the barracks that can still be seen around the Savannah, and a hospital that once occupied the apartments known to-day as Pavilion Court.[13]

Parade on the Garrison Savannah

For some time the area was an insalubrious one and give rise to a high mortality rate among the officers and men of the garrison. The parade ground, however, was later drained of stagnant water, the holes that harboured innumerable crabs were filled in and the whole Savannah levelled to such an extent that it became one of the best sites of its kind in the West Indies. The man who transformed "Crab Town", as it was formerly known, into what it is to-day was Stapleton Lord Combermere who enjoyed the resounding title of Captain General and Governor-in-Chief of Barbados and Commander of the Forces Stationed on the Windward and Leeward Islands.[14]

In the meantime Barbados had become the headquarters of the British forces on these islands. The Lieutenant-General, who directly commanded the forces, resided in Barbados and the troops under him numbered four thousand. He lived in spacious quarters provided in Queen's Park and his residence was known as Queen's House. The soldiers under his command were stationed at St. Anne's Fort and the barracks around the Garrison Savannah. The citadel at St. Anne's provided magazines which stored arms and ammunition for the Imperial troops.

Barbados Museum, originally part of the Garrison Savannah barracks

St. Anne's Fort served as the focal point in the military establishment in Barbados. Communication with important points all over the island was provided by signal stations at such places as Charles Fort, Highgate, Dover Fort, Gunhill, Moncrieffe, Cotton Tower, Granade Hall and Queen's House. The signals conveyed by these stations were used for various purposes such as summoning members to meetings of the Council, giving information about the arrival of merchant ships or sounding the alarm in case of a slave insurrection or a threat of foreign invasion.[15]

Except for a small annual grant paid by Barbados for the benefits it received from the signal stations, the entire expenses for the upkeep of the Imperial troops were met by the British Government. For many years the military works at St. Anne's, the military residences around the Savannah, the Lt.-General's residence at Queen's Park and the signal stations in various parts of the island were maintained at Britain's expense and during most of that period the average total cost of this was £80,000 per annum. This was an addition to its revenue that Barbados enjoyed until the first decade of the twentieth century when the troops were withdrawn from the island.

Early in the nineteenth century Barbados, which took some pride in being called Little England and did not mind being considered more English than the English, seemed greatly worried over Napoleon's threat to invade England. As in the case of the Dutch Admiral De Ruyter, Napoleon's plans to weaken England included a diversionary tactic to attack her overseas possessions. Accordingly, the French Admiral Villeneuve was sent to the West Indies with a fleet of eighteen ships.

Measures were at once taken to defend the Leeward and Windward Islands but the authorities in Barbados realised that the British naval forces in the area were inadequate for the defence of the islands and that Barbados, in spite of the Imperial troops and its militia, was no longer the impregnable island fortress it had been in earlier years.

The Barbadians were therefore greatly relieved when Horatio Nelson sailed into Carlisle Bay with eleven battleships and seven smaller vessels. The celebrated English Admiral did not tarry long but left for Trinidad shortly after on receiving inaccurate information about Villeneuve's whereabouts. It is interesting to speculate that, had Nelson proceeded north to Antigua instead of south to Trinidad, he probably would have caught up with the French Admiral before he departed for Europe. In that case, one of the decisive battles of the world might well have been fought not off Cape Trafalgar but in West Indian waters.[16]

The fact that Nelson was killed in that battle seemed to make a profound impression on the Barbadians. The victory at Trafalgar was celebrated with great joy but the death of the British hero was deeply mourned. A fund was started to erect a statue to his memory and within a few weeks over £2,300 was subscribed for that purpose.

So great was the enthusiasm of the Barbadians that it was subsequently recorded that the statue, erected in Bridgetown in 1813, was the first to be raised to Nelson's memory. Actually, it was the third, the first being erected in Montreal, Canada, and the second in Birmingham, England; but it did precede the Nelson Column which was erected in London twenty-seven years after the construction of the Barbados monument.[17]

By Whose Authority?

In the realm of defence and offence there were three areas in which the House of Assembly exercised a growing influence and

Nelson's Statue, Trafalgar Square, Bridgetown

authority: the organisation of the militia, the building of fortifications and the fitting out of expeditions to the neighbouring islands.

From the earliest years the Governors of the various colonies had been given the authority to organise militias to deal with such emergencies as slave insurrections and foreign invasions. The Assemblies at first had no share in the organisation of such military units. But Barbados did not accept orders from the Governor and his Council with alacrity and quite clearly regarded the actions of the Executive in this respect as arbitrary and tyrannical. Before long, therefore, in the interest of the proper organisation of its defences, the island's Assembly was given the right to pass laws to regulate its militia.[18]

The laws thus passed laid down who was to serve on the militia, how many regiments were to be organised, what uniform and equipment those recruited were to provide for themselves and where and how often the militia men were to turn out for training. Those who were absent from parades, neglected their equipment or disobeyed orders were punished in the manner prescribed by the law of the land.

In the matter of fortifications the Assembly also insisted that Barbados should be protected from any arbitrary acts of the Governor and his Executive Council.

A law passed by the Legislature made the island responsible for the administration of its defences. It required all planters to send a quota of their slaves, appropriately furnished with tools and food, to work on the fortifications. It was laid down how many slaves were to be sent and for how long a period of time they were to work. And if any landowner had too few slaves to be able to spare any, he was required to make financial contributions to the task of fortifying the island. Committees appointed for the purpose in the various sections into which the island was divided, were given the authority to collect the slaves and the money prescribed by law and were entirely responsible for the defensive works of their own divisions.[19]

Some of the Governors objected to this invasion on their sphere of authority. Sir Thomas Robinson, for instance, complained to the Board of Trade in Britain that the islanders regarded it as their province and not the Governor's to order what repairs were to be done to the fortifications. Moreover they threatened, by virtue of a power vested in them by the law of the land, to refuse obedience if the Governor should be so ill-advised as to issue any such orders himself. The Board of Trade gave no aid or support to such Governors and advised, instead, that some way should be found to work harmoniously with the islanders.[20]

Whatever executive authority the Governor and his Council originally had, in the conduct and management of fortifications, had now passed to special committees which were under the control of the Legislature and more particularly of the House of Assembly.[21]

The same trend was clearly evident in other departments of the island's defence services.

If an expedition was to be sent to any of the neighbouring islands, if vessels were to be prepared for the pursuit of enemy craft, or if defence works of a special character were to be constructed, the island insisted that all such undertakings were to be managed by special committees in which its representatives exercised an effective control.

Barbados was agreeable and co-operative, for instance, when it was suggested that an expedition should be sent to Tobago in 1672 and another one to the Leeward Island in 1691. But the Governors, William Lord Willoughby and James Kendall, were told quite plainly that the detailed plans for these expeditions must be entrusted to joint committees drawn from both Houses of the Legislature.

In vain did a Governor like James Cunninghame protest to the Board of Trade in 1780 against this surrender of his "essential rights" in these matters. The Board merely replied by asking him not to interfere with a practice already long established and to seek the co-operation of the Legislature instead of raising controversial issues at a time when the colonies were faced already with a critical state of affairs during Britain's war against the French.[22]

In spite of the frequent controversies between the Governors and the Assembly however, there were two things that the Imperial troops and the local militia held in common. Barbados, though sturdily independent in spirit, was still British to the core and shared the determination of the Imperial Government to keep the island free from foreign domination. And the Imperial troops were as anxious as the militia to keep the island free from slave insurrections, or any threats to the peace and internal security of the island. Thus the Imperial forces and the local militia were closely linked together by common interests. This we shall see later in the measures taken to suppress the Insurrection of 1816 and the Confederation Riot of 1876.

It was a happy omen for the future when the House of Assembly was asked in August 1650 to join in providing for the defence of the island against the threatened invasion by the forces of the English Parliament.[2 3] From that time a pattern was set and a trend established by which the islanders gradually assumed more and more control of their defences. Barbados may have been an almost impregnable island fortress, especially in its earlier years, but the islanders endeavoured at all times, in building their defences, to preserve their freedom from arbitrary and tyrannical acts on the part of the Governor and his Executive Council.

Questions and Exercises to Consider

1. If you were a Barbadian living at this time what would you feel about the Navigation Act of 1651, the mercantile system and the banning of the island's trade with the Dutch?
2. Go on a field trip to one of the forts in the island and reconstruct in your imagination how it must have looked in the earlier years.
3. Draw a plan of St. Anne's Fort, including as much as you can of the military establishment that adjoined it around the Garrison Savannah.
4. Write sentences explaining the meaning of the words "tyrannical", "arbitrary" and "prerogative".
5. In what ways did the Dutch deserve the gratitude of Barbados in the early years after its settlement?
6. Compare the sentiments of the Barbadians in 1813 and those of the present day in regard to the statue of Nelson in Trafalgar Square, Bridgetown. Arrange a debate on the question whether the statue should be removed from its present position.

CHAPTER SIX

The Slave Society

Prosperity and Decline

In 1651 Barbados was said to be the most flourishing island in the British West Indies and during the following decade it enjoyed the Golden Age of its prosperity. The reasons for this thriving condition have already been indicated in an earlier chapter. White indentured servants were still plentiful and African slaves were being imported in steadily increasing numbers. Improved methods of cultivation were employed, the production of sugar increased more than fourfold and the price of that commodity remained at a consistently high level.

Out of these circumstances emerged the planters who made their way to the forefront of the island's affairs mainly at the expense of the yeoman farmers. The pattern of the Barbadian economy suited them well and they took the opportunity to establish themselves in the economic and political life of the colony. The phrase to be "as wealthy as a West Indian planter" may well have owed its origin to the affluence of the Barbadian planter aristocrat.

The 'Golden Age', however, did not last more than a decade.[1] The period of great prosperity was followed by one of decline. A host of evils came upon the inhabitants of Barbados. When the woods were cleared, the cultivated fields were attacked by monkeys and raccoons. The canes were gnawed by rats which had come across the Atlantic as unsuspected passengers on board the English ships. To cope with the rats, canefields were set on fire, but these fires frequently spread when strong winds arose and fanned them out of the control of the planters. And the practice of burning the canes was imitated by the slaves when they wanted to give expression to their bitter resentment against their enslaved condition.

Moreover, the Barbadian soil began to show signs of exhaustion. The land had grown much poorer and produced much less sugar. A strange kind of caterpillar came upon the scene "like the locusts of Egypt" and devoured everything that

63

chanced to come its way.[2] A fire which broke out in 1666 destroyed Bridgetown and this was followed two years later by a drought which was accompanied by one of those epidemics that raged in the island during the latter part of the seventeenth century. Such epidemics, not always clearly identified, were of smallpox, or yellow fever, typhoid, dysentery or elephantrasis.[3]

When this calamitous decade ended, Barbados, with remarkable resilience, seemed about to return to its normal condition. But its efforts to regain a measure of prosperity were frustrated by the renewed conflict between the British and the Dutch who succeeded on one occasion in capturing the whole fleet of ships transporting Barbados sugar to its overseas market.

Nor was this the end of the troubles. In 1675 the island was visited by a disastrous hurricane and few things seemed to survive the ravages of that tempest. In some areas of the island all the sugar works and dwelling-houses were destroyed and few, if any, of the windmills escaped the fury of the high winds. Canes were flattened by the force of the hurricane and some were uprooted from the ground as if by some malignant giant. The pots in the curing houses were all smashed to bits and vessels in Carlisle Bay were driven on to the shore by the gales of the storm. Slaves were diverted to the task of rebuilding the shattered houses and, as a result, the damage to crops of 1675 was followed by total lack of a crop the next year, owing to the lack of an adequate labour force to cultivate the land.[4]

The Plantocrats

In the circumstances described above, it is not surprising that a number of planters emigrated with all their belongings to seek their fortunes anew in other parts of the world. It was only the wealthier planters who survived to enjoy a period of prosperity that started in 1677 and lasted for some years.

The planters and their labour force set to work with remarkable energy and soon it was reported by Governor Atkins that "there is not a foot of land in Barbados that is not employed even to the very seaside".[5] But prosperity was soon again followed by adversity. The price of sugar fell from £4 to £1 for a hundred pounds. This was bad enough, but the situation was made almost intolerable by the ever-pressing burden of the 4½ per cent export duty. To this was added the problems of heavy customs duties imposed on West Indian sugar in England and the

Navigation Acts that terminated free trade with the Dutch and subjected Barbados to the tender mercies of the English merchants. It was a crushing combination and one planter was moved to ask the plaintive question: "What have we done, or wherein have we offended, that we should be used in this manner?"[6]

Thus Barbados continued on its way, with prosperity followed by hard times, with war and the uncertainties it brought and with the Mother Country adhering to a policy that considered her welfare above that of the island. The planters clung tenaciously to their position and their representatives on the Assembly came into frequent conflict with Governors who sought to promote imperial rather than local interests.

The instrument the planters used to protect themselves against the Imperial Government was the House of Assembly. Persons eligible to vote or hold elective office were required to be Christians and British Subjects, owners of at least ten acres of land or proprietors of a house with a taxable value of £10 per annum. In this way, the poorest whites were excluded from the privilege of voting for a representative in the Assembly or of standing themselves for election as such a representative.[7] With the small farmers rapidly disappearing from the island the planters soon gained control of the Assembly. They set themselves up as a planter aristocracy which came to be known as a plantocracy.

Share of Property and Office
(From Census of 1680)

	Big Planters (more than 60 slaves)	Other landholders	Bridgetown house-holders
Number	175	2,417	405
Acres	46,775	40,804	
Servants	1,032	883	402
Slaves	20,289	17,054	1,439
Councillors	10	2	
Assembly men	20	2	
Judges	19	4	
Colonels of Militia	8	0	
Lt. Colonels	6	1	

The issue that brought a memorable clash between the Governor, Francis Lord Willoughby, and the House of Assembly was the 4½ per cent export duty which was imposed on the island's produce in 1663. This duty was to remain in force for one hundred and seventy-five years (until the abolition of slavery) and was to prove a frequent source of conflict between Barbados and the British Government.

It is true that the planters looked forward to the end of the proprietary system. For more than three decades they had resented the fact that they were merely "tenants at will" and that they were under the control and direction of the proprietor of the island. They had long wanted all "proprietary rights, dues and acknowledgements" cancelled and all title deeds to be held as good "in spite of existing defects".[8] The complaints had been in the past that the proprietor, the Earl of Carlisle, and his successors collaborated closely with the British Government to divert the trade of the island to channels that brought advantages to him and that the merchants of London, not the planters of Barbados, benefited from this diversion.[9]

After the death of the first Earl of Carlisle, the rights given to him and his successors over the Caribbee Islands gradually fell into decay. There were several reasons for this. First, there were quarrels among Carlisle's successors. Secondly, the Cavaliers, who sought refuge in Barbados during the English Civil War or were sent out to the island as indentured servants, promoted strong Royalist sentiment in the island. Thirdly, sugar and the economic revolution that followed gave the planters wealth and power and this produced a growing defiance of Cromwell's England and her military resources. And finally, the planters were determined after the Restoration of the Stuarts, in 1660, to resist any attempt to re-establish the old proprietary rights or to revive the regulations under which the island's produce was shipped exclusively to England.

The proprietary system lasted thirty-six years and the planters welcomed its passing because it was "harsh and unsympathetic, greedy and often unjust".[10] The proprietorship of the island would now be abolished and the land titles of the inhabitants would be guaranteed. In return for this, Barbados, like other islands of the Caribbean, was prepared to pay an export duty of 4½ per cent to the Crown.

Yet when the duty was first proposed to the House there was a long and bitter debate that lasted for an unprecedented period of three weeks. The Act providing for the export duty was eventually passed, the Governor making extraordinary efforts to have the will of the King implemented. But almost irreparable damage was done to his reputation in the eyes of the Assembly. For the planters expected that the proceeds from the tax would go to the defence of the island and to meet the expenses of the British officials in their midst. Great was their disappointment when the money raised from the export duty went straight into the coffers of the King.

Two years later it became necessary to replenish the island's supplies of powder, shot and cannon. The money from the 4½ per cent duty was not available for this purpose and Governor Willoughby was forced to call on the House of Assembly to grant the requisite supplies. It is significant that Samuel Farmer, who had already proved himself a hot-headed and contumacious member, was elected Speaker of the new Assembly.

With Willoughby and Farmer, both men of the same temperament, leading the opposing sides, a confrontation was inevitable. The Governor's appeal for supplies was thrust aside and the infuriated Assembly, led by Farmer, presented a petition setting out their grievances against the Governor and the Imperial Government. Farmer bluntly informed Willoughby that "it was a Petition of Right" and that the Barbados Assembly had merely "followed the Example of the Best of Parliaments". [11]

Willoughby replied by dissolving the Assembly and imprisoning the ringleaders, notably Farmer, who refused to submit to his authority. Farmer was required to appear at the next General Sessions and, until the Sessions began, he was ordered to do nothing prejudicial to the Government. Farmer's reply was that he would prefer to "be damm'd and rott" in the prison where he was than to submit to the dictate of the Governor. [12]

To deal with such a turbulent spirit seemed beyond the capacity of Willoughby who therefore hustled him off as a prisoner to England, where he was to be charged with high treason before the King. The fact that the Assembly then proceeded to elect as their Speaker John Jennings, who was even more hot-tempered and obstinate than Farmer, indicated that the members of that body remained unrepentant about the burning issue of the day.

The truth is that Barbados could not afford to pay £7,000 a year through the 4½ per cent export duty, submit to increased customs duties from England and, in addition, assume some of the financial burden for the war in the West Indies. Willoughby's efforts to enforce the authority of the King and impose arbitrary actions on the Assembly were clearly unjustified. The new Governor, William Lord Willoughby, accordingly adopted a conciliatory policy, befriending the indomitable Samuel Farmer, who accompanied him from England to Barbados, and appointing other leading figures in the opposition as members of his Council.

The Grand Manner

His efforts at conciliation did not save William Willoughby from being involved in a number of controversial matters. First, there was the awkward question as to who was to succeed his uncle as Governor. When that question was settled in his favour, another and more important issue arose. In 1670, three years after he became Governor, the House of Assembly gained the right to appoint the Colonial Treasurer. This was regarded as an invasion of the province of the Executive and in 1710 the Council took up the challenge. To win its point, the Assembly went on strike and for two years no laws were passed and no taxes raised. Eventually the Assembly won the day; the matter was referred to Queen Anne who determined the matter in their favour.

Such a development was perhaps predictable. It was intended at the beginning that the Assembly should be only a minor feature in the island's system of government. It could not be denied control over taxation since that was the cardinal principle for which the English colonies in the New World had consistently fought. But it was certainly the intention of the Imperial Government that the Governor and his Council would keep the Assembly firmly under control, with no power to interfere in executive matters.

But this was merely a pious hope on the part of those who overlooked two important factors. The first of these was that all the English colonies in the New World were resolved to follow the English precedent of parliamentary government; the second was that the Assembly in Barbados, as in other territories in the West Indies, regarded itself as the House of Commons of the island. It is significant that, from the time of Sir John Gay Alleyne, the Speaker of the Assembly at the beginning of every session claimed for its members the privileges claimed by the English Parliament:

freedom of speech, freedom from arrest and freedom of access to the Representative in the island of the British Sovereign.

Thus it was that the Assembly steadily extended its authority and influence. Its great bargaining power was that it could refuse the supplies that were essential for the running of the government. In this way it became a potent weapon in the hands of the planters whose interests were fully represented in the deliberations of the Assembly.

During this period the sugar colonies of the British West Indies were merely places of transitory residence for those who invested large-scale capital in the sugar industry. Such capital came from England which was rapidly growing in wealth and seeking places for profitable investment. Large plantations had taken the place of small holdings and the owners of these plantations looked on England as their "home". These were the absentee landlords who made all the money they could from the sugar islands and lived in England in comfort, and at times in luxury, according to the price of sugar.

Barbados seems in some respects, however, to have been the exception to the general rule in the British Caribbean.[13] While in 1645 there had been 11,200 smallholders in Barbados, in 1667 the available land was divided into large estates owned by 745 persons. Moreover, in the hundred years between 1680 and 1780 less than a hundred families owned more than half the land in the island. Yet somehow Barbados managed to escape from the excesses of unrestricted capitalism and absentee landlordism. For in 1765 it was recorded that there were 4,000 proprietors in the island and this, in striking contrast to what happened in other islands, was to have a marked influence on the life of Barbados.[14]

Barbados had now come a long way from the earlier pioneering days. An observer noted in 1658 that there was a great number of fine homes in the island and that many of these were built in the fashion favoured by the English. There was a handsome church in each of the island's parishes and Bridgetown boasted shops and storehouses which were filled with all kinds of merchandise.

The remarks by this observer were confirmed and extended by Père Labat in 1700. He saw houses built in the English style and magnificently furnished and he noted an atmosphere of cleanliness, gentility and wealth which he did not find in other islands. He observed that the shops and merchants' warehouses

Harmony Hall

were filled with goods from every part of the world. He saw goldsmiths, jewellers, clock-makers and other artificers at work and concluded that the "largest trade in America" was carried on here in Barbados.[15]

The planter aristocrats of the day lived in the grand manner. They lived, we are told, like little sovereigns on their plantations, with servants to attend to all their needs in the household and in the field. Their tables were spread with every variety of delectable dish and they served their guests with all manner of local drinks and imported wines. Their equipages and liveries, their coaches and horses, their chairs and chaises were described as "rich", "fine" and "magnificent". Their dress was reported to be fashionable and courtly, their behaviour genteel and polite and their hospitality generous and open-hearted.[16]

Nicholas Abbey and Drax Hall, built in the middle of the seventeenth century, still stand today as monuments to the style of living enjoyed by the planter aristocrats of that time. They belong to the great period of mansion building in Barbados. That period started when sugar was established as the staple crop of the island and lasted until the end of the seventeenth century. Barbados had failed to compete with the tobacco produced by Virginia which was to gain great wealth from this crop. But the island was to derive great affluence from sugar and achieved a position of prestige and importance that the mainland colony did not attain for many years.

Drax Hall and Nicholas Abbey have been described as "the finest British Colonial dwellings in America".[17] Their style of architecture is Jacobean and they are so typical of the period that they closely resemble the mansions built by the English gentry at about the same time (1650). This is scarcely surprising since the rising plantocracy of Barbados was connected with the landed gentry of England. These mansions are interesting and important for two reasons. Their architecture reflects the prosperity of the planters during the golden period of sugar. And they are the only surviving examples of the dwellings that were built during the great era of mansion building in the New World. The great house, once occupied by the Royal Governor of Virginia, was destroyed early in the nineteenth century; while the Province house in Boston, the only mansion that could be compared with its Barbadian contemporaries, suffered a similar fate in 1922.[18]

To judge from its façade, with its three "curly" gables, Nicholas Abbey was probably constructed at a slightly earlier date than Drax Hall. Both mansions were built of coral stone and covered with plaster. Nicholas Abbey is interesting not only for its façade but for its three transverse rear gables, its four chimneys and the formal garden that leads to the mansion in the style typical of the English manor of that period. The architectural interest of Drax Hall lies among other things in its gable windows, its entrance hall and the archway leading to "the great stair" which is recognised as "an excellent example of the best design of the period."[19]

Another mansion that was of the same architectural importance as Nicholas Abbey and Drax Hall was Holborn in Fontabelle Bridgetown. Once the residence of the Governor of Barbados, it was noted for its beautiful setting and its handsome approach. At the entrance was a gateway fitted with iron gates. Immediately behind the gateway were two sentry houses with gun slots in the side walls. An avenue of royal palms led to the two-storey house, with its enclosed vestibule forming the main entrance and its low arcaded galleries surmounted by battlements.[20] Unfortunately, Holborn lost its original character over the years until eventually it disappeared entirely from the scene. The domain once enclosed by walls that ramped up to the gateway at the entrance is now the site of a successful commercial concern.

There can be no doubt that economic wealth, as well as

Drax Hall

Nicholas Abbey

72

political power, were in the hands of a small group of planters who dominated the House of Assembly, controlled all the higher offices in the land and played a major part in the social life of the island.

The Social Hierarchy

By the beginning of the eighteenth century, the foundation of a slave society had been firmly established in Barbados and the island was divided into two main camps, the plantocracy and the African slaves. It has been said that the Barbadian character was formed in this century. The significant migrations of the white population during the seventeenth century had virtually come to an end. After the great shifts of the population, that had taken some 30,000 persons out of the island, the white section of the Barbadian people could be said to have been stabilised by 1715.[21] In addition, there were many Barbadian born slaves. It has been argued that this tended to transform a "plural society" into something approaching a Bajan or "homogeneous unit". But there can be no doubt that this process worked to the detriment of African cultural traditions in Barbados. It was achieved at the expense of African traditions and to the advantage of a European culture that derived much of its strength and status from the power structure controlled by a white minority group.[22]

It would be wrong to assume, however, that the plantocrats and the slaves represented the only divisions in the society, for both of them were subdivided into different social classes.

Among the whites, the owner, if he was resident, or the attorney who acted as his agent, towered above all the other classes in his group. Next in "rank" were the manager and the overseer who were followed at respectable distances by the book-keeper, the tradesman and other more humble white employees on the plantation. A wide gulf separated the great man at the top of the social scale from the poor white who was engaged in the work of the plantation or in cultivating his own smallholding.

Living off the large plantations were a number of whites who formed a small but important middle class. This group represented about 25 per cent of the white population of Barbados. They could be sub-divided into two segments according to the property they owned either in land or in slaves. In the upper segment were proprietors of estates which were less than one hundred acres in extent, clergy, lawyers, doctors, small merchants and members of the civil establishment. In the lower segment were owners of small businesses, tavern keepers, clerks, master craftsmen and, perhaps most important of all, those who owned more than ten acres of land — the "ten acre men" of whose political significance we shall read in a later chapter.[23]

Among the slaves, too, there were distinct social groups. If a slave was a skilled worker, he occupied a position of some importance among his own kind. If he came from princely or other high rank in Africa, he was accorded considerable prestige by his fellow slaves in Barbados. If his master was a man of great wealth, he enjoyed a higher social position than other slaves whose owners were men of lesser substance. Undoubtedly, there was a kind of hierarchy among the slaves. Gang drivers, skilled craftsmen and rangers were groups in an ascending order in the social scale. The class consciousness among the slaves was adopted from their European masters. This system of social stratification has been described as a major development among the slaves in the eighteenth century. The status of a slave was determined not only by his own position but by that of his master. By a process of "conferred élitism" the standing of the slave was enhanced by the personal status of his master.[24]

The lowest position in the social hierarchy of the plantation system was held by the field slave who was the least esteemed man at the bottom of the economic pyramid. Here in the nethermost regions of the society no slave could claim any distinction over his fellows. No one could rise above the rigid confines of this social class, unless he was the 'driver' of a labour gang or an expert in the art of Obeah, claiming supernatural powers.

The owner of the estate (or his attorney) lived in the Great House in almost solitary splendour and in a style befitting his pre-eminent position in the hierarchy. Nearer the factory buildings, the scene of noisy and bustling activity during the crop season, were the smaller houses of the manager and his senior assistants. And, at a considerable distance from all this, were the slave quarters.

The slaves lived in small huts made, at one time, of sticks, mud and thatch. Later, when conditions improved, they were constructed of board and shingled roofs. The huts were separated from each other by a short 'interval' to prevent the spreading of fires and each one was surrounded by a piece of land where the slaves could grow their own provisions and vegetables and raise their own livestock such as hogs and poultry. They were allowed a waistcoat, breeches and a vest of cotton or wool, but these were not distributed frequently enough to meet even their minimum requirements. Accordingly, they sold the produce of their allotments to obtain necessary extra clothing and such items as were considered luxuries by those who shared their spartan lot.[25]

The two most important factors in the successful management of an estate were a high price for sugar and an adequate labour force. If the price of sugar fell and if the number of slaves was reduced to the point of inefficiency, it could mean all the difference between prosperity and bankruptcy for a plantation.

Certainly the slaves on an estate were among its most valuable assets. An adequate supply of labour, it has been claimed, was the key to the entire sugar economy. Unfortunately, one of the problems besetting the plantation was the high mortality rate among the children of the slaves. Efforts were sometimes made to cope with this by offering a bonus of 6s. 3d to expectant mothers and a similar inducement was provided for midwives. But this was not the general practice on the plantations.

Equally disastrous for the sugar economy was the high mortality rate among the slaves themselves. There were many reasons for this. The housing conditions of the slaves were primitive and they were constantly exposed to the uncertainties and hazards of the weather. The slaves, who worked almost continuously in the field, paid a heavy price for this and were frequently ill. And those who worked long shifts, by day and night, to maintain the boiling houses, were usually so reduced in their powers of resistance that they fell victims to one or other of the epidemics that frequently afflicted the island. The death rate was particularly high among these slaves who suffered from long exposure in the field or worked arduously through the night to maintain the unceasing activities of the factory.[26]

Number of Slaves in Barbados, 1683-1753

Year	No. of Slaves
1683	46,602
1710	52,337
1724	55,206
1734	46,462
1748	47,025
1753	69,890

To meet this deadly toll on the slave population, the planters resorted to substantial importation every year. If the planters replenished their labour force every year by bringing in fresh supplies from Africa, there appeared to be no need to improve the living conditions of the slaves. There was no necessity for a programme of amelioration. All they needed to do was to replace those who had failed to survive the rigours of their seasoning period or died from over-work or poor living conditions.

Unending Toil

It may be argued that conditions on the estates were no worse than those which prevailed in other parts of the world in the eighteenth century. In England and elsewhere in Europe, the criminal code was harsh and punitive. Capital punishment was the fate of many who committed minor offences and the soldiers and sailors of leading countries of the world were flogged as unmercifully as the slaves on the sugar plantations in the West Indies. The cruelty that was practised on the estates was characteristic of a harsh and brutal age.

Yet the policy of importing more and more slaves every year to take the place of those who died, was not in the best interest of the island's sugar economy. Newly introduced slaves were usually restless and insubordinate and tended to imbue the rest of the labour force with their spirit. Moreover, when they settled down, they had to be trained in the various skills that were required on a plantation. A wise manager would train them as carpenters, coopers, masons, blacksmiths and wheelwrights, especially if they were replacements for those whose skills had been lost to the estate through premature death. Broken fences had to be mended, roofs damaged by high winds had to be rebuilt and unending attention given to the repairs and maintenance of the slave quarters, the houses of the manager and his staff and the mills and boiling houses that produced the sugar crop and prepared it for the market. In these unceasing tasks, the slaves with special skills could play an invaluable part. [27]

The slaves worked all the year round but were free on Sundays, Good Friday, Christmas, Boxing Day and other approved holidays. On some plantations they were also free on Saturday afternoons. Apart from these days, however, life on the plantation was a continuous round of labour in the blistering sun and the drenching rain.

The most arduous part of the work of the slaves began with the preparation of the land for cultivation. They toiled in the fields from dawn to dusk with a break of two hours at noon. They tilled the soil with hoes for the simple reason that the plough did not provide an even spreading of fertiliser which the land required. Then the slaves began to dig holes at intervals in the land. Some three thousand holes were dug for every acre of land and the labour involved was considered to be of the most debilitating kind. Cane cuttings from a neighbouring field were then placed in each hole and these were covered with several inches of mould. When the young shoots began to appear, mould was added and all the time the greatest care had to be taken with the clearing of the weeds and the nurturing of the suckers. [28]

In due course, the harvesting began and the slaves set about cutting the canes with cutlasses or "bills" and this work was not only strenuous but called for considerable skill. The canes had to be cut low on the stalk, where they were very tough, and the slaves had to exercise the greatest care not to damage the bud from which the "ratoons" were to spring for the following year. The canes thus harvested were then loaded on carts drawn by donkeys or oxen and later carried to the mills by the slaves themselves.

In the factory the work was not as heavy as in the field, but it called for even greater skills. When the canes arrived at the factory, they were fed into rollers which were turned by the windmill. The canes were crushed by these rollers and the juice extracted from them. The crushed canes were transported to the fields where they were dried and then returned as "megasse" which was the fuel used for the boiling process that was soon to follow.

The extracted juice and the fuel were then taken to the boiling house. There the juice was strained into "clarifiers" and the process of removing all impurities from the liquid was begun. The juice was then passed from the clarifiers into a series of copper pots which were kept constantly boiling from a fire that was fed by the megasse. All this while, the slaves had to be vigilantly at work. The fire in the open oven had to be tended day and night, the various pots had to be kept at boiling point and the impurities had to be removed from pot after pot until the process was completed.

At the end of this process, the contents of the final pot were transferred to a vat for the purpose of cooling. This cooling

A mill yard c. 1830 (Edward Suter)

Modern sugar mill

78

marked another stage of production and the sugar crystals emerged after a few days. The contents of the vat were then poured into vessels with perforated holes and these were placed on racks from which the molasses dripped into the waiting troughs below. The last thing to be produced was rum, a lucrative commodity, which was made from the waste matter left over from the preparation of the sugar and molasses. The whole process of manufacture was now completed and the sugar, along with its by-product, was ready to be shipped to the market.

Like the animals on the plantations, the slaves were regarded as property. Cattle, horses and donkeys were valuable to the sugar economy because they helped in the work of production and, moreover, fertilised the land with their manure. "Without Cattle we can't make Sugar," a planter once said, "for it is produced by dung and much labour."[29]

The slaves worked like the beasts in the field. But they had at least one distinguishing asset and this lay in the special skills they brought to the manufacture of sugar and its by-products, molasses and rum. During the eighteenth century, however, shorter working hours, lighter discipline and more humane treatment were not generally speaking regarded as economic virtues. That would appear strange to us in the twentieth century for, apart from considerations of humanity, it clearly did not make economic sense to allow highly skilled labourers to die from over-work and other circumstances and then import more than three thousand inexperienced slaves every year to take their places in the fields and the factory.

The Strains of Society

The circumstances of the slave society in the eighteenth century imposed undoubted strains on all sections of the island's population. Certainly, the plantocrats were well aware of the volcanic nature of the society. Yet they set themselves unflinchingly to the task of perpetuating their family fortunes. The economics of sugar production triumphed over whatever moral scruples they entertained about slavery. The slave system, in the words of the historian, Karl Watson, embraced and devoured them. While they loved the land and invested much of their resources in agriculture, they acquired such faults as "a tendency to stultifying conservatism and class and race arrogance".[30]

There were others, however, who reacted differently and found it difficult, after a period of education abroad, to re-adjust themselves to the melancholy conditions of a slave society. They had looked forward on their return to a tranquil existence in their native land but were sensitively aware that there were storms gathering against the prevailing régime. One of these returning Euro-creoles expressed "an invincible aversion to the system, an aversion which I never conquered". At a later date he was more emphatic in expressing his "repugnance to the system", saying that the soul reviles with horror from "the sight of surrounding objects and flies and then inevitably falls, the species debased".[31]

Such sensitivities were not shared by all the planters. Yet they were all affected by the atmosphere of fear and insecurity that prevailed in the society. In spite of the restrictions of the existing régime, there was "a viable slave culture" in the island. In their leisure time the slaves could decide how best to use their energies. Music and dancing were their favourite recreations. They would watch a cock fight at one plantation or attend a dance at another. They would gather in assemblies where they beat drums, blew horns or used other loud instruments.[32]

Most of the planters accepted these activities as harmless pastimes. They held the view that the slaves worked better the following day after diverting themselves the night before. Yet every aspect of the slave law in the British Islands, as Elsa Goveia has written, was primarily concerned with the subordination and control of the slaves.[33] And Barbados was no exception to the general rule. The early slave laws of the island, which proved difficult to enforce, sought to prevent the slaves from leaving their plantations at any time, especially Saturday nights, Sundays or "other holidays" unless they had passes from their owners. The use of drums, horns and other loud instruments were prohibited. The beating of the "Koromantin drum" was especially feared because its "terrors" threw the white inhabitants into a state of "panic".[34]

The comparative tranquillity of the island gradually made this aspect of the slave law a dead letter. Time was to show, however, that the old fears of the planters were not entirely groundless. For it was during the week-end dances, which gave them the chance to gather together, that the slaves were able to recruit supporters and plan their strategy for the great uprising that took place early in the nineteenth century.

Questions and Exercises to Consider

1. What is a land title? Get the necessary details from the Registry or the Archives and draw up an imaginary one conferring a title on a colonist in the seventeenth century.
2. What light does the 4½ per cent duty throw on the attitude of the Imperial Government towards its colonies?
3. What powers did a colonial governor have in the seventeenth century? Why did the Barbados House of Assembly show such a spirit of independence? What factors enabled the House of Assembly to frustrate the intentions of the Imperial Government?
4. What does the phrase "to slave" at anything mean? In what way did the work of a slave on a plantation justify this usage?
5. From the table on page 65 make any deductions you can about the power which property conferred on the Barbadian of 1680. In discussion, examine what might be considered the sources of power in modern Barbados.
6. What is meant by "a viable slave culture"? What activities of the slaves indicated that they had such a culture?
7. What is the meaning of the word "productivity"? Would you say that the diversions of the slaves in their leisure time would tend to increase their productivity? Is the question of work and leisure also a problem today?
8. Explain the meaning of the words "social stratification". Draw a diagram showing how the Barbadian society was divided in the eighteenth century.
9. What do you understand by such terms as the "culture" of a European, the "culture" of an African, a "plural" society and a "homogeneous" community?
10. Write a dialogue in which a field slave instructs a "green" or inexperienced slave about the work he must do on the plantation.
11. Find out about the different types of drums made in Africa. Why is a drum so much a feature of Afro-societies?
12. Pay a visit to Drax Hall and Nicholas Abbey. Find out all you can about their style of architecture and why they are regarded as the finest buildings in the British Caribbean of that time. What can you discover about other long-standing buildings such as Pilgrim (now Government House), Harmony Hall in St. Michael and Nicholl's House in Lucas Street?

CHAPTER SEVEN

The Humanitarian Movement

A Gloomy Situation

One of the most remarkable persons in Barbados during the second half of the eighteenth century was the aristocrat and radical, Sir John Gay Alleyne. Coming on the scene at a time when the ever-recurring battles between the House of Assembly on the one hand and the Governor and Council on the other hand had been virtually ended, he gave his attention to improving the methods of procedure of the Lower Chamber. As Speaker, he presided over the deliberations of the House for a period of thirty years and succeeded in making it a more effective instrument of government.

Alleyne's career derives an even greater significance from the efforts he made to arouse the social conscience that was soundly asleep in the island. He lived at a time when the old order, destined to give way to the new only in the early decades of the nineteenth century, was stoutly defended by his compeers. In this climate of opinion, he stood apart from his contemporaries. When drought afflicted the poor and distressed, he spoke with moving sympathy on their hardships and privations. When an attempt was made to increase the manumission fee on female slaves, he strongly objected on the ground that such a measure would impose an unwarranted restraint "upon the justice and gratitude" of those who owned them.[1] And at a time when the institution of slavery was strongly entrenched in the island, he would express regret over the melancholy necessity that made him an owner of slaves.

Clearly, Alleyne was an interesting combination of conflicting interests. But he went on his way, undeterred by the criticisms of his peers. He spoke on the condition of the poor whites and the free coloured people and emphasised that these represented classes in the Barbadian society who could rightly claim "the equal protection of wise and equitable laws". He declared that slavery placed an immense debt on men of his class "to clear the obligation of human nature" and looked forward to the day when the system would be consigned to the limbo of forgotten things. [2]

Certainly he was not happy about the condition of the slaves. Harsh treatment, poor rations and overwork had increased the death rate among the slaves. Epidemics of one kind or another, drought and the ravages of storm and tempest caused greater suffering and raised the slave mortality rate to an even higher level.

Nor was the spiritual condition of the slaves any less gloomy than their material situation. They clung as best they could to the basically African system of Obeah, with its magico-religious beliefs and practices, until it was banned by the laws of the island. Neglected by the Church of England, they turned to such other Christian churches as could give them attention. The Roman Catholic Church, which played a vital part in other territories, had almost ceased to function in Barbados since the seventeenth century. The Baptists, notable for their role in Jamaica and other parts of the West Indies, did not succeed in establishing themselves in Barbados during the years of slavery. The Methodists, who came to Barbados in 1788, encountered so much hostility that they had to confine their activities almost entirely to Bridgetown and had little success in reaching the slaves on the plantations.

With the Moravians, however, it was a happier story. They came to Barbados in 1765 and set up their first mission at Sharon in the parish of St. Thomas. This was followed by a second

The Sharon Moravian church

mission at Mount Tabor in St. John, while a third was established at Bridgetown in 1835. Since their moral conduct was deemed "irreproachable" and their manners "quiet and inoffensive", they managed to secure the co-operation of the planters in their missionary work among the slaves.[3]

Anglican Experiment

In face of the inactivity or indifference of the major Christian Churches, the Codrington bequest was the one bright spot in an otherwise gloomy situation. Christopher Codrington was a Barbadian planter who died in 1710, at the comparatively early age of forty-two and bequeathed his property of 800 acres and 300 slaves to the great Anglican missionary organisation known as the Society for the Propagation of the Gospel. That bequest was established as a foundation for Christianising and educating the Negro slaves.[4]

The significance of the Codrington legacy was emphasised by Bishop William Fleetwood in terms of unmistakable clarity. The Negroes, he said, when he delivered the S.P.G.'s Annual Sermon in 1711, "were equally the Workmanship of God with themselves" (the planters). They were endowed "with the same faculties and intellectual powers" and possessed "bodies of the same Flesh and Blood, and Souls certainly immortal." It has been claimed, not without justification, that by these remarks the Bishop proclaimed "the charter of liberties for the Negro race" in Barbados and in far-ranging countries of the world.

"If all the Slaves throughout America," continued the Bishop, "and every Island in these Seas, were to continue infidels for ever, *yet ours alone must needs be Christians.* We must instruct them in the Faith of Christ, bring them to Baptism, and put them in the way that leads to everlasting Life. This will be preaching by *Example,* the most effectual way of recommending Doctrines, to a hard and unbelieving World, blinded by Interest, and other Prepossessions."[5]

To people of the present century, the notion that the slaves should be converted to Christianity and educated and equipped with appropriate skills may seem to be in no way revolutionary. At a time, however, when the murder of a slave was punished only by a fine of £15, the concept entertained by the S.P.G. was regarded as radical and dangerous to the prevailing social order of Barbados. Indeed, the views of the Society and of the average

Barbadian planter were poles apart. The former looked on the slave as a person with an immortal soul. The latter viewed him as a piece of property, a chattel, a tool to be used in the economic machine of the age.

For more than a century before emancipation, the S.P.G. was engaged in promoting a humanitarian culture in the island of Barbados. During that time the Society worked within the plantation system, seeking to make money for the purpose of improving the schools on its Barbadian estates and furthering the welfare of its slaves. To the planters of the day, the Society was an instrument of radical reform and its programme a revolutionary one. To them the Codrington experiment was the first step to freedom, as indeed it was. Once it was conceded that the slave possessed an immortal soul, his emancipation would follow by a process of inescapable logic. First, the Society established the idea that the slave could be a Christian. Then, as the years went by, the more radical view was accepted that slavery was contrary to the spirit of Christianity.

It is not surprising, therefore, that the Society incurred the hostility of the planters of the island who did not share Codrington's vision and humanitarian zeal. They regarded the Codrington experiment as "a piece of Religious Knight Errantry".[6] Moreover, they were joined in their opposition to the Codrington movement by local Anglican clergymen, not a few of whom owned land and slaves and shared the views of the island's plantocracy.

It may well be regarded as a tragedy that the Non-conformist missionaries were not allowed to work in Barbados as they were in other territories of the Caribbean. In vain did men like Dr. Beilby Porteus, Bishop of London and Diocesan of the Established Church in the West Indies, attempt to inspire his clergymen with the spirit of missionary enterprise. His unquenchable zeal was not emulated. He had no effective authority over the Anglican clergy in the area and the Established Church had to wait until the nineteenth century before the necessary changes in its policy were adopted.[7]

There are many things that could be said against the missionaries by the radical spirits of a later age. They taught the slaves to accept the existing social structure and emphasised the notion of subordination to that structure. They urged the slaves, as St. Paul urged them in his day, "to obey their masters in all things, not answering again, not purloining, but showing all fidelity, as becometh Christians".[8] They preached to their black converts that they should submit to the slave system and not promote ideas of enmity against their masters. As far as they could, they suppressed all African customs and traditions that were not accepted by Christianity on the ground that such customs and traditions were relics of "heathenism".

The truth is that the missionaries worked not for a social change but for a spiritual transformation of the West Indies. They repudiated the notion that the Christian belief was "beyond the intellectual and moral capacity" of the blacks. They stressed their belief that a universal brotherhood was possible among all Christians, both black and white. They secured the assistance of blacks and whites in the work of conversion and they afforded opportunities for all their members — and this included slaves — to "rise to positions of trust and responsibility" within their churches. Thus the slaves were given their first chance in British West Indian history to participate in a form of social organisation in which they could attain a measure of social recognition and find some scope for individual talents and satisfy their desire for self-expression.[9] Thus it may be said that while they accepted the existing social order, the missionaries introduced new values in that order of society. The limited success of the S.P.G. in the eighteenth century could have been greatly enhanced if it had been strengthened by the zeal of the Nonconformist missionaries in the British Leeward Islands.

The Reform Movement

In the meantime, the great reform movement was gathering momentum in the world beyond Barbados and the West Indies. The humanitarians in Britain were pressing forward in their campaign, during the late eighteenth and early nineteenth centuries, to restrict the labour of women and children, to improve working conditions in the factories and enact liberal measures for prison reform, poor relief and popular education. With all the far-reaching victories they won, however, none was perhaps more significant than one of their earliest triumphs, the abolition of the trade that trafficked in human beings, transporting them from their native Africa to work in the plantations across the Atlantic.

The first blow in the campaign against slavery was struck by the Quakers as far back as 1671. In that year George Fox, their founder, spoke to the Quakers during a visit to Barbados and called on them to treat their slaves well and free them "after a considerable term of years".[10] Less than twenty years later, the Quakers in Pennsylvania declared that "Those who steal and rob men and those who buy or purchase them" were all alike to be censured. And at a meeting in London in 1727, they warned their members against "reaping the unrighteous profits arising from the iniquitous practice of dealing in slaves".

But the Quakers were persecuted in seventeenth century Barbados for their criticism of the local whites, for their refusal to pay for the maintenance of the Anglican clergy, for their failure to play their required part in the militia, and their attempts to Christianise the slaves after Fox's visit to the island. As a result of this persecution, they scarcely survived as an active community in the eighteenth century.[11] Thus it was that, except for the limited activities of the Moravians and the work of the S.P.G. on the two Codrington plantations, the slaves continued to languish in their condition of material and spiritual neglect.

In the outside world, however, the forces that were working for amelioration of the slaves' condition and their eventual emancipation were given an impetus from various sources during the closing decades of the eighteenth century. John Wesley attacked the slave régime in his publication *Thoughts on Slavery*. Adam Smith struck at the economic foundations of the institution when he declared in his *Wealth of Nations* that it was no longer a profitable enterprise. Tom Paine delivered a trenchant assault on the slave system in his tract, *African Slavery in America*. Bishop Warburton proclaimed from his pulpit in England that "the infamous traffic for slaves directly infringes both divine and human law". Clearly, the slave trade had become an anachronism in an age that was being activated by the spirit of the French Revolution.[12]

Perhaps the most important single event in the humanitarian movement was the success of Granville Sharp in securing the freedom of a slave, Jonathan Strong, who had been brought to England by a Barbadian planter, David Lisle. This occurred in 1765 and led Sharp to the rescue of other slaves in similar circumstances. Then in 1772 Sharp, thanks mainly to his unwearying persistence, won a great triumph. In that year, the Chief Justice of England, Lord Mansfield, declared, in the case of another slave, James Somerset, that all slaves in that country must be recognised as free men. That celebrated judgement not only amounted to the abolition of slavery in the British Isles but paved the way for its abolition throughout the British Empire some sixty years later.

Sharp was soon joined in his agitation by James Ramsay, Thomas Clarkson and other humanitarians. Undoubtedly, the greatest convert to the movement was William Wilberforce, who became its champion in the British Parliament. Year after year, Wilberforce introduced measures for the abolition of the slave trade but these were rejected at each session either by the House of Commons or the House of Lords. It was perhaps predictable that the rising tide of Liberalism in Britain was temporarily checked by the excesses of the French Revolution and the slave insurrection in St. Domingue in 1791. But that tide could not be permanently stemmed and in due course the humanitarians won a resounding victory when the slave trade was abolished by the British Parliament in 1807.

Among Wilberforce's stoutest opponents, both in and out of Parliament, was the Society of West India Planters and Merchants who fought tooth and nail against his propositions in the House of Commons. After the success of his campaign, the Society resolved to contest his seat for Yorkshire. Two opponents entered the arena, one of them being Henry Lascelles, owner of sugar plantations in Barbados, who declared he was ready to sacrifice his landed property in the tropics if, by doing so, he could unseat Wilberforce.[13] But the challenge to the champion of the abolition movement did not succeed and Wilberforce retained his seat in the House of Commons.

The Aftermath

By no one was the progress of the humanitarian movement in Britain followed more closely than by the slaves in Barbados. They gathered in small groups throughout the island to listen to those among the free coloured people who read to them about the momentous debates that were taking place in the British Parliament. They learnt of the work of the abolitionists and particularly of Wilberforce's speeches in the House of Commons and they came to regard him as the Moses who would lead them out of their captivity into the land of freedom. Not surprisingly, there was an unusual stirring among the mass of the slave population and this gave rise to no little misgiving and apprehension among the planters.

The progress of the abolitionist movement itself was regarded by the planters with growing concern and alarm. They already had a number of problems and difficulties to bewilder them. Among the calamities that afflicted them was an increase in the damage done by rats and this was followed by a plague of sugar ants. Barbados, in the words of a contemporary historian, was visited by "tribes of vermin" more destructive than "the locusts and caterpillars of old" and was "reduced to a state of comparative poverty".[14] In the midst of all these tribulations, a law was passed in 1766 allowing creditors to seize the slaves of those who owed them money and these slaves were dragged to the market place where they were sold to local planters or exported to other colonies.

Moreover, the American Revolution deprived the island of important supplies after 1775. Items such as lumber, flour and Indian corn went up double and treble the pre-war prices when the island's legal trade with New England was ended. Alternative sources in British North America could not supply cattle, lumber, staves and foodstuffs in sufficient quantities to meet the island's requirements. The planters could not benefit appropriately from the increased prices for sugar in 1776 and 1777 because they were growing less sugar at the time and more provisions. And the natural calamities, from which Barbados was already suffering, reached their peak when the hurricane of 1780 wrought almost irreparable damage to the island.[15]

Nor did the health conditions in the island help to mitigate the situation facing its inhabitants. In the decade before 1783, the slave population dropped by more than ten thousand, a decline that was attributed to the ravages of the hurricane, the outbreak of smallpox and yellow fever and the planters' inability to maintain their "stock" of slaves through importations. It may be noted that during this period the mortality rate among the British soldiers stationed in Barbados reached unprecedented heights, with 185 deaths per year per thousand, rising to a maximum of 413 per thousand in the year 1796.[16]

To counter some of the arguments of the British abolitionists, the planters of Barbados turned to the task of ameliorating the condition of the slaves. The latter were provided with increased rations of food and better supplies of clothing. And the Legislature in 1805 passed an Act repealing one of the old statutes which laid it down that the murder of a slave was punishable merely by a fine of £15. This measure, which made such a murder a capital offence, was welcomed by the Chief Justice of the island, John A. Beckles, a white Barbadian, who described it as the "repeal of an act which for a century past had been a disgrace to the code of laws."[17]

In view of the increased price of slaves and the rising costs of production, the planters directed their attention to another vital matter. In the earlier years of the slave régime, sexual irregularities and profligacy produced a number of inevitable results. There were countless still-births and miscarriages, the birthrate was low, and the number of deaths among infants was notoriously high. Since the labour force now had to be replenished by the natural increase of the slaves and not through importation, greater care was given to pregnant slaves and measures adopted to reduce the high infant mortality. These were among the most important social benefits resulting from the abolition of the slave trade.

The 1816 Insurrection

Three weeks after the abolition of the slave trade, the African Institution was formed for the main purpose of ensuring that the Act abolishing the trade was strictly enforced. It at once won the support of the British abolitionists and received generous sums of money from the leading families of England, and from poorer people in church and chapel collections, to assist in the carrying out of its ambitious programme of preventing the evasion of the abolition measure, extending a similar reform to other countries of the world and promoting the civilisation of Africa.

The African Institution kept the issue of the slave trade alive by its unremitting agitation and in due course measures were passed by the British Parliament declaring that anyone who engaged in the trade was guilty of a felony and later such an offence was deemed an act of piracy. In spite of all its efforts, however, there was little evidence to support the view that the abolition law was frequently and deliberately violated.[18] Nevertheless, the Institution managed to convince the abolitionists that violations of the law were occurring on a considerable scale and that such violations could only be stopped by compulsory registration of all the existing slaves in the West Indian colonies.

At the instigation of the African Institution, a registration system was introduced in Trinidad by an order in council in

1812. Then a bill was prepared, under the auspices of the Institution, to introduce a similar system in other colonies of the British Caribbean. That bill was presented to the British Parliament in June 1815 by Wilberforce, who had given his hearty support, right from the outset, to the movement launched by the African Institution.

The Slave Registry Bill sparked off a sharp controversy in the West Indies. The planter opponents were articulate and vociferous, displaying a notable unanimity of opinion. Not the least among the opponents were the planters of Barbados who maintained that no slave had been smuggled into the island since the abolition of the slave trade in 1807. Moreover, they took their stand on a constitutional principle, submitting that what was done in Trinidad by an order in council could not be done in Barbados with its elected assembly. The levy of fees for registration, they argued, was a form of direct taxation by the Imperial Government and this would "subvert their constitution and destroy their best and dearest rights".[19]

As the opposition of the planters increased in bitterness, the slaves grew more and more suspicious of their masters' motives. They became restless, entertaining the erroneous idea that Wilberforce's bill sought to provide not for the registration of the slaves but for their emancipation. They believed that the day of freedom was at hand and that the planters were refusing to grant the boon contemplated by the British Parliament. It is noteworthy that there was a similar consensus of opinion in Trinidad and Jamaica. Indeed, in all the territories of the British West Indies the slaves seemed to be asking the same question: "Why Bacchra no do that the King bid him?"[20]

There had been no servile revolt in Barbados since 1702 and this may have given rise to a false sense of security among the planters. To the superficial observer there seemed to be no premonition of the impending insurrection. There had been some improvement in the condition of the slaves in recent years and the island had been blessed for some time with good rainfall that produced adequate supplies of corn and ground provisions.

Those who looked below the surface, however, saw an unusual stirring among the slaves. It was not their physical condition but their rising and unfulfilled expectations that kindled a spirit of growing unrest among them.[21] They were heartened by the humanitarian movement in England and the speeches of Wilberforce in the House of Commons. They were exhilarated by

Negro Dance in Dominica, 1779 (A. Brunias)

the achievement of Toussaint L'Ouverture, who had changed the French colony of St. Domingue to the black republic of Haiti, and were clearly resolved to follow the example of the great leader of that revolution.

The comparative tranquillity in the island for more than a hundred years was soon to prove deceptive. The relaxation of the early slave laws enabled the leaders of the slaves to move from one plantation to another and to plan their revolt. The mastermind behind the uprising was Washington Francklyn, a free mulatto, who was slated to be head of the Government if the revolution succeeded.[22] Among his chief lieutenants who were active in the field, agitating the cause of the revolt, were Cain Davis and John Richard Sarjeant, both from St. Philip and both free coloured men; Bussa, an African and a "ranger" or headman of Bayley's Plantation; Roach, a free coloured man from St. Philip; Jackey, a black driver and John Ranger, a black labourer, both from Simmons's Plantation; and Mingo, a black ranger from Byde Mill.

These men met and talked on numerous occasions, especially at week-end dances. They discussed the existing situation and prepared their plans over a period of more than two months. During a dance on Good Friday night, April 12th, 1816, Bussa and Sarjeant held a crucial conversation. In the meantime, the leaders had warned that the houses of all the Negroes who did

A. It was about twelve o'clock that we met with a large body of the insurgent slaves, in the yard of *Lowther's* Plantation (several of whom were armed with muskets), who displayed the Colours of the St. Philip's Battalion (which they had stolen), and who, upon seeing the division, cheered, and cried out to us, " Come on !" but were quickly dispersed upon being fired on.

Q. Did you preside at the Board of Field Officers when a slave by the name of Robert (belonging to *Simmons'* Plantation) was upon trial? and was the annexed Confession made before you?

A. The annexed Confession was made before the Board, and signed by myself and the other members.

The Confession of ROBERT, *a Slave belonging to the Plantation called* " Simmons'̱:"

Who saith, that some time the last year, he heard the negroes were all to be freed on New-year's Day. That Nanny Grig) a negro woman at *Simmons'*, who said she could read,) was the first person who told the negroes at *Simmons'* so; and she said she had read it in the Newspapers, and that her Master was very uneasy at it : that she was always talking about it to the negroes, and told them that they were all damned fools to work, for that she would not, as freedom they were sure to get. That, about a fortnight after New-year's Day, she said the negroes were to be freed on Easter-Monday, and the only way to get it was to fight for it, otherwise they would not get it; and the way they were to do, was to set fire, as that was the way they did in Saint Domingo. Further saith, that Jackey, the Driver at *Simmons'*, said he would send to the other Drivers and Rangers, and to the head Carters about, and to Bussoe (at *Bayley's*), to turn out on Easter Monday to give the Country a light, and let every body know what it was for : and that John (at *Simmons'*) was the person who carried the summons from Jackey : that Jackey was one of the head men of the Insurrection, and that he had heard him say he was going to point out a good great house to live in, but he did not say which : that Jackey sent also to a free man in *The Thicket* (who could read and write), to let the negroes at *The Thicket* know, that they might give their assistance. That he does not recollect the man's name, but if

Extract from Report of the Select Committee of the House of Assembly not follow them would be burnt down. Sarjeant told them "they must fight for their liberty in the same way they had done at Saint Domingo".[23] Cain Davis proclaimed that "the Negroes were all to be free, that the Queen and Wilberforce had sent out to have them freed . . . He had seen it in the Newspapers . . . that they must fight for it; that he was ready to do so with them, as he had some children who were slaves; he had a cornstalk heap at his house and would set it on fire as a signal for them to begin".[24]

Bussa and Jackey spent the whole of Sunday, April 14th, issuing detailed instructions to the slaves on their plantations. At about 8 o'clock that night, two cane fields and various trash heaps were set on fire as a signal that the revolt had begun. The fires spread from the parish of St. Philip to those of Christ Church, St. John and St. George. News of the insurrection spread rapidly and provoked first shock and consternation among the planters. "What I have been for some months dreading has at length come to pass." Thus wrote Robert Haynes, a prominent planter, a member of the House of Assembly and General of the Militia.[25]

At about 1.30 on the morning of Easter Monday, April 15th, the alarm was sounded in Bridgetown by the firing of a cannon. Martial law was proclaimed and a combined force of regulars and militia set out for the disturbed areas under the command of Colonel Edward Cobb, commanding officer of the garrison at St. Anne's Fort. Against such a combined force the slaves never had a chance. Before the insurrection was suppressed, a great deal of damage was done. Fires broke out in numerous plantations, which were sacked by the insurgents, one-fifth of the island's sugar crop was destroyed and the loss of property was estimated at £179,000. It is noteworthy that only one white was killed, a member of the militia. But about 176 slaves were killed in the fighting and some 214 were later executed after trial by court martial. Bussa and others died on the field of battle and Francklyn "who was to be Governor" and "live at Pilgrim"[26] was hanged like a common criminal.

Again an acrimonious controversy arose between the planters in Barbados and the abolitionists in Great Britain. The latter claimed that the insurrection was due to the conditions under which the slaves lived and worked, while the former maintained that the slaves were misled by the pernicious propaganda of the humanitarians.

In the event, the British Government decided to postpone

direct action on the registration of slaves and called on Barbados and other colonies to pass their own slave registry bill. At first Barbados was disposed to continue its opposition to a measure which its legislators considered was unnecessary. But John Beckles, father of the Chief Justice, who originally led the opposition to the measure, now persuaded his colleagues to change their stance. Like his son before him, he pointed out that the island's slave laws were "a disgrace to our code" and, though these laws were not all acted upon, he emphasised that they should be deleted from the statute book of Barbados.[27]

The Legislature of Barbados accepted Beckles's advice and the peace and tranquillity of Barbados was restored. The honour of the country, as a largely self-governing colony, was saved and the humanitarians were satisfied, for the time being, with the progress they had achieved in an important area of reform.

Questions and Exercises to Consider

1. As a class exercise, arrange a press conference where Christopher Codrington is interviewed by others in the class on the Codrington experiment. Consult *Barbados, Our Island Home* and *Builders of Barbados* by F. A. Hoyos.

2. Arrange a class debate on the question whether the missionaries were justified in preaching subordination of the slaves to their masters.

3. Imagine you are Cain Davis and make up a speech exhorting the slaves to rise in revolt.

4. Enact a scene with the slaves plotting the Insurrection of 1816 and devising their strategy.

5. From the extract (page 93) what can you deduce about the causes of the Insurrection? What part did the Militia and the Imperial Troops play in supressing it?

6. Go to the Reference Section of the Public Library and ask to see the Lucas MSS. Read Nathan Lucas's account of the uprising.

CHAPTER EIGHT

The White and Coloured Classes

The Poor Whites

In an earlier chapter we noted that there were two main divisions in the Barbadian society, the white plantocracy and the African slaves. One segment of the white community was represented by the poor whites who had survived the consequences of the sugar revolution and formed a group that was separate and distinct from the other classes in the social order of Barbados. Although their lot was little better than that of the slaves and inferior to the more prosperous of the free coloured people, they kept very much to themselves, remaining distant and aloof from other underprivileged groups in the community.

Attempts to encourage white immigrants to come to Barbados in order to halt the steady decline in the white population of the island, proved of little or no avail. For one thing, it was by now bruited abroad that Barbados was no place for white servants, and secondly, the planters preferred to use their own labour force rather than employ whites who for various reasons could no longer match the vigour of the African slaves in a tropical climate.[1]

The Act, which was passed in 1702, for the settlement of the militia in the island was in some ways a boon to the poor whites. Every man who served in the militia was given a house to live in and an acre or two of land to grow his own requirements of ground provisions. But this arrangement, while it gave the poor whites a sense of security, encouraged them to lead a life of aimlessness. They were content to eke out a living through subsistence agriculture, venturing out from time to time to help in harvesting the sugar crop or in performing occasional tasks on the plantations.

One account in the early nineteenth century painted a very unfavourable picture of this group of Barbadians. The laws of the island laid it down that every plantation was required to provide one member of the militia for every sixty acres of land. Yet these employees, it was reported, "owe no fealty to the landlord, make him no acknowledgement and entertain no kind of gratitude towards him". The writer added that, except for their service in the militia, "the greatest part of them live in a state of complete idleness and are usually ignorant and debauched to the last degree". Yet, in spite of all this, the writer concluded "they are as proud as Lucifer himself, and in virtue of their freckled ditch-water faces consider themselves on a level with every gentleman in the Island."[2]

The truth appears to be that the poor whites had become physically incapable of competing in the labour market with the slaves or the free coloured people. And their physical degeneracy became more marked as the years went by. They probably suffered more than any other group from hookworm, with all the debilitating effects of anaemia, emaciation and faulty growth. They had neither the strength nor the inclination to work effectively in any branch of agriculture, particularly in the strenuous task of digging cane holes. Their condition was in-dicated as a research group reported years later, by shortness of breath and palpitation of the heart and there were other symp-toms, notably on their skin, tongue and lips, that seemed to show that they were enervated not only by the tropical climate but by the ravages of the hookworm disease.[3]

The degeneracy of the poor whites appeared to be not only physical but moral and intellectual. They were not only idle, but indolent, not only ignorant but improvident and intemperate. Their appearance was a strikingly pathetic one. "Their hue and complexion", wrote an observer, "are not such as might be ex-pected; their colour resembles more that of the Albino than that of the Englishman when exposed a good deal to the sun in a tropical climate; it is commonly sickly white or light red, not often of a healthy brown". They bore the marks of physical frailty, being described as slender, loosely jointed and with little muscular development.

Clearly they were the creatures of circumstances that extended over a number of generations, going back almost to the begin-ning of the island's settlement. And the observer expressed the melancholy conclusion that, in brief, "their general appearance denotes degeneracy of corporeal frame and reminds one of exotic plants vegetating in an uncongenial soil and climate."[4]

Later, the condition of the poor whites was to deteriorate still further. When the militia was dissolved — a step that was con-sidered necessary after emancipation — the whole bottom seemed to drop from their world. For they now had no useful function to perform and no longer enjoyed the benefits resulting from military service. In these circumstances, they drifted still further away from the normal activities of the society. Some would walk all over the island, begging for alms, and most if not all of them continued to sink still lower into the depths of poverty, privation and degradation.[5]

The Yeomanry of Barbados

Another section of the white population was the yeoman class who enjoyed a far happier lot than the redlegs of Barbados. Once the economic backbone of the island, they had been almost extinguished as a class in the years following the sugar revolution but they made a good recovery in the eighteenth century. They established themselves again as yeoman farmers, cultivating their modest holdings and earning the name of "ten acre men". They did not belong to the aristocracy or the *nouveau riche* and they were certainly not members of the ruling class. By virtue of their increasing property, wealth and education, they became the landowning middle class of Barbados.

At first, the yeoman class posed no threat to those who controlled the power structure of the island. With the beginning of the nineteenth century, however, the politics of change began to have a marked influence on the Barbadians. And the catalyst of that change was the yeoman class under the leadership of James Sarsfield Bascom. They laid no claim to be classed "among the richest or the greatest" but merely wished to be considered as "the yeomanry of Barbados".[6] They banded themselves together in a party which they called the "Salmagundi" and started their own newspaper, the *Globe*, in October 1818. The aristocracy went by the name of the "Pumpkins" and they, too, had their newspaper which was known as the *Western Intelligence*.

The Salmagundi were strongly opposed to the "exalted notions"[7] of the aristocracy and presented the first real challenge to the latter's position of privilege and power. But the liberal principles they professed soon landed their newspaper into trouble with the law. On one occasion, the Governor of the day, Lord Combermere, ordered some companies of the militia to assemble in Trafalgar Square to lend dignity to a special religious service he proposed to attend in St. Michael's Cathedral. Soon after the regimental order was issued, it was criticised by the *Globe,* which declared that its purpose was not to create insubordination in the regiment but to "oppose oppression and resist tyranny". The editor, Michael Ryan, explained that the militia was organised for "the protection of the country and its laws" and not to "dance attendance on those who delight in a red coat". It was urged that those responsible should not take advantage of the law and, "instead of encouraging the men in their duty, make it disgusting to them by the petty tyranny which they attempt to practise".[8]

The House of Assembly, which was controlled by the Pumpkins, at once issued instructions for the prosecution of the *Globe* for a libel on its honourable members and for seeking to incite sedition against the Government. The reaction from the Salmagundi was equally prompt and unanimous. They proclaimed Ryan as a martyr in the public cause and held a number of meetings at which they censured the proceedings against the newspaper's editor.

In the event, Ryan was acquitted and was borne in triumph through the streets of Bridgetown. Among those who took part in this demonstration were two magistrates, or justices of the peace, J. B. Lane and Cheesman Moe, who sat on the Bench when the verdict was returned. A few weeks later, they were deprived of their commission on the charge that they vacated the Bench on that occasion and joined in the tumultuous demonstration instead of helping the Chief Justice to restore order in the Court of Grand Sessions.

The election of 1819 was fought on the lines of party politics and ended in a notable victory for the Salmagundi who won a majority of seats in the House of Assembly. John Beckles, who as Attorney General had prosecuted Ryan and was attacked as the leader of the reaction, lost his seat in the Assembly, a position he had held for thirty-seven years. Lane and Moe, who had been dismissed from the magistracy, had the satisfaction of being elected to the House. And Bascom, who did not contest a seat in 1819, was elected two years later and started on a career that was to make him "the terror of the House".[9] In 1821, too, Michael Ryan was appointed printer to the House of Assembly.

The irruption of the yeoman class into the House of Assembly was a sign of the times. The social conscience was stirring after the insurrection of 1816. Amelioration and amendment of the slave laws were in the air. The plantocracy entered into a period of decline, seemingly unaware of the shape of things to come,

and looking with disdain on "a doating old Man" like Joshua
Steele who purchased 1,068 acres of land, extending over the
parishes of St. John, St. Philip and St. George, and sought "to
reform the evils of slavery" by trying "to secure voluntary labour
from the blacks by giving them sums of money above their
customary allowance, and land as well".[10]

What concerned the plantocracy at the time was that their
position was threatened by the rise of the white yeomanry.
Property was being more widely distributed and small planters
were acquiring more than ten acres of land. Starting from
humble origins and with little or no education, they were making
their way to social prestige and political office. Now they were
substantial citizens and could claim a number of educated men
in their ranks.

But the Salmagundi were not destined to hold the centre of the
stage for long. For a while they controlled the majority in the
Assembly, though this was not as significant as it would be today,
in view of the powers then enjoyed by the Governor and the
Council. Yet they were soon to be left behind in the rush of
events. There were those among them who did not sympathise
with the aspirations of the free coloured people and later found
themselves out of step with the Liberals led by Samuel Jackman
Prescod. For they were middle class reformers and not plebeian
revolutionaries and they lost their identity when they drew closer
to their aristocratic opponents as the day of emancipation
approached.

The Free Coloured People

Perhaps the most interesting group that emerged during the
régime of slavery was that of the "free coloured people". The
latter were usually of mixed racial ancestry, being the products
of white fathers and black mothers. The co-habitation of white
masters with their female slaves was a custom that was not in-
frequently practised in slave societies throughout the New
World.

During the seventeenth century, the free coloured people
represented only a tiny minority of the island's inhabitants. Their
numbers increased in the second half of the eighteenth century,
but it was not until the early decades of the nineteenth century
that they became a significant portion of the population.
Predictably, this increase became a source of uneasiness and

The Barbados Mulatto Girl (A. Brunias)

apprehension to the ruling class of Barbados. It is noteworthy that until 1721 they enjoyed the right to testify in legal cases involving whites and were able to give evidence in cases where their free status was contested. But after that date this right was withdrawn and during the hundred years that followed they were engaged in a struggle to regain the vital right to testify.

The census of 1802 disclosed that there were 1,155 adults and 1,013 children among the free coloured people, making a total of 2,168.[11] This represented a considerable increase on earlier figures which never reached the 1,000 mark. In the twenty-seven years following the census of 1802, the number of free coloured people rose to 5,146 and on the eve of emancipation, five years later, it approached the figure of 7,000. Thus it was that during the early decades of the nineteenth century the free coloured people had more than trebled. This section of the community had by then become a significant portion of the population, at a time when the number of whites was declining mainly through emigration in search of better opportunities in other countries.[12]

While natural increase was a significant factor in the growth of the free coloured people, there is little doubt that manumission played an even more important part in that growth. The first manumission of slaves (these were the Amerindians who had been imported into Barbados) occurred early in the 1650s.[13] But the cases in which slaves gained their freedom through this process were rare in the early history of the island. After the slave conspiracy to revolt in 1692 (the first was in 1675) a law was passed, giving freedom to any slave who informed on those who were plotting any insurrection or rebellion against their masters.[14] But this meant little to the slaves for, apart from the planned uprisings in 1675, 1692 and 1702, the only slave revolt that really took place was the insurrection of 1816.

The usual form of manumission was through the wills and deeds of those who owned slaves. Where a slave had given faithful service as a domestic, he could be rewarded with freedom for his fidelity. This would account for some of the black members of the freed population. Where a woman slave had a sexual relationship with her master, she could be given her freedom as a favour. There were not a few instances where owners were so captivated with the charms of their slave mistresses that they gave them and their children the cherished prize of freedom. This was regarded as "the only adequate reward for such an endearing service".[15]

If a slave killed an enemy in defence of the island he could be rewarded with his freedom. Since Barbados, except for Ayscue's attempt, was never invaded by an enemy, this law was a dead letter. But there were also cases where slaves won their liberty through self-purchase and then proceeded to purchase their kinsmen out of bondage.

At first no attempt was made to control the process of manumission. But in 1739 a law was passed requiring owners to pay fees on manumitting their slaves.[16] The reason for this legislation was to restrain owners who freed their slaves, when they were old and infirm, without providing for their support and maintenance. Such owners were now required to pay £50 for the support of any slaves they manumitted so that they would not become a burden on the community. But there can be little question that the purpose of the manumission fee was to control, if not check, the steady increase in the number of the free black people.

The Civil Rights Struggle

The law of 1721, mentioned above, prevented the free coloured people from enjoying the rights and privileges of full citizens. They could not play an effective part in the politics of the country. They were not eligible to vote, to hold elective office or serve on juries. A person who owned ten acres of land or possessed a house with a taxable value of £10 per annum could be enfranchised. In earlier years such a provision had disfranchised women, Jews and the poorest of the poor whites. Now it was laid down in 1721 that no one could be enfranchised unless he was white.[17]

Again, since the law of 1721 denied them the right to testify in the law courts, the free coloured group were unable to protect themselves adequately against assault and theft and thus ensure the security of their person or property. There were, it is true, a number of privileges and responsibilities which they shared with the white section of the community. They were required to pay taxes and serve in the militia. They could own and carry firearms, possess or bequeath property and travel freely in the island or abroad. Unlike Jamaica, Barbados did not prevent its free coloured people from undertaking any occupation of their choice or place any limits on the amount of land they could own or inherit from whites.[18]

Perhaps the most important right the free coloured group enjoyed was that which enabled them to form their own associations, hold public meetings and petition the legislature. A petition was drawn up and presented by the group in 1799 and this was probably the first move in a civil rights campaign that was to continue for more than a hundred years. The petition pointed to the necessity of their right to legal testimony so that they could live "under the protection and security or the law". It is significant that the petition did not suggest measures for improving their status, expressed their awareness of their "subordinate state" and undertook to "use our constant endeavours by every act of gratitude, obedience and loyalty, to endear ourselves to all in authority". [19]

The free coloured people were clearly divided between progressives and conservatives. With the progress of the British reform movement and the change in the climate of opinion, the progressives became more influential in their councils. At one time the conservatives expressed themselves as opposed to the campaign of the British abolitionists but this was repudiated by the progressives. Eventually an act was passed, in 1817, granting the free coloured people the right to legal testimony. One of the main arguments for its acceptance was that, during the insurrection of 1816, those who were to benefit under the new Act had shown "the greatest attachment and fidelity to the white inhabitants of the Island". [20]

In 1829 another petition, couched in less conciliatory language than those of previous years, asked that the free coloured people be granted the right to vote, to be elected to public office and to serve on juries. Samuel Jackman Prescod, then a young man of twenty-two, made his forceful appearance in public life and called for a more militant stand on the question of civil rights. When a law was passed in 1831, granting the free coloured people full legal equality, there was much rejoicing among them, but Prescod convincingly pointed out that because of certain provisions "the Assembly had only added insult to past injuries". [21]

The household qualification had previously been £10 and this still applied to those who enjoyed the right to vote before 1831. But it did not apply to new freeholders whose property qualification was raised to £30 by the new Act. Up to the time of emancipation the House of Assembly was unwilling to remove a piece of legislation that was glaringly discriminatory to the free coloured people.

Property and Wealth

The free coloured people kept away from plantation work because to them it bore the stigma of slavery. But they readily engaged in small-scale agriculture, sharing with the poor whites the privilege of being "militia tenants" on the estates. There were limited opportunities for owning land of their own. Yet, in spite of the difficulties and disabilities they faced, it is remarkable that some of them, admittedly few in number, rose to become plantation owners in the closing decades of the eighteenth century and the early part of the nineteenth.

Jacob Belgrave owned a plantation in St. Philip of 98 acres, with 94 slaves as its labour force. That plantation, now known as Summervale, was inherited by a son who increased it to 144 acres and added five slaves to its labour strength. Another son, Jacob Belgrave Jr., owned two plantations with a total of 480 acres and 306 slaves. These were Graeme Hall in Christ Church and Stirling in St. Philip. Robert Collymore was the owner of Haggatt Hall in St. Michael, a plantation which then comprised 368 acres and 90 slaves. Another wealthy member of the free coloured group was Amaryllis Collymore who left a property called "Lightfoots" and 60 slaves to be divided among her eleven children.[22]

Other members of the free coloured people engaged in the skilled trades and in the internal marketing system, where they sold food crops and small livestock, sometimes operating as receivers of stolen property. A considerable number of the group opened shops as soon as they acquired the capital they needed, but few of these were able to move from their small businesses to large-scale enterprises. Yet it is remarkable that some achieved success in a wider field.

Joseph Rachell, who was born a slave, was a black merchant in Bridgetown, owned a great deal of property and operated on a large scale. Actually, he gave employment to some white people and was known to help white planters and merchants when they could not cope with their financial problems. Thomas J. Cummins was another coloured merchant who held an almost unique position as the agent for a plantation the owner of which was a white man. Thomas Harris and Samuel Francis Collymore were also prominent merchants who attracted substantial business by their special talents.

Perhaps the outstanding person among the wealthy coloured men in the island was London Bourne whose business interests were not confined to Barbados but extended far afield. He owned three stores in Bridgetown and was widely respected for his honesty and his integrity. He had business agents in England, set up a branch establishment in the City of London and employed Englishmen to attend to his multifarious concerns.[23]

Nor were the women of the free coloured group without success in their own fields of endeavour. Some of them did a considerable business in retail shops and from the profits they made they were able to acquire property and save enough money to purchase and manumit their slave children.

But the greatest success attained by the free coloured women was in the realm of taverns and inns that did a prosperous business in Bridgetown. Among the most celebrated of these women was Rachael Pringle Polgreen, who was the daughter of a Scotsman and an African woman. She was purchased and freed by a British naval officer, became his mistress and the house where he set her up was later known as the "Royal Naval Hotel". When she died, she left as estate of 19 slaves and property consisting of "houses and lands".[24] Other women who followed in Rachael's footsteps, attaining a large measure of prosperity, were Nancy Clarke, Mary Bella Green, Betsy Lemon, Hannah Lewis and Betsy Austin.

While all the taverns did not function in the same way, the main attraction in these houses was undoubtedly the practice of prostitution. The owners of these taverns saw to it that their female employees, usually slaves, were the most beautiful they could get. In the words of a contemporary, these "attendants" were allowed one "privilege" — "that of tenderly disposing of their persons", since this offered them the only hope of "procuring a sum of money, wherewith to purchase their freedom". And this practice was so common among them that "neither shame nor disgrace attaches to it; but, on the contrary, she who is most sought becomes an object of envy and is proud of the distinction shewn her".[25]

By a variety of ways the free coloured people were able to acquire wealth and property. Those who could afford it adopted the life style of the wealthy whites, living like black and coloured aristocrats. They lived in houses that were as well appointed as any, rode their horses and drove their carriages, adopting the habits and manners of the more affluent members of the society.

106

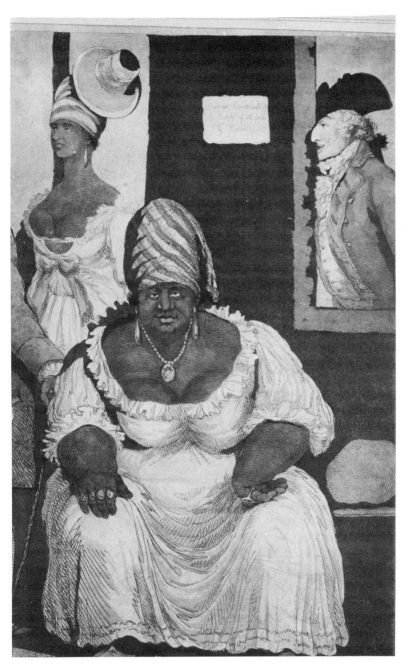

Rachael Pringle Polgreen

But the success of the individuals mentioned above cannot conceal the fact that the rest of the coloured community lived in straitened circumstances, if not in extreme poverty.[26]

Questions and Exercises to Consider

1. How would the "ten acre men" (white yeomanry) relate to the big planter, the "red legs", the free coloured people and the African slaves? Have a group discussion with each of these groups explaining their position in the society.

2. How far was the irruption of the yeoman class into the House of Assembly due to the stirring of the social conscience after the Insurrection of 1816?

3. Place the following events in the right order of time: the St. Domingue Revolution, the Charter of Barbados, the abolition of the slave trade, the commencement of St. Anne's Fort, Chief Justice Mansfield's Judgement, De Ruyter's attack on Barbados, the Slave Registry Bill, the erection of Nelson's statue.

4. What is meant by a "plebeian revolutionary"? How does he differ from a "middle class reformer"?

5. Were the free coloured people an important section of the island's population before Emancipation? From what disabilities did they suffer?

6. Compare the disabilities of the free coloured people in Barbados with those endured by the free coloured in St. Domingue.

7. Explain the meaning of the phrase "the process of manumission". What was done to control this process and why?

The Road to Freedom

Amelioration

Following the triumph of 1807, the British humanitarians, after a short lull, turned their attention with increasing fervour and pertinacity to the removal of the evils attendant on slavery. It had been hoped that the institution of slavery would die a natural death after the abolition of the slave trade. But that was not to be the case. Before long, therefore, the humanitarians openly proclaimed that they would aim at two objectives. They would agitate for the immediate improvement in the condition of the slaves and at the same time they would seek to attain their freedom in the shortest possible time.

Two significant events occurred in 1823, a year that was to prove eventful in many respects. The African Institution was absorbed by the Society for the Mitigation and Gradual Abolition of Slavery which now led the fight against the plantation labour system throughout the British Dominions. And Wilberforce, now bowed with the infirmities of age, handed over the leadership of the abolitionist cause to his friend and disciple, Thomas Fowell Buxton. The movement to free all enslaved blacks within the British Empire was now fully launched.

The new Society declared that slavery was "opposed to the spirit and precepts of Christianity as well as repugnant to every dictate of natural humanity and justice". And Buxton, emulating the zeal of his mentor, proclaimed that the aim of the society was "the extinction of slavery — nothing less than the extinction of slavery, in nothing less than the whole of the British dominions".

Supported by the Society and its numerous branches in Britain, Buxton moved swiftly forward in his agitation against slavery. The first shot in his campaign was the celebrated resolution he moved in the House of Commons declaring that slavery was "repugnant to the principles of the British constitution and of the Christian religion; and that it ought to be gradually abolished with as much expedition as may be found consistent with a due regard to the well-being of the parties concerned".[1]

Influenced by the remarkable debate that followed, George Canning, on behalf of the British Government, presented a number of proposals that were aimed at "ameliorating the condition of the slave population in his majesty's colonies".[2] The stage was thus being set for a complete victory for the emancipationists. No-one was more vividly aware of this than the Society of West India Planters and Merchants who at once proceeded to draw up a "Plan for the improvement of the Condition of the Negroes".[3] The programme of reform they drew up was incorporated in a despatch of the Secretary of State for the Colonies, the Earl of Bathurst, and circulated to the British colonies. The Bathurst proposals, which bore a close resemblance to those of the West India Planters and Merchants, were as follows.

1. The slaves should be given religious instruction and the British Government, if necessary, should provide financial support for clergy and teachers under the control of a bishop.
2. Sunday markets should be abolished and some other time should be set aside for the slaves to do their business.
3. The whipping of female slaves should be abolished.
4. Floggings should be administered under the supervision of responsible persons. All such punishments, exceeding three lashes, should be recorded and quarterly returns of these records should be made to local magistrates.
5. The slaves should be given a nine-hour day and the whip should no longer be used as a stimulus to work in the fields.
6. The evidence of slaves should be accepted under certain conditions.
7. Slaves should not be sold for the payment of debts and slave families should not be broken up by any sales.
8. Marriage should be properly encouraged and slaves should have the right to purchase their own freedom and that of their legitimate children at appraised prices.
9. Manumissions should be made easier and less expensive.
10. Savings Banks should be set up to enable slaves to accumulate money to purchase their freedom.[4]

The purpose of the Society of West India Planters and Merchants was to avert the danger that lay ahead. They hoped that, by adopting a policy of amelioration on a liberal scale, the planters in the colonies would be able to stem the headlong rush of the emancipation movement. The only way the situation could be saved, they felt, was "by doing ourselves all that is right to be done — and doing it speedily and effectively".[5]

The local planters, however, did not see it this way and nowhere in the British Caribbean was the plan of the Society generally accepted.

The Planters' Attitude

The proposed reforms met with little favourable response in Barbados. The island's Council asserted that the amelioration programme would sever the bond uniting master and slave and was therefore unacceptable to the Legislature. They declared that there was no need for amelioration and that the description by the humanitarians of the condition of the slaves was based on abolitionist propaganda, bearing "no more resemblance to the actual state of things in this country than a caricature commonly does to the object which it is meant to ridicule".[6]

Two decades previously, Lord Seaforth, then Governor of Barbados, drew attention to the condition of the slave population and "the many instances" in which they had been "treated with great inhumanity". In a letter to Earl Camden, the Governor related the "wanton acts" of cruelty that had been committed upon the slaves in the island. It is true that this letter was written on November 13th, 1804, a few years before the reform measures, noted in an earlier chapter, were adopted in Barbados. Yet it has been claimed that Lord Seaforth's recital of cruelties in his letter was unduly influenced by "the philanthropic fervour of the reporters" of the House of Commons debate on the slave trade.

Whatever may be said of Lord Seaforth's letter, there is little doubt that the address delivered to the Legislature in 1824 by another Governor, Sir Henry Warde, was an exaggeration of the true position. "It is my firm conviction," said the Governor on that occasion, "as far as it has come within my observation to judge, that the slaves as a body throughout the colony were uniformly treated with kindness, lenity and liberality; and to which their appearance of cheerfulness and happiness may fairly be attributed".[7]

The remarks of Joseph Sturge, the humanitarian who visited Barbados in 1836, were probably nearer the truth than either Lord Seaforth's or Sir Henry Warde's comments on the slave régime in the island. The slave code was harsh, probably the harshest in the British West Indies, but it is doubtful whether the island's record was "stained" with more than "comparatively few cases of individual cruelty".[8] Looking back over the recent years of the slave régime, Sturge declared: "In the management of their slaves, as slaves, the Barbadians excelled. Like good farmers they bestowed the same attention upon them as upon their cattle; and if the Negroes had been animals and not men, their success would have done honour even to their humanity. Their aim was to keep them in the highest working and breeding condition, in which they succeeded; and though ever reputed the strictest disciplinarians, yet theirs was the only sugar colony where the population rapidly increased".[9]

The slave laws had been consolidated in Barbados in 1817 but this was not regarded as satisfactory and by 1824 the Bill to ameliorate and amend these laws had not yet been placed on the island's statute book.[10] Indeed, the Bill failed to pass in 1824 and did not become law until the following year when considerable modifications were added to the measure.[11]

The attitude of Barbadian legislators to the proposed reforms is indicated by the remarks in the House of Assembly that they were "a mere catalogue of indulgencies to the Blacks".[12] They opposed the proposal to prohibit the flogging of female slaves. "Our black ladies," said Renn Hamden, a member of the Barbados Council,"have rather a tendency to the Amazonian cast of character; and I believe that their husbands would be sorry to hear that they were placed beyond the reach of chastisement".

Hamden was an articulate champion of the views of the planters. He led the opposition against the proposal to abolish the Sunday market on the ground that Barbados could not afford to lose any more of its already reduced income. The removal of the whip would be the end of discipline "and then adieu to all peace and comfort on plantations". And to those who exposed the irony of slave owners expatiating on their rights and privileges, he gave the unabashed reply: "Look to history and you will find that no nations in the world have been more jealous of their liberties than those amongst whom the institution of slavery existed".[13]

The views expressed by the planters in Barbados were shared by their counterparts in other territories of the Caribbean. In Jamaica it was maintained that giving the slaves "time for religious duties" would only encourage them in idleness. The Bill seeking to grant the slaves the right of testimony was rejected by thirty-six votes to one. The claim of the British Government to legislate on internal matters in the colonies was challenged and one member of the Assembly wanted to know what right the King of England had to Jamaica "except that he stole it from Spain".[14]

In Trinidad, the proposal for a nine-hour day was denounced as "a most unjust and oppressive invasion of property"; while in British Guiana the holder of the newly created post of Protector of Slaves remarked, as late as 1832, that "there is no protection for the Slave Population. I am desperately unpopular."[15]

Clearly, what was said of the Barbadian planters in 1833 by Governor Sir Lionel Smith could be applied to their fellows in other parts of the West Indies. "The love of power of these planters," wrote Smith, "over the poor Negroes, each in his little sugar dominion, has found as great an obstacle to freedom as the love of their labour".[16]

Missionary Martyrs

As the abolitionist movement gathered momentum in Britain, a critical and dangerous situation developed in Barbados. The planters blamed the British humanitarians for misrepresenting their case in the outside world. And they accused the non-conformists, and more particularly the Wesleyan Methodists, for exciting the slaves in the West Indies and giving rise to expectations that could not reasonably be fulfilled. They declared that the Methodists were "in league with the Anti-slavery Society" and these accusations were especially damaging at a time when "public opinion was inflamed" by the reports of the British Parliamentary debates, initiated by Buxton, on the issue of slavery.[17]

As in 1816, there was an ominous stirring among the slaves in the island. Rumours spread among the slave population that their freedom was soon to be granted and the Governor, Sir Henry Warde, was moved to issue a proclamation on June 10th, 1823, warning them not to believe such rumours but to regard as their enemies the "designing men" who spread the "various unfounded reports".[18] The situation was made more acute when the news was received in the island that the slaves had risen in revolt in Demerara.

On July 7th, 1823, instructions from Lord Bathurst reached Demerara in respect of certain measures to improve the condition of the slaves. These instructions excited "great alarm

Planter and Slave (from *A Voyage in the West Indies,* John A. Waller, 1820)

114

and feverish anxiety" among the white section of the population. This reaction was noted by the domestic slaves and speedily reported to the field slaves. The intelligence soon reached all the slaves that their freedom was at hand and for seven weeks nothing was done to relieve "the inquisitive anxiety of the slave population". On August 18th, the insurrection broke out. The Rev. John Smith, who had been a missionary in the colony for seven years, was arrested on the charge of exercising a subversive influence over the slaves. He was tried by a court-martial and sentenced to be hanged. During the time when he awaited execution, he was imprisoned in abominable conditions that accelerated the fatal progress of the disease from which he was suffering.[19]

News of the Demerara insurrection arrived in Barbados on August 30th. For some years the white section of the Barbadian population had been directing their suspicion and anger against a Methodist missionary in the island, William James Shrewsbury. The opportunity was now taken to fan the hostility against the missonary into "a fierce flame". It was falsely stated that both the Methodist clergymen in Demerara had been imprisoned and that they were "deeply implicated in the insurrection".[20]

Shrewsbury first came to Barbados early in 1820. He made himself unpopular by the forceful and pungent language he used to reprove sin in whatever quarter he found it. Along with a fellow missionary, he wrote a letter to England in March 1820, explaining the situation in the island as they saw it.

The fear of God is hardly to be seen in this place. The free black people who live in town are, many of them, exceedingly given to profanity, especially the watermen; for they swear and blaspheme the name of God almost with every breath . . . As regards the moral condition of the slaves, that is nearly the same; polygamy, fornication, adultery, blasphemies, lying, theft, quarrelling and drunkenness — these are the crimes to which the generality are addicted. They live and die like the beasts of the earth . . . We are happy, however, to find a few honourable exceptions.[21]

While reporting their gratitude at being welcomed by several planters to their estates, the missionaries drew attention to the melancholy plight of the slaves.

The Island is divided into eleven parishes, and there is a church erected and clergyman appointed to each; but it is a rare thing to see a slave within the church walls . . . Not that they are prohibited from going to church—the clergymen would be glad to see them attend; but no man compels, no man *invites* them to come in. They are lost and no man goes to seek and save them; they are as much disregarded and neglected as if they possessed no immortal souls.[22]

Later Shrewsbury was able to make a more favourable report to the London Missionary Society part of which read as follows:

The wilderness begins to bloom as the rose . . . the work of grace is becoming deeper in almost every heart. The classes and prayer-meetings are well attended; the spirit of grace and supplication rests upon us . . . Several very wicked young men have been truly converted to God.[23]

But not all the very wicked young men had been converted from the error of their ways. Coloured women who had lived with white men hearkened to Shrewsbury's preaching and gave up their life of concubinage. This more than anything else had inflamed the anger of their paramours against the missionary and they were resolved to get even with him for his "bold and withering denunciations of vice". By 1823 the storm of wrath that had been accumulating for some time broke upon his head. His letter of March 20th, 1820, was revived and misquoted and garbled versions circulated throughout Bridgetown. It was made out that he had traduced the character of all self-respecting Barbadians and that, moreover, he had urged the slaves, if they could not obtain their freedom in any other way, to rise and take it by force.[24]

Soon the missionary's enemies took to overt action. First, an organised attack was mounted on his congregation. That was on Sunday, October 5th. Then a Secret Committee of Public Safety was formed and persons invited to take part in an enterprise they had in mind. By October 19th and 20th that enterprise was accomplished. Shrewsbury's chapel was demolished, not one stone being left upon another, and the following day the missionary and his wife were forced to embark on a schooner that took them to St. Vincent.

Enlisting the Church

The Smith outrage in Demerara won friends for the cause of Emancipation "in every corner of England".[25] The same may be said in the case of Shrewsbury. Buxton brought a motion before the House of Commons and papers laid before that chamber showed that a shameful riot had taken place in Bridgetown, much property had been destroyed and the perpetrators went unpunished, continuing "their terrorism and defiance of the law". Canning, the Secretary for Foreign Affairs, joined in the debate and so did Henry Brougham, who had previously spoken on John Smith's tragic death. The motion, amended by Canning, was accepted by the House and Buxton was able to say, with great satisfaction, that he had obtained "the declaration of the Commons of England that we will have religious toleration in the West Indies. . ".[26]

The outrages committed against the non-conformist missionaries drew attention to the apathy and indifference of the Anglican Church. The Bishop of London, Beilby Porteus, saw the opportunities that awaited the Established Church in the West Indies over which he had some episcopal control. He entertained "large and generous ideas"[27] for the slaves. In 1783 he addressed the S.P.G., as Bishop of Chester, and urged that the slaves on the Codrington estates be given religious instruction; and for many years after he was actively interested in promoting the welfare of the general slave population. Through his efforts, from 1792 to 1806, better trained clergymen were procured for the West Indies, but this programme soon lapsed. Some attention was paid to education. Up to 1812, there were no schools for the slaves in Barbados except on the Codrington estates. But after the insurrection of 1816, an aroused social conscience brought about some improvements in education for the children of the underprivileged. In 1818 the Colonial Charity School was founded for coloured and black children and the following year the Central School in Bridgetown was opened for the children of the poor whites. These two schools owed a great deal to the interest of the Governor, Lord Combermere.

Unhappily, the "ample designs"[28] of the Bishop of London were gradually reduced. The Church of England's interest in the slaves and their education was not maintained. It relapsed into the condition of apathy, where, as the Church of the planters, it turned its back on the spiritual condition of the slaves.

It was in these circumstances that Canning took a decisive step, that of strengthening the Anglican Church in the West Indies. Two dioceses were established in the area and funds to pay for their administration were provided by the British Government. Christopher Lipscomb was appointed Bishop of Jamaica, the Bahamas and Honduras, while William Hart Coleridge was made Bishop of Barbados, the Leeward Islands, Trinidad and Guiana.

With the appointment of Coleridge, a new era began in the history of the Anglican Church in Barbados. "It seems the strangest thing in the world," said one of the appeals that had been sent to England over many years, "and it is thought history cannot parallel it, that any place which has received the Word of God so many years should still remain together in the wilderness as sheep without a shepherd."[29]

Coleridge turned his attention to the main task that awaited him, the christianising and education of the slaves. But his efforts were extended to all sections of the island's population. He emphasised the pastoral nature of the work the clergy were required to perform. He insisted that the goodwill and co-operation of the planters must be enlisted in the work of the Church among the slaves. "I need not remind you," he said in one of his addresses to the clergy, "that in every attempt of ours to ameliorate the spiritual condition of the Slave Population, we must, as much as possible, carry the influence of the Planter along with us."

He made it clear that both masters and slaves had to be prepared for the new order of society that was inevitable in Barbados and the West Indies. "Every soul is God's property; every soul in your parish must be your care. The soul of the master, and the soul of the slave, will equally be required at your hands."[30]

In Barbados he worked as indefatigably as in the other territories of the vast area he was called on to administer. In the eighteen years of his episcopate, he increased the number of Anglican clergy from fifteen to thirty-one. He multiplied the places of worship in the island. The eight schools he found (six for whites, one for 'coloured' and one on the Codrington estates) he increased to eighty-three and the number of children on the roll rose from five hundred to seven thousand.[31] And, after the hurricane of 1831 struck the island, he set out, with infinite patience, to repair the vast damage that had been done to the churches and schools he had painstakingly constructed.

The spirit that guided Coleridge in his work was indicated in one of his Charges to the clergy of the diocese. "Once convince people," he said, "that you have their interest at heart, and that the saving of a single soul is more to you than all the treasures of the world, and your work is more than half accomplished. The

Negro especially is peculiarly susceptible to kindness; he will throw himself unreservedly on an affectionate Minister, with all the confidence and docility of a child; he is now eager for instruction, and though among the wheat we must expect some chaff, yet the Minister will gather in all that he finds and having done his utmost, leave to God and His Holy Angels at the last day to winnow the good from the bad."[32]

Twin Disasters

As Emancipation drew nearer, Barbados was afflicted with a number of problems. The cost of producing sugar, when added to freight charges, was greater than the average price that was sometimes paid for the product. The planters of the island had to face competition from the East Indies, Cuba and Brazil. In addition, there were the new colonies that had been acquired by Britain after the Napoleonic Wars in 1815, St. Lucia, Trinidad and Tobago and the three territories of Guiana, Demerara, Essequibe and Berbice. The increase in the quantity of sugar available to Britain led to a decline in its price. Moreover, there was the beginning of competition from beet sugar which was to become a source of great anxiety later in the century.

Nor was this all. The preferential tariff given to the British West Indian colonies was reduced and their molasses was excluded from Britain's distilleries. Moreover, as the Barbadian planters submitted to a committee of the House of Commons, two-thirds of the land of each estate in the island was used for the cultivation of provision crops. This was a sensible arrangement since it saved a great deal of money owing to the high prices paid for imported foodstuffs. But it meant a substantial reduction in the sugar crop, the production per slave becoming much less than in other territories. In the circumstances, the planters maintained, a strong case could be made out for the abolition of the 4½ per cent duty which had long been a burden to the island.[33]

To the planters, the "twin disasters" that visited Barbados at this time were the hurricane of 1831 and Emancipation a few years later. The Great Hurricane brought heavy losses in life and property. The number of persons killed was 1,591 and the amount of damage done was estimated at over £1,600,000. Yet, with the peace that prevailed after the Napoleonic Wars and the resumption of normal trade relations, Barbados rapidly

119

recovered from the difficulties that beset the island. Indeed, there was an interesting belief among the inhabitants, as recorded by a contemporary, that hurricanes were not altogether unmixed evils.

Though so destructive in their immediate operations, [he wrote] hurricanes are not purely evil in their consequences; there is reason to believe that they have often been beneficial. After some of them, especially the last that occurred in Barbados, the seasons were more favourable, vegetation more active; there was improvement in the health of the people, certain diseases even disappeared; benefits, in the opinion of many, more than compensating for the instant losses sustained.[34]

It is certain, however, that such improvements as were recorded would scarcely have been possible but for a number of vital factors. Among other things, the British Government and private citizens gave substantial sums of money to help in the work of hurricane relief. And the island benefited not a little from the temporary suspension of customs duties.

Equally interesting was the view held by some Barbadians that the other "twin disaster", Emancipation, also did Barbados a great deal of good.

And what the hurricane did for the physical atmosphere of Barbados, [wrote the same observer] emancipation effected for its moral and domestic atmosphere; it purified that in a remarkable manner, and to the matron ladies and their daughters, always exemplarily correct, was an incalculable comfort. Licentiousness, whatever it may have been before, acquired new ideas of correctness and purer tastes and habits, all of an elevating kind and favouring the development of the higher energies.[35]

There were many, however, who took a gloomy view of the situation facing Barbados on the eve of Emancipation. These resisted the trend of the times and took whatever opportunity they could to maintain "the distinctions they deemed necessary to their safety". Thus in 1827 the Rev. W. M. Harte, Rector of St. Lucy, was accused of "inculcating doctrines of equality" among the slaves, doctrines which were considered "inconsistent with their obedience to their masters and the policy of the Island". Harte was cited before three magistrates and the jury declared him "guilty of misdemeanour". He was sentenced by the magistrates and ordered to pay a fine of one shilling. But he was supported by Bishop Coleridge and unconditionally pardoned by the King.[36]

By 1830, the emancipationists, complaining that nothing was being done to improve the condition of the slaves, moved more vigorously to the offensive. They called upon the British Government to free all the slaves by an act of parliament. The following year the British Government issued instructions to the crown colonies, Trinidad, St. Lucia and Berbice, to restrict the punishment of the slaves, establish a nine-hour day and provide better quarters and more generous allowances of food and clothing.

The reaction in the West Indies was predictable. The planters complained belligerently that their rights were being destroyed and the slaves assumed that their freedom had been granted and was being withheld by their masters. It is not surprising that the slaves rose in a formidable revolt towards the end of that year. What happened in Barbados in 1816 and in Demerara in 1823 now occurred in Jamaica late in 1831.

It was a time of excitement and apprehension in the West Indies. The hostility of the planters, the restlessness of the slaves and the calls by Buxton and Brougham in the House of Commons for the end of slavery, all combined to produce a tense situation in the area. Proclamation after proclamation was issued to calm the prevailing anxiety. Indeed, all the signs seemed to indicate that the dawn of freedom would be marked by wild delirium, violence, bloodshed and carnage. And Barbados did not escape the infection that was sweeping through the Caribbean.

Hurrah for Jin-Jin

In the end, however, the voice of reason and moderation prevailed. Emancipation was a social revolution of the first magnitude and has rightly been described as "one of the landmarks of the history of human progress".[37] Yet it was effected without disorder and bloodshed. There were many causes that contributed to this happy event but not the least was unquestionably "the strengthening of the Church just nine years previously".[38] The Anglican Church, as revitalised by Coleridge in Barbados and other territories, played a notable part in ushering in the new order without the wild excesses that had been predicted by the prophets of doom.

It is not surprising that, when the day of freedom arrived, the Bishop was able to report favourably to the Society for the Propagation of the Gospel:

800,000 human beings lay down last night as slaves, [he wrote] and rose in the morning as free as ourselves. It might have been expected that on such an occasion there would have been some outburst of public feeling. I was present but there was no gathering that affected the public peace. There was a gathering, but it was a gathering of old and young together in the House of the Common Father of all. It was my peculiar happiness on that ever memorable day to address a congregation of nearly 4,000 people, of whom more than 3,000 were Negroes just emancipated. And such was the order, the deep attention, and perfect silence, that you might have heard a pin drop. [39]

The newly emancipated slaves had their own way of celebrating the occasion. Mention has been made in an earlier chapter that there was a viable culture among the slaves in Barbados. They loved dancing and music and indulged in other pastimes to divert themselves after the exhausting toil of the field and the factory. In spite of the dominance of European values and customs, they succeeded in preserving something of their African cultural traditions. Though their customs and art-forms were largely submerged, they managed to preserve part of their heritage by handing on some of it from generation to generation through secret meetings, ceremonies and rituals. [40]

One of the most pronounced characteristics of the Africans through the years was their love of music and their practice of suiting a song to every significant occasion. Something of the culture of the slaves has come down to us in the folklore and folkways from which originated the Barbadian folk music and folk song. However rude and primitive it may sound to the sophisticated ear today, the folk song of these early years was the poetry and the music of the poor and underprivileged. And nothing that has come down to us is more significant than the folk song *Lick and Lock-up* in which the newly freed slaves celebrated their liberation.

1. The Queen come from England
    To set me free
    Now lick and lock-up done wid
    Hurrah for Jin-Jin. [i.e. Queen Victoria]

Chorus
> Lick and lock-up done wid
> Hurrah for Jin-Jin
> Lick and lock-up done wid
> Hurrah for Jin-Jin.

2. They sell me mudda fuh six bit piece
   Hurrah for Jin-Jin.
   Now lick and lock-up done wid
   Hurrah for Jin-Jin.

3. God bless de Queen fuh set we free
   Hurrah for Jin-Jin
   Now lick and lock-up done wid
   Hurrah for Jin-Jin.[41]

Questions and Exercises to Consider

1. What is the meaning of "amelioration"? Imagine you are a West Indian planter living in England and write a letter to a Barbadian newspaper explaining why and how the condition of the slaves should be improved. If you were a Barbadian planter how would you reply?
2. Write a speech a member of the Barbados House of Assembly might have made against the amelioration proposals. Bring out in the speech what is implied in the words of Governor Sir Lionel Smith about the Barbadian planters.
3. Compare the views of Lord Seaforth, Sir Henry Warde and Joseph Sturge on the condition of the slave population. Do any of these seem (a) objective, (b) biased, (c) exaggerated. What factors do you need to consider in order to detect bias in a statement?
4. Why were the Wesleyan missionaries unpopular in Barbados? Why was it so difficult for missionaries like Shrewsbury to succeed in Barbados? Compare his fate with that of John Smith of Demerara.
5. Imagine you are Shrewsbury and prepare a sermon to be delivered to your congregation on the moral evils of the Barbadian society.
6. What is a "social revolution"? Emancipation has been described as a social revolution of the first magnitude.

Arrange a class discussion on the reasons for and against this view.

7. Imagine you are Bishop Coleridge and write out the kind of sermon you would give to the newly freed slaves on the day of their emancipation.

8. Carry out some investigations and find out which were some of the schools founded by Bishop Coleridge. From what sources in Barbados would you expect to find information about the work of Bishop Coleridge?

9. How do you think the comment by Coleridge on page 118 would be received today? Write an imaginary letter to the press and comment on this speech.

10. Is the Barbadian folk song an art form? Make a class collection of folk songs and find out from them what you can about the life and views of the slaves or ex-slaves.

11. How would you interpret the words of the song "Lick and Lock-up done wid"? What light does it throw on the period?

CHAPTER TEN

The Fall of the Planter Class?

Emancipation

It has been claimed that Emancipation brought the old order to an end, completed the downfall of the planter class in the West Indies and sent the old plantation system, "that magnificent structure", tottering to irretrievable ruin.[1] That may have been true in certain territories in the British Caribbean but it certainly was not true of Barbados.

Contrary to what had been predicted by the prophets of doom, the white section of the Barbadian population did not emigrate en masse. The work of cultivating the sugar estates went on as before. The cost of producing sugar did not rise on the scale expected by the faint of heart. Indeed, the production of sugar increased rather than diminished and the trade prospects of the island improved rather than declined. Barbados was faced with difficulties from time to time and there were periods when the sugar industry seemed to be threatened with bankruptcy. Yet it cannot be said that Emancipation, in the case of Barbados, "brought to a dramatic close the golden era of Caribbean History". In no way can it be said that the planters of Barbados ceased to play leading roles after the abolition of slavery.[2]

Crop, Profit and Taxation for a Barbadian Plantation
(453 acres, 200 Negroes, 90 Cattle)

Year	Hogsheads	Net Profit £	4½ per cent Duty £	Tax Percentage
1827	60	787	61	8.00
1828	105	1,090	78	7.25
1829	81	298	45	15.00
1830	83	210	42	20.00

The reasons why the situation in Barbados differed from that prevailing in other territories in the West Indies will be made clear in the course of this chapter.

The Emancipation Act was passed on August 28th, 1833, a month after Wilberforce died. It became effective on August 1st, 1834. For the purpose of carrying out the provisions of the Act, Barbados was united with three of the neighbouring islands, St. Vincent, Grenada and Tobago. One Governor-General, Sir Lionel Smith, was appointed for the whole group and was stationed in Barbados. Three Lieutenant-Governors were placed over the other islands. These officials were paid by the British Government, the purpose of this being to keep them independent of local influence.

The legislation emancipating the slaves included the following provisions: -

1. A sum of £20,000,000 was granted to the West Indian planters by the British Government to compensate them for the financial loss they incurred through Emancipation. Barbados' share of this was £1,721,345. 19s. 7d. sterling.[3]

2. Bondage was forever abolished as from August 1st, 1834 and children under the age of six years were given their immediate freedom.

3. The slaves generally were not to receive their full freedom immediately. A period of apprenticeship was introduced and this period was to last six years in the case of field labourers and four years in the case of domestic servants.

4. The working week for the former slaves, now apprentices, was reduced to forty-five hours and Sunday labour was abolished.

5. Wages were to be paid for work that exceeded 40½ hours a week and apprentices could purchase their own freedom before the period of apprenticeship was completed. But full freedom was to be secured, without payment of any kind, after that period was over.

6. Special magistrates were to be appointed and their salaries paid by the British Government to make sure that the provisions of the Emancipation Act, in respect of apprenticed labourers, were properly observed.

7. Allowances that were formerly granted to the slaves were to be continued under the apprenticeship system.

The grant of £20,000,000 from the British Treasury was of great help to the planters. The fact that it was raised to this figure from the sum of £15,000,000, originally proposed, was due mainly to Sir Thomas Buxton. The latter, still the champion of emancipation, now became the advocate of compensation. He believed that the planters could not fairly be asked to bear the whole burden of financing the great reform measure and incurred the strong displeasure of his more radical colleagues by pressing for adequate compensation. [4]

Apprenticeship

Under the apprenticeship system, the West Indies were supposed to derive three advantages. In the words of one authority, it was designed (1) to provide an easy and peaceful transition from slavery to freedom, (2) to guarantee an adequate supply of labour for the plantations for some years and (3) to train the apprentices for the responsibilities of free citizenship. [5]

Nevertheless, Antigua alone in the British West Indies rejected the apprenticeship system and went on straight to complete emancipation. The reasons for this unique decision can usefully be mentioned here.

In July 1834 a planter of Antigua, John Dunscombe Taylor, declared that he could no longer provide for his slaves. When summoned before the island's Council, he showed convincingly that the merchants of St. John's refused to give him credit owing to the uncertain situation facing Antigua on the eve of emancipation. He testified further that there were other planters in the island who were in the same predicament.

Two months later, Taylor presided over a meeting of planters in St. John's and a number of important decisions were made. It was resolved that a period of apprenticeship would serve no useful purpose in Antigua; that it would be expensive and have an adverse effect on the relations between masters and apprentices; that the transition from slavery to complete freedom would be peaceful, mainly because of the work of the non-conformist missionaries who had taught the slaves the value of certain social institutions; that the discussion of emancipation and its terms, if prolonged, could give rise to unrest and rebellion; that they should press for immediate and complete freedom, if they were granted compensation at the rate of £30 per slave and were relieved from the payment of the burdensome 4½ per cent tax.

Predictably, the planters of Antigua were concerned over the prospect of obtaining labour and the level of wages after emancipation. They were as much concerned about the eager expectations of the slaves as with "the uncertainties of business and the lack of credit prevailing in the island during 1833". There is little evidence to indicate that the meeting at St. John's was "convinced by any moral arguments against slavery". It seems fair to say that the passing of the resolutions proposed at the meeting was due more to economic realities than to humanitarian considerations. [6]

It may well be that in Barbados, as in Antigua, there was no need for the apprenticeship system. And the same thing may be said of St. Kitts. For in both Barbados and St. Kitts conditions were in many respects similar to those in Antigua. In all three of these islands the slave population was sufficiently developed and did not need any special training under the apprenticeship system for the responsibilities of citizenship. Secondly the proportion of the productive land outside of the sugar estates was small and gave the ex-slave little opportunity to find employment apart from sugar cultivation. And thirdly, the planters of Barbados and St. Kitts, like the planters of Antigua, might well have been convinced that they could cultivate their estates cheaper by free labour than slave labour. [7]

Certainly, Barbados did not share the problems of other territories in the Caribbean. There were no mountains, as in Jamaica, where the slaves could move away from the shadow of the plantation to establish their own settlements. There were no crown lands, as in Trinidad, which the former slaves could occupy and claim as theirs, organising their own communities of smallholders. There was no bush land, as in British Guiana, where the newly emancipated could set themselves up as owners of productive property. In Barbados, the ex-slaves had few, if any, alternatives to continuing to work on the sugar estates.

The apprenticeship system was rigidly and severely administered in Barbados from the outset. [8] Friction was, therefore, inevitable and this embittered the relations between masters and apprentices. Indeed, neither side was satisfied with the administration of the system. The apprentices did not enjoy the right to dispose of their own labour to any employer of their choice. The planters complained that the system cost them a lot of money and did not give them adequate returns for such expenditure. Certainly, there was considerable strife and discontent on all sides and the special magistrates whose function it was to deal with the many complaints that arose from the system rarely satisfied either the employer or the apprentice. Before

128

long, it was generally admitted that the apprenticeship system was a failure.[9]

Robert Bowcher Clarke, then Solicitor General, pointed out to the House of Assembly that the working of the system did no good to the reputation of the Barbadian planter. In view of the bitter attacks that were made on the fair name of the island, particularly by Sir Thomas Buxton, Clarke felt that the best way to deal with the strictures, was to proceed at once to the abolition of the apprenticeship system. He declared that it was his "deliberate conviction" that the house should without delay provide for the complete emancipation of the slaves on August 1st, 1838. The matter was promptly taken up by the House. A number of opposition resolutions, moved by F. Hodgkinson on April 24th, were eloquently opposed by Clarke, who won the day by eleven votes to seven. James Sarsfield Bascom, who had consistently supported Clarke in his efforts to shorten the period of apprenticeship, at once gave notice that a Bill should be introduced to end the apprenticeship of praedial labourers on the first day of August 1838. He also moved that a committee be appointed to prepare such a Bill. Unfortunately Clarke just at this time fell ill with scarlet fever. His illness undoubtedly delayed the work of the Committee and the House did not consider the matter again until May 15th. In his absence Bascom took charge of the Bill and declared that he was "proud to be an instrument, though an humble one, in aiding to destroy the last link of slavery".[10] But the measure terminating apprenticeship on the proposed date was not really a satisfactory one. While the Antigua Abolition Act had granted the ex-slaves conditional residence on the plantation for a period of twelve months, the Barbados Act limited such conditional residence for the ex-apprentices to three months. Moreover, it made the latter responsible for the upkeep of their poorer relations. Governor McGregor was perhaps justified in informing the Secretary of State that the imperfections of the measure were due to Clarke's continuing indisposition.[11]

When Clarke resumed his duties in the House, he took the opportunity to press for the removal of the 4½ per cent duty which had long afflicted the planters of the island. Many attempts had been made to abolish this iniquitous duty. It had recently been described by Lord Brougham "as a tax beyond others the most injurious to the subject in proportion to the benefit it produces to the Government of any recorded in the history of taxation".[12] Yet all the petitions and memorials to have it repealed had proved to be fruitless. Clarke perceived, however, that the crisis through which the island was passing was the appropriate occasion to make another appeal to the British Government. And his instinct proved to be right. On August 14th, 1838, an act was passed by the Imperial Parliament, abolishing the 4½ per cent duty. The tax on the exports of the planters which had been in force for one hundred and seventy-five years was thus removed and its place taken by a duty on essential items consumed by planters and labourers alike.

Located Labour

Before long there was some deterioration in the labour situation in the island. Labourers moved from one plantation to another, seeking kindlier employers or higher wages. Other labourers began to emigrate to such territories as Trinidad or British Guiana. The rain did not fall copiously and this decreased the output of sugar and the cultivation of ground provisions. It seemed clear to the planters that something had to be done to stabilise these unstable conditions. In due course, the place until recently held by the apprenticeship scheme was taken by the located labourer system. The latter was introduced by the Masters and Servants Act of 1840 which was to remain in force for nearly one hundred years.

The located labourer system may be said to have evolved from the apprenticeship scheme. Labourers appeared to be willing, at least at the beginning, to remain on the sugar plantations if they could receive some guarantee of security in return. And the planters, untroubled by the almost feudal character of the system,[13] were willing to enter into a relationship with the labourers who thus provided a stable labour force.

Under the new system, the labourers were allowed to remain in the houses and allotments they occupied during slavery and under apprenticeship. For these houses and allotments they paid rent either in money or in labour. In addition, they were required to give their labour to the plantation for five days a week. For this labour they were paid a fixed rate of wages. That rate was usually about twenty or thirty per cent lower than the level of wages paid in the common market.

The located labourer system was a constant source of friction and litigation. Sometimes the labourers tried to get away from their location to work for higher wages further afield. Sometimes

Wages in the 1840's

Territory	Wages	Allowances	Benefits
Antigua	9d	Cottage and grounds	Medical attention
Barbados	9d	Cottage and grounds	
British Guiana	2s	Nil	
Dominica	9d	Cottage and grounds	
Grenada	8d	Cottage and grounds	
Jamaica	1s.8d	Cottage and grounds	
Montserrat	4d	Cottage and grounds	
Nevis	Nil	Nil	Small share of estate produce
St. Kitts	1s.0d	Nil	
St. Lucia	1s.6d	Cottage and grounds	
St. Vincent	8d	Cottage and very small grounds	
Trinidad	2s.0d	Nil	

the planters would try to involve not only the labourers but all their families in the system. If the labourers did not perform satisfactorily the services required of them, they could be ejected from their allotments. The planters had to give four weeks notice of this ejection and the crops of the tenants were then taken over at a value appraised below what they were really worth. If the tenants gave notice, their growing crops were taken over without any payment.

The inequities of the system were criticized in season and out of season by the *Liberal*, a radical newspaper which was edited by Samuel Jackman Prescod. The planters maintained that the evils of the system were more apparent than real since they seldom resorted to the power of ejection. But Prescod replied that the power inherent in the system was such that it forced the labourers to submit to the obligations laid down by the law of the land. The articles in the *Liberal* were noted for their lucidity and one of them so impressed the Secretary of State for the Colonies, Sir E. Bulwer Lytton, that he ordered it to be printed for the information of the House of Commons.[14] In spite of all efforts, however, to have the Masters and Servants Act repealed, the located labourers system remained in force and continued to supply a stable labour force for the sugar plantations.

New Villages

There were other circumstances that ensured the planters a full reservoir of labour. In Jamaica, Trinidad, British Guiana and the Leeward Islands rapid strides were made in the development of villages at an appropriate distance from the shadow of the sugar plantations. Free villages were set up among the hills of Jamaica, in the forest areas of Trinidad and up the rivers and on the abandoned estates of British Guiana. In Barbados the situation was markedly different. There were few, if any, areas of arable land available to satisfy the land hunger of the emancipated slaves in the island.

It is true that two years after complete emancipation some one thousand smallholders possessed plots of land that varied in size from one to nine acres. But the evidence indicates that this group of landowners came into existence before full emancipation was attained in 1838. It consisted of poor whites, free coloureds and free blacks who were already free-holders and small landowners by that time.[15]

Some progress, however, was made after emancipation. At first there were some clusters of smallholdings in districts like Foul Bay, St. Philip. Yet the difficulties in acquiring small plots of land seemed almost insurmountable at the time. A Police Magistrate reported in 1842 that little progress was made by the ex-slaves in obtaining freeholds because of the untoward circumstances that faced them. "The reason is obvious;" he added, "there is not in the whole island a spot of waste land fit for cultivation; and as the land is principally divided into plantations, the proprietors are not likely to sell off small plots for that purpose; and there being no public lands available it is plain that freeholders to any extent cannot be established in this country."[16]

The first major breakthrough in the prevailing system was due to the "charity or philanthropy" of two planters, Reynold Alleyne Elcock and Peter Chapman. As a result of Elcock's bequest, the labourers on his estate at Mount Wilton in St. Thomas were able to purchase small portions of the plantation. That occurred in 1841-42. Elcock's philanthropy led to the establishment of a free village at Rock Hall near the parish church of St. Thomas. Peter Chapman, some fourteen years later, divided his estate at Enterprise in St. George into one and two acre lots and offered them for sale at £70 per acre. Though all the land was not sold off, mainly because of the price, nevertheless Chapman's subdivision of his estate was responsible for the development of Workmans in St. George as a free village. [17]

Few planters followed the example of Elcock and Chapman at this time. Resistance to change remained almost insuperable. Yet there were some successes owing to the intense land hunger among the ex-slaves and the habit of thrift they developed which enabled them to buy land even at high prices whenever a planter here and there decided to sell off small portions of his estate. Thus did new villages begin their existence, such as Arthur's Seat, Redman's Village, Arch Hall and Melrose in St. Thomas and Good Intent, Ellerton, Sweet Bottom, Newbury and Jehovah Jirah in St. George. [18]

Nevertheless, the situation in Barbados remained largely unchanged for some years. Ownership of land was almost entirely the monopoly of the plantations. The planters were in the main unwilling to sell off land because this monopoly gave them a control of labour. This, added to the located labourer system, gave them a reliable supply of labour which was a vital ingredient in the efficiency of the sugar industry.

The New Middle Class Emerges

While the planters and the labourers were trying to adjust themselves to a new relationship after emancipation, the third main social group, formerly known as the free coloured people, were seeking to integrate themselves in the changed order of society.

Before and after emancipation the latter suffered from cruel and degrading discrimination in a variety of ways. Racial distinctions were rigidly enforced against them in the largest religious denomination in the island, the Church of England. They were confined to certain seats within the churches and were not allowed to take communion at the same time as the white members of the congregation. They were excluded from the ministry of the Church and from leading positions and posts of responsibility. Moreover, no provision was made for a change in the future, for up to 1837 "no coloured student has yet been admitted within the walls of Codrington College". [19]

Equally discriminatory were the practices in the schools. Coloured teachers received smaller salaries than white teachers and were permitted to teach only coloured children. Although their parents paid taxes, coloured children could not attend the parochial schools which were financed from public funds.

Nor were such distinctions confined to the institutions of the Church and education. The free coloured people could not serve on juries, give evidence against whites, exercise the vote or gain admission to "public situations of honour and profit". They were required to serve in the militia but their units were segregated from the whites and they could not be promoted to commissions even in the coloured units.

In 1831 the franchise was extended to them. Yet even in the twilight of slavery the plantocrats were not disposed to grant the free coloured people any real concessions. Anyone, irrespective of race, could vote if he owned twn acres of land. But since few coloured people owned so much land the law of 1831 was a hollow mockery of their aspirations. Those who owned a house of a certain annual taxable value were declared eligible to vote, but this value was three times higher than that laid down for whites in the previous law of 1721. It is not surprising that the new act providing for increased property qualifications was strongly criticized by Prescod, who described it as "a mockery of their wrongs" and as adding "insult to past injuries".[20]

In spite of the disabilities they endured, the free coloured people appeared to have no "fellow feeling with the slave". Indeed, the élite of the group held marked conservative views and seemed indifferent if not actually opposed to the notion of emancipation. Concerned as they were with their own efforts to attain the rights and privileges enjoyed by the whites, they strove to distinquish their status from that of the slave and showed little or no enthusiasm for the liberation of their less fortunate brothers.[21]

If is significant, however, that with emancipation this group was to abandon the policy of exclusively seeking their own selfish interests. It is true that the élite seemed more concerned to perpetuate their special position, a position they saw threatened by the recently emancipated slaves and by the lower sections of the coloured community. But the group as a whole was to adopt a more liberal policy.

That this view prevailed among the group was due to the leadership of men who became prominent in the press and politics, in religion, commerce and social welfare. Among these were men like Prescod, Anthony Barclay, Joseph Hamilton, Joseph Thorne, Nat Roach and London Bourne. They made the coloured people a cohesive community and sought to build their own institutions within their group. They trained their followers in habits of hard work, sacrifice and self-help and, in all their efforts to promote their welfare, they demonstrated their attachment to representative institutions. While the free coloured people had seemed opposed to the campaign for the abolition of slavery, after emancipation they took the recently liberated slaves under their wing and persuaded them to accept their habits, their life style and their philosophy. That was the great contribution they made to the stability and progress of the island as a whole.

We have noted in an earlier chapter the emergence of the yeomanry of Barbados, that section of the white population which became the land-owning middle class of the island and enjoyed a brief period of ascendancy, in the House of Assembly. Now, in the period that followed emancipation, we see the gradual development of a more significant middle class. "The day that proclaimed slavery extinct and the labourer free", the leaders of the free coloured people declared hopefully in 1838, "indissolubly links him with us in one common body, with interests and rights the same as ours to be advanced or retarded in his progress by whatever advances or retards us."[22]

One of the main events at this time was the foundation of *The Times,* the first coloured newspaper in the history of this island. This was followed by the *Liberal,* which was edited by Prescod for 25 years. In 1843 Prescod was elected the first coloured member of the House of Assembly, undoubtedly a victory for the new middle class. In the press, and in the Legislature, Prescod fought for the rights and privileges of the coloured people as well as for the integration of the former slaves into the new coloured community. But he went further. James Bascom and his party of white yeoman farmers were no more. Prescod allied himself and his group with the "Ten Acre" men and thus it came about that, although he was the only coloured member of the House, he was soon the accredited leader of a Liberal party consisting of nine men.

The object of all this was to form a grand alliance against the planter class who still dominated the political, social and economic life of the island. Prescod's aim was not so much to destroy the plantocracy, as to force them, through the island's representative institutions, to abandon all measures of class legislation and to plan for society as a whole. The policy of the middle class, now composed of white, black and coloured people, and the guidance of their leaders, was to give the island a welcome measure of stability for the next forty years.

It may well be, however, that this stability was attained at the cost of progress in an important area of social welfare. In other territories of the Caribbean, the growth of free villages and other significant social changes were attended by growing tensions and even open confrontation. In Barbados, however, the situation was quite different during the forty years after emancipation. There was no relaxation in the plantations' control of the land reserve. There was no rapid expansion of free villages, as in other parts of the West Indies. Barbados continued the even tenour of its life in the forty years following emancipation owing to the nature of its leadership, the attitudes of its middle class and the thrift and industry that brought its labourers through a period of hardship and privation.

Meeting the Challenge

In the meantime, the planters of Barbados braced themselves to meet the sea of troubles that seemed to beset them on all sides. Cotton had long been one of the island's staple products, but this had to be abandoned because of the grave threat that was posed by the cotton producers of the U.S.A. Sugar produced by slave labour in the East Indies and beet sugar grown in several countries of Europe encroached on the traditional markets that Barbados had long enjoyed. The population of the island had steadily increased from the beginning of the nineteenth century until it had doubled itself by the middle of that century.[23] Perhaps the greatest peril during this period was the passing of the Sugar Duties Act by the Imperial Parliament in 1846, for this act reduced the preferential duties on colonial sugar, exposed the West Indies to serious competition from their foreign rivals and imperilled their market in Britain. While the planters of Barbados were almost over-whelmed with gloom, there was rejoicing among her rivals in Cuba, Brazil and Louisiana. For these countries produced sugar in ever-increasing quantities, continuing to use slave labour and enjoying the advantages of greater capital, central factories, larger plantations, modern machinery and a more efficient management.

Bankruptcy stared the planters in the face and they could not have survived the hazards of the time but for a number of events and developments. The increased supply of sugar in other parts of the world was offset by the increased demand for sugar everywhere. The planters of Barbados reduced the cost of production by employing fewer labourers in the off season. They planted an increased acreage in canes and doubled their production of sugar between 1838 and 1852. Perhaps the most important factor in their survival was the improved methods of sugar cultivation that were introduced in the island.[24]

The white population of Barbados was, comparatively speaking, larger than any similar group in other parts of the British West Indies. A marked advantage enjoyed by the island was that its leading figures consisted more of resident proprietors than absentee landlords. They formed a closely knit group and their agricultural societies knew the value of research and experiment. Not the least significant of their enterprises was a monthly periodical, *The Agricultural Reporter,* which, in spite of a limited circulation, was a publication of undoubted merit.

The work of improving the methods of sugar cultivation went steadily ahead. Chemicals and green manures were used. The practice of mulching became more widely spread. The sytem of "jobbing out" fields to the labourers to be weeded by the week was introduced. The plough was substituted for the hoe. So favourable was the progress that *The Agricultural Reporter* could write, with great satisfaction, about "the comparative steadiness of our labour market, the destruction of devil's grass, the beautiful thyme-bed appearance of our fields and, under providence, the unprecedently large crops that have crowned our efforts".[25]

The planters carefully planned their cultivation to suit the

Cost of producing one cwt. of sugar in the West Indies, 1848
(Selling price in London 22s.6d per cwt.)

	s	d
British Guiana	25	0
Trinidad	25	0
Jamaica	22	7
St. Vincent	19	2
Grenada	16	2
St. Kitts	16	2
Antigua	15	4½
Barbados	15	4½

vagaries of the seasons and they also gave their attention to better methods of manufacture. Steam engines were substituted for windmills. The vacuum pan, as an improved means of evaporating cane juice, became the accepted thing. "Invaluable adjuncts to the production of good sugar", such as precipitators and centrifugal dessicators, were being so rapidly adopted that anyone who did not provide himself with such means and appliances was regarded as "a very slow coach indeed".[26]

Such were the circumstances that were favourable to the success of the agriculture pursued by the planters of Barbados. In 1840, according to a contemporary return, there were 1,874 landed properties in the island. Of these, 1,367 were smallholdings of one to nine acres and 508 ranged from ten to eight hundred and seventy-nine acres. Seven years later, the number of landed properties rose to 2,998. The larger estates averaged one hundred and seventy-four acres. They were large enough to call upon all the resources of the planters in skill and capital for their successful cultivation and not so large as to be beyond their competence to manage them profitably.

The planter lived in a large house that was usually "a very comfortable abode" and "a pleasing object", whether constructed of stone or wood. It was accounted somewhat Oriental in its appearance "from the galleries and verandahs" with which it was surrounded and "its light decorations, if any, and bright colours". Sometimes the air of coolness would be enhanced by "the pleasing shade and verdure of a grove or shrubbery" and more rarely its approach would be dignified by "an avenue of stately cabbage palms, or of a narrow strip of dense wood".[27]

From such a commanding position, the planters applied themselves to three things in the management of their estates. First, they produced as much sugar as possible to make the plantation a profitable concern. Secondly, they reserved a part of the estate as pasture land for the maintenance of their livestock. And thirdly, they cultivated a crop of ground provisions both for themselves and for their labourers and this became a matter of growing concern as the population of the island increased by leaps and bounds.[28]

Thus did the planters pursue their system of agriculture. Their methods and their skill enabled them to survive at a time when bankruptcy was bringing ruin to many of their fellows in other territories of the West Indies. Certainly, if the planter class in the period immediately following emancipation was overthrown in the other plantation colonies of the British Caribbean, their counterparts did not suffer a similar fate in the island of Barbados.

Questions and Exercises to Consider

1. What do you understand by the system of apprenticeship? Why was it not adopted in Antigua? Should Barbados and other territories in the B.W.I. have followed Antigua's example?

2. Draw a plan of a plantation, showing the manager's house, the overseer's quarters, the slave compound and huts, the sugar mill, the porportion of land given to sugar cane, pasture land and provision grounds.

3. What were the improved methods employed on the plantation in the nineteenth century? How did they help the Barbadian planters survive when almost all of their fellow planters in the area were going down in ruin.

4. Go on a field trip to a plantation and make a rough plan of the buildings and compare it with the traditional plan of a plantation in the nineteenth century. List the changes you notice.

5. See if you can find areas where land was occupied by workers under the Located Labour system.

6. In what ways do you consider that the absence of free villages might have contributed to an absence of tension in Barbados in the nineteenth century?

CHAPTER ELEVEN

Education and the Church

Slow Progress

Progress in the field of education was slow in the earlier years of the history of Barbados. That was the period when the children of the well-to-do, on reaching the age of twelve years, were sent to England for their education and no thought was given, except by Christopher Codrington, to the instruction of the children of the slaves. This was a policy that enjoyed the approval of the planters as a whole and was condoned by the clergy of the Established Church.

Those who benefited from the island's first progressive step in education were the children of the poor whites. The needs of these children were met by a number of small private schools that were established in various parts of the island. Gradually, over a period of a hundred years, schools of this kind were found in each parish. As far back as 1686, the first charity school for poor white children was set up in the parish of St. George. This was due to the generosity of two planters, John Elliot and Rowland Bulkeley, who contributed the land and a sum of £1,000 for the building of the school. Unfortunately, this school does not exist today since it was destroyed by the hurricane of 1780. [1]

The year 1686 was important for another event. In that year, Colonel Henry Drax, son of Sir James Drax, the great pioneer in the establishment and organisation of the sugar industry, left a will bequeathing the sum of £2,000 for the foundation of a school in Bridgetown. It was an ambitious scheme under which the bequest was to be increased, through grants from the Vestry and other donations, to the substantial total of £20,000.

It was stated by an educator in the *Barbados Diocesan History* that the will making this request had disappeared, leaving no trace behind, and that the executors under the will had probably diverted the sum bequeathed to their own personal uses. [2] Fortunately this statement has since been proved to be inaccurate and the will is now safely deposited in the Barbados Department of Archives.

To the names of John Elliot, Rowland Bulkeley and Henry Drax must be added that of Francis Williams. In 1709 he gave a hundred acres of land in the parish of Christ Church for the building of a charity school for the children of the poor whites. A hundred years were to pass before the foundation stone was laid and the school, which was then erected, was destroyed twenty-two years later by the hurricane of 1831. A second foundation stone was laid the following year. The laying of the first foundation stone in 1809 marked the beginning of the history of the institution which later developed into the two schools now known as the Boys' Foundation and the Girls' Foundation.

Thomas Harrison, a merchant of Bridgetown, was the founder of Harrison College which was to acquire, in the years ahead, the reputation of being one of the leading secondary schools in the island. Its inception was due to the generosity of the man who was once Churchwarden of St. Michael and gave up half of the commission he received for "collecting and disbursing parish funds" for the purpose of establishing a charity school. Subsequent churchwardens followed his example and Harrison's aim was happily achieved in 1733 when the school was opened "for the poor and indigent boys of the parish".[3]

The most famous of the public benefactors in the cause of education was undoubtedly Christopher Codrington. As recorded earlier in this narrative, he was the first to insist that the slaves be instructed in the precepts of Christianity and to establish a school for the education of their children. At first, it was not thought practicable to establish the missionary college envisaged by Codrington and a school, known originally as the Codrington Grammar School and later as the Lodge School, was established in 1745 to provide secondary education for those who intended later to undergo training for the missionary purpose intended by Codrington's will. The execution of that will along the lines requested by Codrington was to prove a matter of considerable controversy, as we shall see later in this chapter.

A Quickened Pace

The early decades of the nineteenth century were to see a quickening in the pace of educational development in Barbados. The revolt of the slaves in 1816, as has already been noted, gave rise to a new spirit in the land and more attention was given to the task of ameliorating the conditions of the underprivileged.

141

One of the significant achievements of this time was the establishment of the first public school for coloured boys, in 1818. The cost of building this school was met by public subscription and the Church Missionary Society provided a grant of £100 for a Master. A Colonial Charity School, as mentioned in an earlier chapter, was also established in 1818 for the instruction of the children of black· and coloured people. It is interesting to note that of the eighty-nine pupils attending this school, thirty-two were the children of slaves.

Another important event at this time was the foundation of the Boys' Central School in Bridgetown in 1819. This was designed to replace the school for poor whites then existing in the parish of St. Michael. A grant of £800 was given by the Government who required the new school "to educate, clothe and board two children from each parish, two nominated by the Freemasons and two by the English Charitable Society".[5] The establishment of this school was interpreted as the fulfilment of the intention expressed in Henry Drax's will and was later called Combermere School, as a tribute to Lord Combermere, who had shown a great interest in the project and laid the foundation stone of the building.

With the arrival of Bishop Coleridge in 1825, a greater impetus was given to the movement for progress and reform in education. Within two years, the first public school for coloured girls was established. This school, like the one for boys founded in 1818, was destroyed by the hurricane of 1831, which was responsible for destroying much of Coleridge's work. But the Bishop was not easily daunted and the two schools were soon rebuilt.

In the same year, the Girls' Central School was established in Bridgetown. Both the Boys' Central and the Girls' Central Schools were designed at first to provide a primary type of education. Some years later, an attempt was made to raise the curriculum of the Boys' Central School to a higher level, but this was not successful. There was general dissatisfaction with the facilities for secondary education in the island but reform in this area had to wait for half a century before it was implemented. It was at this later stage that Queen's College emerged from the Girls' Central School and soon won acceptance as one of the leading secondary schools in Barbados.

It was in the field of primary education that Coleridge exerted himself most and gained his conspicuous successes. In a sense, the way had been cleared for him by Lord Combermere and an association of clergy and laymen which had been formed in 1818 under his patronage. This association was given the official title of "The Barbados Society for Promoting Christian Knowledge" and played an active part in the foundation of the Boys' and Girls' Central Schools. In 1825, after the arrival of Coleridge, it divided itself into "The Barbados Society for the Education of the Poor", which gave its attention mainly to the progress and welfare of the Central Schools, and the "Diocesan Committee" which applied itself to the propagation of Christian knowledge throughout the island. [6]

Circumstances were undoubtedly favourable for the success of Coleridge's work in Barbados. The ideas prevailing in England during the Age of Reform were bound to have an impact on Barbados and other territories in the British Caribbean. The spirit that gave rise to the movement for progress and reform constrained the British Government to meet the demand for popular education in England. A sum of £30,000 was granted in 1833 to provide facilities for English primary education. In 1835 the reform movement reached out to the West Indies when £30,000 was granted to these colonies for the education of the recently emancipated slaves.

Barbados was in a good position to make the best possible use of its share of the Negro Education Grant. In Trinidad, St. Lucia and Grenada, where the British Government was inhibited by its anti-Catholic prejudice, little was done by way of that Grant to establish a system of public education. In Barbados, where the Anglican Church was the Established Church, there was no such difficulty during the ten years the British grant was made available to the West Indies. In any case, except for the Wesleyans and the Moravians, no other denominations received financial help and, accordingly, there was no split in the resources being made available for education by the British Government.

The money obtained under the Negro Education Grant was added to Church funds already existing and Coleridge was able to continue his work for education, a brief record of which has been given in an earlier chapter. It is interesting to note that many private schools continued to function in the island. These, added to the schools under the management of the Church of England, brought the total number of schools in the island to two hundred. It was an impressive total, though it should be borne in mind that many of the private schools were small and inefficient.[7]

A Crucial Controversy

When the S.P.G. set out to execute the will of Christopher Codrington, they first accumulated money and then erected the buildings that were to house the proposed missionary college. The difficulty that faced them at the outset was that there were few, if any, students to take up the places in the college.

Their obvious course then was to "grow a body of candidates from which to select their students".[8] To this was due the origin of the Codrington Grammar School which functioned with a varying degree of success until the beginning of the nineteenth century when a new scheme was introduced by the "President" of the school, the Rev. Mark Nicholson. Under this scheme twelve boys were selected from "the upper classes" and given free board and lodge at the school. The Codrington Trust Fund paid the President of the school £40 per annum for each of these boys and when they reached the age of eighteen years they were sent, if they satisfied the requirements of an examination, to one of the English universities "to study one of the learned professions". For this purpose they were awarded an exhibition for £100 per annum for four years.

This arrangement was clearly contrary to the intention of the Codrington bequest. The exhibitions thus awarded did not require the beneficiaries to undergo any special course of training as candidates for Holy Orders. Accordingly, in 1829, Bishop Coleridge abandoned the system devised by Nicholson. The same year the grammar school was moved to the site it now occupies as the Lodge School, the intention being that it should be "strictly subsidiary to Codrington College". Students from the school desiring to study for Holy Orders were given exhibitions that enabled them to be educated at the College free of charge.[9]

This system was in accordance with the terms of Codrington's will and remained in operation until Coleridge's resignation from the bishopric in 1842. But it was not accepted by those who had benefited from the previous system. After Coleridge's retirement and just before the arrival of Richard Rawle as Principal of Codrington College, an attempt was made to revive the plan that had given the sons of "the Barbadian gentry" an opportunity to study for a profession at an English university at the expense of the Codrington bequest.

144

Of the said Sarah my wife unto my said sister Mary Jackson and
to her heires Executors and assignes fforever Item I nominate
and Appointe Benjamin Nuthall Coexecutor with these two
Executors named in my will and give him ten pounds thorofore
to be by him retained any thing in my will conteined to the
Contrary thorof notwithstanding and this I declare to be part
of my Last will and testament conteined in One Shoot of paper
and have to the same sett my hand and Seale the day and yeare
ffirst above written Robert Cooke Signed Sealed and published
by the said Robert Cooke to be part of his Last will and testament
in the presence of us who have sett Our names as witnesses
hereto in the presence of the said testator after the interlineation
Joseph Brittaine Eliz ___ ___ Whitehand Joon: Smith ___ Item
will that instead of ten pounds a poore to be retained by my three
Executors fforthoir Care I will and desire they should retaine
to themselves fforthoir trouble Fifteen pounds a poore
and I desire this to be a further part of my Last will and to be
taken as such Robert Cooke Signed by the testator as part
of his will in the presence of us Jose ___ Brittain Elize ___ ___
Whitehand Joon: Smith

Probatum fuit huiusmodi Testamentum
apud London Coram prehonorando viro domino Carolo Hedges
milite Legum doctore Curia prerogativa Cantuariensis magistro
Custode sive Commissario legitimo Constituto decimo quinto
die mensis ffebruarij Anno domini (Stylo Angliae) Millesimo
Septingentesimo decimo Juramentis Johannis Cumberland
Samuelis Eades et Benjamini Nuthall Executorum in dicto
testamento nominatorum Quibus Commissa fuit Administratio
Omnium et singulorum bonorum Jurium et Creditorum dicti
defuncti de bene et fideliter Administrando Eadem ad sancta dei
Evangelia vigore Commissionis Jurat Exam

In the Name of God Amen
the twenty second day of ffebruary in the ffirst yeare of the reigne
of Our Soveraigne Lady Anne by the Grace of God of England
Scotland ffrance and Ireland Queen Defendor of the ffaith etc
Annoq, domini 1702/3 Christopher Codrington of Dodington in the
County of Gloucester Esquire and Cheife Governour
of Her Majesties Leward Islands in America doe make and declare
this to be my Last will and testament I recommend my Soul to
the good God who made it hopeing for Salvation through his
mercy and the meritts of his Son my worldly Estate I thus dispose
of Item I give my nearest kinsman Lieutenant Collonell
William Codrington all my Estate in and about Dodington
aforesaid provided and upon condition that he pay to All Souls
Colledge in Oxford ten thousand pounds Sterling in manner
ffollowing viz two thousand pounds within one yeare after
my decease and the summe of two thousand pounds yearly

Extract from Codrington's will

The leader of those who wanted the College to revert to the arrangements organised by Nicholson was Robert Bowcher Clarke, now knighted and Chief Justice of Barbados. The latter contended that the system which had been in force before 1829 had given "great satisfaction to the community", enabling many persons of "slender means and with large families" to educate their sons in the liberal professions. It had provided the island with "living examples of persons educated under it" who had turned out to be "most honourable proofs of the excellence of the principle and the complete success of its working".[10]

The Chief Justice expressed regret that all this had been changed since 1829 when "the Institution, as a charity, became exclusively confined to the Established Church". He submitted that the Trustees were maintaining an awkward position if they argued that after a lapse of 120 years the Founder's Will was only now being carried into effect for the first time. Turning his attention to the provisions of that will, he insisted that it was a violation of the terms of the Trust to limit the exhibitions to those intending to study for Holy Orders. The Trust was intended to advance the study and practice of physic and chirurgery as well as of divinity. From this he deduced that the exhibitions could be granted to those who intended to take up medicine as a profession. He then proceeded to the quite astonishing conclusion that those intending to embrace law as a profession were also entitled to benefit from the Fund. The change introduced since 1829, he submitted, was "most injurious to the laity" and had produced "no compensating gain to the clergy". He concluded that the existing system, re-introduced by Coleridge in 1829, was an "entire failure" and called attention to the fact that there were only eight students at the College and two boys at the grammar school.[11]

The successor of Bishop Coleridge, Thomas Parry, entrusted Rawle with the task of defending the College against the Chief Justice and the influential party that supported him both in the island and in London. Rawle's first step was to clarify the interpretation of Codrington's will. He pointed out that Codrington had bequeathed his property to the S.P.G. whose "object and operations have ever been *exclusively missionary*". The will laid it down that professors and students should be maintained on his estate in Barbados and not in England. He alluded to the "Vowes of obedience, poverty and chastity" in the clause of the will which demonstrated that the institution envisaged by the Founder should be "characterised by economy and religious discipline" and not be concerned with "the social accomplishments" on which the Chief Justice had placed so much emphasis. He added that the main concern of the students at the College was the study of divinity. A knowledge of medicine was also prescribed so that the students might have "the better opportunities of doing good to men's souls while they are taking care of their bodies".[12]

To Rawle the controversy was a matter of life and death for the College over which he had recently been appointed to preside. To him it was inconceivable that the missionary institution so clearly projected by Codrington should revert to what it had been before, a grammar school for the sons of planters. The Chief Justice remained convinced of the excellence of the former arrangement and hinted that, if it was not re-introduced, the question would be referred to the Court of Chancery. The fear that this Court would pronounce in favour of the Chief Justice and his supporters induced the S.P.G. to appoint a Commission, with the Governor and the Chief Justice among its members, "to investigate the affairs of Codrington College and report thereon".[13]

Rawle was astounded that "the blarney of the lawyer" had blinded the eyes of the "good and wise men" who composed the Society. He lost no time in addressing "a firm and decided protest" against the appointment of such a Commission and this was accompanied by a statement that he would immediately resign from the post of Principal if the true intentions of the Founder were so flagrantly violated.[14]

In the end, Rawle won the day after a long and exhausting battle. His objection to the appointment of the Commission was upheld. There was to be no departure "from the plain meaning of the Founder's Will". Gratified by the decision of the Society, Rawle settled down to the work ahead of him. And he was fortified by the hope that, if the Society would "but act in the spirit of their present profession", a new era would begin in West Indian education, both lay and clerical.[15]

Developing the Curriculum

The controversy between the Chief Justice and Richard Rawle throws an interesting light on the prevailing system of education in the island and the nature of the Barbadian society. Clarke frankly maintained that Barbados was grievously in need of "a high class school" such as the Lodge School had been at one time and not "a low class college"[16] such as Codrington College had become.

During the period from 1819 to 1829 the Lodge School was in "a class by itself". It enjoyed great benefits from the funds left in the Codrington will. It was a school for the sons of gentlemen and those who did not enjoy such social status were discouraged from attending it. Alone in the British West Indies before emancipation, Barbados could boast of "a superior Grammar School". Its course of study was similar to that "cultivated in Grammar Schools in England" and included Latin and Greek. Thus it provided for the education of the upper classes in Barbados. Unfortunately for those who supported the school as a "Superior Grammar School", it suffered a serious setback when the Codrington funds were once again applied to their original purpose. It lost most of its prestige as a school for the sons of gentlemen.[17]

Rawle had maintained that if the upper classes wanted their own "high class school", this should be provided by the House of Assembly in which they were amply represented. If that was not done they could continue their practice of sending their children to upper class schools in England and to the Universities of Oxford and Cambridge. This was not the ideal system since, as was the case with Jamaica, the education they received in Great Britain did not qualify them for useful employment in Barbados. Except for those who were trained in the learned professions, they did not usually return to "their inheritance in the West Indies".[18]

After the retirement of Coleridge, the work of education in Barbados lost much of the impetus he had given it during his episcopate. The clergy, who had responded to his lead soon relapsed into the apathy that had traditionally characterised them as a body. And during the period, when the Negro Education Grant was discontinued and before funds were provided by the local legislature, the various educational institutions began to weaken and languish.

Rawle set to work on the missionary College, as envisaged by Codrington. He established its course of study as the "elements of Theology, Classical Learning, Logic and Mathematics, with lectures from a Professor of Medicine in Anatomy, Chemistry and Physiology". He had declined the appointment as Principal

148

Codrington College

of St. Bree's Theological College with a salary of £1,500 per annum and, believing that he was guided by the hand of God, accepted the post at Codrington College at a salary of £700 per annum. Such was the financial condition of the College that, on his arrival, he offered to accept a reduced salary of £600. He was appointed simply to teach divinity but soon took on the additional task of teaching mathematics in view of the state of the College funds. Before long, too, he accepted responsibility for the teaching of classical studies at the College. By 1847, he had the duties of the chaplaincy of the Codrington estates added to those he had already assumed.

The reduction of the sugar duties had an almost ruinous effect on the estates which supported and maintained the College. Rawle saw that the College could make no real progress until something was done about the market for sugar. The most he could do for the present was to restrict the scope of the College to

149

a small scale, perform his duties as well as he could in the circumstances and practise prudent measures of retrenchment until there was some improvement in the general situation facing Barbados and the West Indies.

Rawle also saw clearly that, if he was to be of much use in these parts, it could only be "by forwarding the education of the mass of the people".[19] As he surveyed the scene, he was appalled by the "wretched state of education" in the island. "The Negro schools are utter failures;" he wrote at the time, "because the masters are untrained and it is nobody's business to provide forms, desks, or books of any kind. Four walls and a man inside, two benches, a book and a half and perchance half a slate, constitute what is called 'a school' and the Negroes are complained of because they don't send their children, or, if they send them, don't pay a shilling a month. They prefer sending them to little private schools, like our dames' schools, and rightly so".[20]

The Principal at once set to mending matters. He busied himself with the school on Society Hill, becoming not only the schoolmaster but the "school-furnisher" as well. Working almost every day in the week, he brought the school "from the lowest state of debasement" to a condition where it could be compared, in point of efficiency, with the English National Schools. But in the matter of the number of children crowded into a given space it could not be rivalled by any of those schools. It had been emphasised before that the main objective of primary education should be to inculcate the principles and promote the influence of Christianity. The authorised version of the Bible was to be read and taught and the other branches of instruction should be reading, writing and arithmetic. It was feared that education would be prized as "the means of enabling the child of a labourer to emancipate himself from the pursuits in which his parent had been engaged".[21]

Rawle's influence is clearly seen in the Act passed in 1858 to provide for a more extensive and general education of the people of Barbados. The Holy Scriptures were to be taught as well as reading, writing and arithmetic. But instruction was also to be given in the elements of Grammar, Geography, History and Music.[22]

Attention was also given to the schools for black children on the Codrington estates and much-needed improvements were introduced. The Middle School at St. Mark's was soon going vigorously forward. Model infants' schools were established wherever possible in spite of opposition from parents who were "absolutely averse to all the fun and amusing instruction which characterises such establishments at home".[23]

The Schoolmaster General

Rawle's reputation as a reformer in education soon spread far and wide in the island. He set to remodelling the Boys' and Girls' Schools in Bridgetown and was made responsible for their staffing and curriculum. He was called on to look after primary schools up and down the island and established model infants' schools to train the very young in the habits of work, study and wholesome discipline. In the meantime, he re-organised the Lodge School for the education of the sons of the gentry but on a different plan from that proposed by the Chief Justice. By 1850 it was reported that, in spite of Rawle's many preoccupations, the number of students at the College had risen to twenty-two and the number of boys at the grammar school had increased to forty. And in 1852 the Bishop of Barbados was able to report that there were several coloured boys at the school and a number of coloured students at Codrington College. It was now designed to provide secondary education for the children of the middle class both white and coloured and its course of instruction included the elements of a good English and Classical education.[24]

To execute the far-ranging duties he was called on to perform, Rawle assumed "the office of schoolmaster general" of the island.[25] He persevered in his work in spite of the lethargy of those in high places who were oppressed by the financial condition of the island and "the lamentable attitude" of the clergy in general who were "the most apathetic of the community in this matter".[26] Moreover, he had to assume the duties of "drill sergeant and bugleman to the hitherto undisciplined corps of pedagogues". To mend this state of affairs, he arranged a course of lectures and practical training in the "most essential points of school-craft" and secured the appointment of a board for the examination of teachers and the inspection of the schools.

While the clergy and laity of the Established Church remained cool to his proposals, the teachers proved to be enthusiastic and readily responded to Rawle's invitation to attend a training course at the College during their holidays. They had been treated with "undeserved and most disheartening neglect and chilling indifference" by those who should have supported them in their efforts at self-improvement. Their "scanty stipends" were six months in arrear, yet several of them attended the training course at their own expense. For no-one seemed interested enough to "pay the few shillings required for their board". But they were all eager to learn what a school ought to be and how they should teach their subjects as skilled craftsmen. After the introductory lecture in the first training session, Rawle asked them to make a list of the subjects they taught. At the end, when he was leaving the lecture room, with the lists in his hand, one of the teachers rushed after him and said: "Please, sir, I forgot: I'se perfect in grammar".[27]

With unwearying diligence, Rawle proceeded in his self-appointed tasks for nearly two decades. Gradually his work won the recognition of the authorities.[28] The first Government grant for primary education, £750, was made in 1846. This was doubled four years later and an Education Committee appointed to control public education. Soon the grant was raised to £3,000, and ten years after Rawle retired, in 1864, owing to ill-health, the Government Grant rose to £9,200. By that time the system Rawle had originated was going steadily forward. Infants' schools, primary schools, middle schools, grammar schools, teacher training and higher education at Codrington College—these were his objectives and he succeeded far more than circumstances seemed to promise at the beginning of his time in Barbados.

Significant Improvements

In the meantime, there was a growing demand for 'middle class' education in the island of Barbados.

In 1858 an Act was passed making it lawful for the Education Committee to spend a sum not exceeding £300 in any one year, out of the education grant, to support and assist any school which was established for the education of the middle classes. Some eleven years later, the Education Committee resolved to re-organise Harrison's Free School as "a first grade secondary school". It was considered that a good grammar school in Bridgetown would be of great advantage to the island generally and the Committee therefore offered the school £200 out of the grant of £500 provided for the aid of 'middle class' education.

This offer was made on the condition that the local Legislature would authorise "at least an equal liberality" and the Vestry of St. Michael would give a yearly grant of £100.[29]

It is clear that there was much dissatisfaction with the facilities for secondary education in the island. When the S.P.G. in 1869 announced its decision not to employ any portion of the Codrington Trust Funds in support of the Lodge School, it was felt the only way the school could free itself from debt and "continue the effective discharge of its functions" was by obtaining financial assistance from the island Legislature. A petition from the Council of Codrington College declared that there was no doubt about "the great usefulness of the Lodge School in the past" or of its "capabilities for good in the future". The petitioners submitted that their arguments would be further strengthened by the encouragement that was soon to be given by the Government to "Middle Schools in different parts of the Island".[30]

It was fortunate for Barbados that the successor of Thomas Parry was John Mitchinson who was consecrated Bishop in Canterbury Cathedral in June 1873 and came out to Barbados two months later. A winner of three firsts at Oxford University and a former Headmaster of King's School, Canterbury, he was well aware of the trends of educational reform. The Education Act of 1870 had laid it down that every child in England should be given the elements of a sound education and Mitchinson was soon to demonstrate his firm conviction that such a policy should be followed in Barbados.

His reputation as an educationist had preceded him in Barbados and he had no difficulty, soon after his arrival, in persuading the Governor, Rawson W. Rawson, to appoint a commission to enquire into and report on the whole question of education in the island. The appointment of that commission, with Mitchinson as its chairman, proved to be one of the most important events in the history of Barbadian education.

The significance of the report of the Mitchinson Commission is indicated by the nature of its recommendations. Infant and primary schools were to be clearly distinguished from each other. Schools fees were to be reduced and the salaries of teachers increased. The colour distinctions maintained in certain schools were to be abolished. The employment of children under the age of twelve years, unless they had attained the essential elements of education, was to be made illegal. The work of training teachers, which had been started by Richard Rawle, should be carried forward by a wider system organised under government auspices.

Other recommendations submitted by the Commission produced equally significant results. Harrison College, hitherto known as Harrison's Free School, the Lodge School, which had recently been closed, and Queen's College, formerly the Girls' Central School, were re-organised as 'first grade schools'. A number of 'second grade schools' were established at a level between the 'first grade' and the primary schools. Herein lay the origin of the Alleyne, Parry and Coleridge Schools in the northern parishes and the Girls' and Boys' Foundations Schools in Christ Church, with the Alexandra and St. Michael's Girls' Schools following in due course. To bridge the gap between the secondary and primary schools, exhibitions were provided to enable all who showed promise to avail themselves of the best education the island could offer. [31]

There were other areas in the field of education to which Mitchinson directed his attention. Through his influence in Barbados and abroad he secured the affiliation of Codrington College to the University of Durham in 1875. He thus placed Barbados in a unique position as the only territory in the British West Indies in which facilities for education were offered from the infant and primary level to that of the university. In addition, his initiative in financing a scholarship to Pembroke College, Oxford, from his income as a Fellow of that College, led to the inauguration of the Barbados Scholarship in 1879. The highest academic training could thus be provided both in the island at Codrington College and in the leading universities of England.

Mitchinson was not the man to suffer fools gladly or to say smooth things to those with whom he disagreed. He possessed neither the conciliating genius of Coleridge nor the patient persistence of Rawle. While the latter complained of his frustrations only in private letters to friends in England, Mitchinson proclaimed his discontent on whatever public occasions he considered appropriate. He criticised the laity of the Diocese for not taking an interest in the pastoral work of the Church. He chided the clergy for practising excess of ritual and neglecting the vital functions of the Church. He assailed the upper and middle classes for their lack of interest in the progress of the island's schools.

On the upper classes he was particularly severe, censuring them in terms of unmitigated contempt. On one occasion, in

February 1876, when he was conferring a number of honorary Durham degrees, he commented "on the lack among the upper classes in the community of that higher culture which develops breadth of thought and largeness of view, and the absence of which exhibits itself in an odious self-complacency and narrow prejudices, the offspring of besotted ignorance". He then proceeded to compare them to the white snails of Hans Andersen who, living under burdock leaves upon which the rain drops pattered, flattered themselves that the world consisted of white snails and that they were the world.[32]

It is not surprising that Mitchinson felt constrained to resign from the office of Bishop of Barbados eight short years after he assumed it. He could not disguise from himself nor did he allow any of his clergy to conceal it from him that his episcopate had been "in many respects, notably in some of its most important enterprises, a failure"; and this failure, he added, must owe its origin "partly I doubt not through errors and failures of my own, partly from causes beyond my control".[33]

Mitchinson may not have succeeded in promoting that revival of church life which he ardently desired to attain. But there can be no question that he was in the van of educational progress in his time and that his labours in this field were to produce significant reforms and improvements in the educational system of Barbados. He laid it down that infant and primary schools were to provide the elements of a sound education. "Second-grade" Secondary Schools were to offer such training as would fit their pupils to play a useful part in the more practical enterprises of the community. "First-grade" secondary schools would be the gateway to the learned professions at Codrington College and the most highly reputed universities in England. Special facilities by way of exhibitions and scholarships would enable the most gifted children to proceed from the lowest to the highest rungs in the educational ladder. Thus provision was made for the children of the labouring class, the middle class and the upper class of the island.

Undoubtedly, the new system was unduly influenced by the demands of a class conscious society. Yet, by the facilities and improvements it offered, it provided opportunities, however limited by our present-day standards, for the upward social mobility of the people of Barbados.

Questions and Exercises to Consider

1. Why did the earliest schools provide education only for the poor whites? Why were the coloured children excluded?

2. Why was the Church of England considered to be the white man's Church before Coleridge's time? Do you think that Coleridge made up for the neglect of the Church of England in the past?

3. Examine Codrington's will (see excerpt) and explain what he had in mind in the matter of education. In regard to the interpretation of the will:
   (a) set out the arguments of Robert Bowcher Clarke;
   (b) set out the arguments of Richard Rawle.
   Which of these seems to be the correct interpretation of the Founder's intention? Use the facts to support your ideas. Arrange a debate on this issue.

4. Why was Rawle called the "schoolmaster general" of the island?

5. What do you understand by the words "a landmark in the history of Barbados"? Could Bishop Mitchinson's Report on Education be considered such a landmark? Do you think that the time is right for another Commission like that to examine all aspects of our present system of education? What recommendations would you like to see made?

6. Visit Society Church (now called Holy Cross Church) and look at Rawle's burial place. Why was the Church called Society Church?

CHAPTER TWELVE

The Confederation Crisis

Crown Colony Rule

In the early years of their settlement, the colonies of the British Caribbean were invariably granted the rights and privileges of self-government and representative institutions. They were given the right, subject to certain limitations, to manage their own affairs through elected assemblies. But with the change of West Indian society, there was a change in the policy of the British Government. As the colonies moved from the status of free and vigorous communities to that of slave societies, Britain began to have second thoughts about the old representative system of government.

It is true that after the Treaty of Paris in 1763 elected assemblies were given to Grenada, Dominica, St. Vincent and Tobago. Before long, however, voices were raised, urging that the West Indian colonies should be governed by a form of despotism, benevolent despotism, and it was argued that the most effective system of government would be a Governor and a Council under the immediate appointment of the Crown. It is significant that, when Trinidad, British Guiana and St. Lucia were captured by the British in the late eighteenth and early nineteenth centuries, these colonies were established as Crown Colonies under the direct control of the British Government.

The trend to assume direct responsibility for the colonies was thus begun and this trend was strengthened with the approach of emancipation. For with the abolition of slavery, it was considered that the assemblies were now merely bodies operated by a small section of the citizens. They were no longer representative but oligarchic institutions. And the fear was entertained that, under the new order of society, the assemblies, elected on a narrow racial and property basis, would be selfish and intolerant in regard to the interests of the newly emancipated class of citizens.

Britain felt constrained, therefore, to think more than before along new constitutional lines. The old assemblies, it was felt, would have to go and single chamber legislatures established in their place. The majority of the members of this single chamber would be nominated by the Crown and the Governor would be able to rely on the support of the legislature for whatever measures were devised for the people of the West Indies. That was the advice given by Henry Taylor, one of the chief advisers of the Colonial Office.

The circumstances of English party politics prevailing at the time, however, made it difficult to implement the policy recommended by Taylor. Those who were in favour of introducing this policy were the Whigs led by Lord Melbourne. The latter were particularly dissatisfied with the Jamaica Assembly because of the illiberal course it followed in the years immediately following emancipation. They wanted to abolish that Assembly but they feared the opposition they would encounter from the Tories. For the latter were determined to uphold 'representative' government in the West Indies even though the existing system was a mockery of representative government.

As it turned out, the Whig Government decided in 1839 not to abolish the Jamaica Assembly but merely to suspend it for five years. Even then the Bill to suspend the Jamaica Constitution passed the House of Commons only by a small majority of five votes and, as a result of this, the Melbourne Government resigned. The Jamaica Assembly was thus saved — for the time being.

By the middle of the nineteenth century the Colonial Office made tentative efforts to introduce the policy recommended by Taylor. The first move in this direction took place in 1848 in the Turks and Caicos Islands, though the change adopted there was not significant. In 1854 a series of constitutional changes were introduced in the Virgin Islands, and in 1863 the Council and Assembly of Dominica were merged in one chamber of nineteen elected and nine nominated members. [1]

It was not until the Morant Bay Uprising in Jamaica in 1865 that the old representative system was seriously challenged. The oligarchs of that island, faced with a situation that seemed beyond their control, voluntarily abdicated the powers they had long enjoyed. The Assembly, to which they had clung tenaciously for many years, was abolished. On June 11th, 1866, an Order in Council was issued by the British Government setting up a nominated Legislative Council and the Crown assumed the duty of governing Jamaica by direct rule. [2]

Under the new system, the Crown took on the function of representing "the lower classes". In the words of Lord Carnarvon, Secretary of State, to Governor Strahan of Barbados, it assumed "that direct protection by the Crown of the unrepresented classes, which takes the place of representation, and which is afforded by the constitution of a Crown Colony".[3]

Having started with really significant changes in Jamaica, the Colonial Office procceeded to apply its new policy in territory after territory in the West Indies. That policy was adopted in various stages. The first step might be to merge the Council and the Assembly into one body, to change the legislature from a bicameral one to a single chamber, consisting both of elected and nominated members. That had been done in the case of Dominica. The second step would be to reduce the number of elected members with the object of giving the colony a nominated majority. The third and final step would be to dispense with the elected members altogether and make the legislature a completely nominated one. That was the system established in Jamaica.

Antigua lost her elected Assembly in 1865 and the Assemblies of St. Kitts and Nevis went the same way in the following year. Montserrat, British Honduras, Grenada, St. Vincent and Tobago all suffered the same fate, with the Crown Colony system taking the place of the old representative form of government. So rapid were the constitutional changes in the West Indies that by 1875 the only colonies that retained the old system were the Bahamas, Bermuda and Barbados.

A Difficult Situation

Actually, Barbados did not seem to be in a condition to face the struggle with the Colonial Office that was now looming ahead.

The first five years after complete emancipation in 1838 were marked by the vagaries of the weather and the uncertain condition of the labour market. The decade that followed saw a steady increase in the production of sugar, rising from 33,111 hogsheads in 1847 to 50,778 in 1858.[4] During the thirty years after this period there was no spectacular advance in sugar production; indeed, the industry appeared to be stagnant. Yet not a few of the planters appeared satisfied with the prevailing state of affairs. There was labour in abundance, manure was applied in increasing quantity and windmills were being replaced by steam factories. It was claimed that one planter, with an estate of a hundred acres, was able to bring up eight children, even sending one of them to be educated at the University of Oxford.[5]

Such comparative prosperity, however, was not universal in the island. There were planters who were overwhelmed by the difficulties of the period. Thousands of acres were sold in chancery during the years 1856, 1857 and 1859. Other planters, unable to meet their commitments, were forced to mortgage their estates to merchant creditors both in England and in Barbados.[6]

The most important event during this period was the outbreak of cholera in 1854. The recorded excess of burials arising from cholera was 7,000, but it was officially reported that about 11,000 were interred without any record of their burial. Governor Rawson declared that this was not an exaggerated estimate, but fell short of the actual figures. For the total number of deaths in 1854 was 22,736 which was more than 20,000 in excess of the previous year. Those who suffered most from the pestilence were the black and coloured people of the island. Few whites of the upper and middle classes were struck down but the poor whites of the Scotland District were reported to have suffered severely from the epidemic.[7]

The census of 1851 revealed that Barbados had 135,939 inhabitants. Of these, 15,824 were white, 30,059 were coloured and 90,056 were black. In spite of the ravages of cholera, however, the upward surge of the black section was such that by 1861 the total population had risen to 152,727, and of this number 16,594 were white, 36,128 were coloured and 100,005 were black.[8]

In the following decade there was again only a moderate increase in the population owing to another factor, emigration. According to the census of 1871, there were 161,594 people in the island but to this was added the 447 men and the one woman who were on board vessels in the harbour of Bridgetown. Of this total 16,560 were white, 39,578 were coloured and 105,904 were black. During the greater part of this period, and particularly in 1864-5, significant numbers of black and coloured people emigrated from Barbados to British Guiana, Dutch Guiana, St. Croix and Antigua.[9]

In these circumstances, Governor Rawson was moved to say that pestilence or emigration was, apparently, the alternative to starvation, in the event of one or two unfavourable seasons occurring at the end of the next decade.[10]

During this period the located labourer system was rigidly applied and the penal clauses were astonishingly severe. Prescod, who had fought to prevent such abuses, died in 1871 after a number of years on the Bench of the Assistant Court of Appeal. As editor of the *Liberal* and later as judge of the Appeal Court, he had tried, not without success, to mitigate the worse aspects of the located labourers system, and to compose the differences between the middle and lower classes, irrespective of colour. Now, with his influence removed, the stratification of Barbadian society hardened and the opportunity lost of forming a grand alliance against the ruling class. And, as the economy of the island stagnated, the strains and stresses of the economic situation in Barbados fell on those who were least able to bear it, the labouring masses of the island.[11]

In the circumstances, it might be supposed that something would be done to alleviate the lot of the poorest section in the community, that some facilities would be provided for the emigration of the able-bodied and some form of poor relief granted to the aged and the infirm.

But little positive action seems to have been taken in this direction. Wages for the 19,000 employed in the sugar industry remained at the level they had long been and would long continue to be. The wage of an agricultural labourer remained at 1/- a day during the crop and 10d during the rest of the year, with a lower rate for women and a still lower one for children. The cost of food, clothing and shelter was low, it is true, but there was no security for such wages as they received since these could be reduced by fines and deductions.

Few or no facilities were provided for emigration for the simple reason that this would interfere with the stability of the island's labour market. Nor was the provision of poor relief any more satisfactory, the planters being unwilling to spend large sums on this during such an uncertain period. A Joint Committee of the Council and the Assembly declared its unwillingness in 1869 to speak disparagingly "of what is now done in this matter in the rural parishes", but they could not "refrain from saying that in their opinion more ought to be done, and that there should be a more organised, a better defined, and more uniform system of relief throughout the island".[12]

The Burning Issue

In spite of the circumstances facing Barbados, the Colonial Office might well have expected resistance to the plan to introduce the crown colony system of government to the island. For those who controlled the power structure in Barbados had recently shown once again that they possessed a sturdy and intransigent spirit.

When the British Government in 1870 discontinued its annual grant of £20,000 to support the cause of religion in the West Indies, they asked the West Indian legislatures to provide for the disestablishment and disendowment of the Anglican Church. Rawson was instructed to have an act introduced in the Barbados legislature for such a purpose, but the opposition was so strong that he urged the Colonial Office not to press the matter. Barbados felt that she had not been "separately consulted" on the issue and resented the idea of being forced to accept a general policy that was being aribitrarily imposed on her neighbours. In the event, when the Imperial Grant was withdrawn, the Barbados Legislature passed an act in 1872 re-establishing the Church. The Bishop, archdeacon and clergy of the Church of England were placed on an official list and certain conditions were laid down for appointment, tenure and dismissal in respect of the payment of stipends and the enjoyment of parsonages. This step was unique in the West Indies and was regarded as "a very remarkable assertion of independence". [13]

The Governor, who was sent to persuade Barbados to accept the new Colonial Office plan, was John Pope Hennessy, a brilliant but impetuous Irishman. He may not have thought at the outset that his task would be difficult. For the principle of closer union already appeared to be working in several departments of West Indian life. The forces in the Windward Islands were under the command of a General in Barbados. The Bishop of Barbados was the head of the Anglican Church in the Windward Islands. Codrington College, Harrison College and the Lodge School received students from neighbouring territories which had no good schools in their midst. The Chief Justice of Barbados presided over a Common Court of Appeal for the Windward Islands. Moreover, the Colonial Bank of Barbados, the Mail Packet, the Telegraph System and the Barbados Mutual Life Assurance all performed services that helped to unite the island with some of the principal territories in the West Indies.

At an early stage, therefore, the new Governor propounded the Six Points which he thought had the approval of leading members of the Council and the Assembly. They were as follows:

1. That the Auditor of Barbados should be appointed Auditor General of the Windward Islands, his salary and clerical staff being increased, but such additional expense to fall entirely on the other islands.

2. That the power of transporting prisoners from Barbados to other islands and receiving prisoners from the other islands should be secured to the Government-in-Chief.

3. That the new Lunatic Asylum should also be open for the reception of lunatics from the other islands.

4. That a similar arrangement should be made about a common lazaretto.

5. That there should be a Chief Justice of the Windward Islands and a remodelling of the judicial system based on the necessity of centralising it.

6. That there should be a police force for the Windward Islands.

There seems to have been a great deal of agreement with the Six Points but the Governor was probably not aware of the fear prevailing in the island, that these proposals would be "the thin edge of the wedge" which would eventually lead to the abolition of the elected Assembly and the imposition of a crown colony system of Government.[14] At first he tried to charm the House of Assembly into a state of rationality. He sought to persuade them to accept the plan in a spirit of sweet reasonableness. In his first address to the legislature, he spoke of the Assembly, which had recently been dissolved after a brief session, saying: "No Assembly in Barbados has had so brief a session. Yet for the short period of its existence, I cannot find any legislative body in the history of this colony, that displayed more of the business-like qualities of true Parliamentary life."[15]

Then he continued: "As Governor-in-Chief, I shall have to ask you to consider . . . some plans by which I hope to render more efficient certain departments of the general administration of the Windward Islands." But, after this cautious approach to the burning issue of the day, he quickly re-assured the Legislature: "In an old and contented community like this, I believe that a Governor should not under-rate local experience; that he should not lightly disregard the conservative spirit of the local traditions . . . and above all, that he should scrupulously respect the constitutional rights and privileges of the local legislature."[16]

As the weeks passed, however, it became clear to Hennessy that Barbados would not easily acquiesce in the instructions he had received from the Colonial Office. The Barbadians became increasingly suspicious that the Governor had been instructed to implement the general policy that had been imposed on other territories in the Caribbean. As the elected assemblies in those territories were being gradually abolished, it became painfully clear to them that a similar fate was intended for the Barbados House of Assembly.

Hennessy had come to Barbados at the beginning of November 1875. On February 28th, 1876, he sent a message to the Assembly, requesting it to meet on the following Friday, March 3rd, so that he could communicate to honourable members certain Letters Patent from Her Majesty the Queen and address them on matters of public importance.[17] On March 2nd, a meeting was held in Bridgetown and the Barbados Defence Association was launched. The main resolution passed at the meeting declared:

That the policy, which has been adopted by the Colonial Office towards this Island, and the measures which its emissaries are resorting to in their endeavours to carry out that policy here renders it incumbent on the inhabitants of Barbados to form an association which shall have for its object the preservation of their 'Constitution', the protection of their interests and the maintenance of order, and a good understanding between the different classes of the population.[18]

When Governor Hennessy had been on an earlier visit to St. Lucia, he spoke to the Administrator, Des Voeux, with astonishing frankness. He intended to base his methods in Barbados on a famous passage from the Latin poet, Virgil, which was freely translated by Des Voeux to mean: "If I cannot bend the whites, I shall stir up the blacks."[19] The Defence Association seemed to have no difficulty in reading the Governor's mind. They had rightly anticipated that Hennessy was about to throw down the gauntlet. On March 3rd, he set out on a bold manoeuvre to convince the House of the wisdom of the Colonial Office's policy or to appeal beyond them to the mass of the people in Barbados. He said that it was clearly desirable that the wishes and objects of Her Majesty's Government should be made known to the people, seeing that the changes proposed were intended to benefit "the people as well as the other classes".

He called attention to the words of the Bishop and the leading ministers of the Wesleyans and Moravians who had said to him: "In all our experience we have never seen a community in which there existed such intense and apparently hopeless poverty as in this."[20]

The Governor then pointed to the benefits of the Confederation plan:

> Our redundant population will find a natural outlet in the neighbouring islands when by a uniform political system, the same laws, the same tariffs, and constant means of rapid communication, the now unoccupied Crown lands and half-tilled estates will be available for their labour, and they can come and go to the various islands as readily as they now pass from parish to parish in Barbados.[21]

To the Assembly and its supporters, the Governor's address was a challenge they could not ignore. The Defence Association held numerous meetings, stressing the grave perils that would follow if the Governor's scheme was adopted. They proclaimed that Confederation was "damnation not salvation", that it would bring with it "starvation, increased taxation and oppression". The campaign mounted by the Association carried conviction to the merchants, their clerks and their porters in Bridgetown and to the planters in the rural areas. But it did not convince "the black and coloured working classes" who seemed to have been favourably impressed by Hennessy's arguments. Certainly they shared his view that "no intelligent person will take the serious responsibility of standing between his poorer countrymen and the wise policy of the British Government".[22]

Upheaval

Thus began the great debate which was to spread throughout the island. The country became sharply divided between the 'haves' and the 'have-nots', between the upper classes and the masses. The heat and intensity of the argument were to increase until law and order were temporarily overthrown by riot and civil commotion.

Hennessy was accused of visiting Long Bay Castle in St. Philip in the earlier months of the year. There he took the occasion, it was alleged, of spreading his views among the shop-keepers, the yeomen and the labourers. He entertained "persons of that class" at luncheon and tea and spoke to them on political matters, seeking to convert them to the cause of confederation. Next, in the "process of stumping the country", he transferred his headquarters to Blackman's in St. Joseph where he made similar efforts to enlist support for Confederation. The fact that the most prominent agitators later came from St. Philip was attributed to the Governor's appeal and the "considerable impression" he made on them.[23]

The Chief Inspector of Police was considered by the oligarchs to be notoriously partisan to the Governor's scheme. And Sergeant Deane of the Central Station was regarded as typical of the spirit that animated the Police Force. Less than two weeks after the Governor's address, the Sergeant was seen addressing a mob at the Station. He castigated "the d---d worthless white people in the island who were opposing Confederation because they wanted to keep the Negroes down". And he expressed the hope that the people would not listen to "what the white vagabonds were telling them, for the Island would have Confederation notwithstanding what the white vagabonds were doing to oppose it".[24]

With the hardening of attitudes on both sides, the Defence Association stepped up their meetings. They called on all their supporters to rally to the defence of the ancient constitution and the island's representative institutions now gravely imperilled by the Colonial Office plan. They resorted to the Press to rally support to their side. On one occasion the Muse was invoked in the *Agricultural Reporter* to exhort the "patriots" to their best efforts:

> Let every patriot in his heart
> Resolve to do a manly part
> To stem the current of the hour
> Though "lobbied" by imperial power.
>
> Let every man but firmly stand
> Upon the Charter of the land,
> Nor Britain's might shall dare to wrest
> The Charter from a freeman's breast.[25]

And one wag was moved to say that the hottest arguments could be heard in the Ice House, one of the most popular restaurants in Bridgetown.

But the situation soon began to take a sinister turn. So disorderly was the populace in the Public Building yard and the corridors of the Chamber that the Council could scarcely conduct its business on one occasion. Later, the meetings of the

Defence Association were broken up and the first outbreak of violence took place on Easter Tuesday, April 18th, 1876. The first act of violence occurred at Byde Mill, a sugar plantation that extended into the parishes of St. Philip, St. John and St. George. Two brothers by the name of Dottin entered the estate yard, one brandishing a sword and the other waving a red flag at the end of a long cane. An attempt to arrest one of them failed. Thereupon he blew a conch shell and the plantation labourers promptly turned out and began raiding the potato fields.

The following day was comparatively quiet but on April 20th there were serious riots in St. John, St. George and St. Joseph. The rioting continued until Saturday, April 22nd, and by that time eighty-nine estates had been attacked. The damage was done by about a thousand persons under the leadership of the Dottin brothers. But it is noteworthy that scarcely any physical violence was done to white people and little or no resistance offered to the police or the soldiers. [26]

In the course of the suppression of the riots, eight people were killed and thirty wounded. With the exception of the Chief Inspector of Police, no white person was on the casualty list. Yet the situation was menacing enough and at the peak of rioting hundreds of whites sought refuge in the ships in Carlisle Bay or in the Garrison buildings or other places where they could be protected by British soldiers.

It is remarkable that, in all these proceedings, the rioters gave the impression that they had the Governor's permission to do the things they did. They did not set fire to estate houses or take life because Hennessy had told them to do no such thing. "The Governor says we must not set fire nor take life, but take everything else". This was instruction given by the leaders to their followers. At another place, they were heard to say: "We cannot break locks, or enter buildings, nor shed blood, unless we are attacked first, and then we will slaughter as we go". Before digging up the eddoes or potatoes, they would announce that they were doing the business of John Pope Hennessy. The procedure they followed appeared to be so satisfactory that at one estate they openly called upon God to bless the Governor. [27]

The Compromise

The remarks made by Hennessy in his first address to the House of Assembly had been used as evidence against him when he was being weighed in the balance. And now the claims of the rioters were quoted to show that the Governor was an irresponsible agitator. While Lord Carnarvon declined at first to remove him at the request of the House, Hennessy was later transferred to the governorship of Hong Kong. It was evident that there had to be a separation of the oligarchs and the Governor on the ground of incompatibliity of views and temperament.

For some months after, all was quiet on the Colonial Office front. The Barbadians received the impression that their fate was being settled in London without any attempt to consult them. As tempers cooled and passions subsided, there grew a feeling that there must be some way out of the impasse between the Colonial Office and the House of Assembly. The man who pointed the way was W. C. (later Sir Conrad) Reeves.

Hennessy had criticised the wasteful method of financing public works by irresponsible boards. Reeves, who was to show a genius for compromise, took up the point and suggested a solution to the problem. That speech read in part as follows:

If the Executive Council is to have the sole control of the departments so far as it involves the expenditure of money raised by taxes levied upon the people, then the people must have control in the Executive Council commensurate with the great issue at stake. They must not only share power with the nominees of the Crown sitting in that Council, but the real balance should be in the hands of the representatives of the people. In other words, the Executive must carry out to its legitimate extent the constitutional principle laid down by itself and he ought to call to his Executive Council, say, three members of this House, and one unofficial member of the Legislative Council. [28]

That speech was made on May 4th, 1876, and was forwarded soon after by Hennessy to the Secretary of State. It suggested a modified form of responsible government and that suggestion, with some changes and amendments, was carried into effect when the Executive Committee Act was passed in 1881. Under this act, it was provided that four members of the House and one member of the Legislative Council should work with the Executive Council to prepare measures requiring legislation and attend to other purposes of government. This was rightly regarded as a great triumph for the representative principle. For, under the new arrangement, members conducting government business were not government officers responsible to the Crown but representatives of the people, responsible to the electors. [29]

But there was another matter on which Reeves was acutely sensitive. Hennessy had made the charge that all talk of government by the "people" was a farce so long as the qualifications for the franchise allowed only a small section of the population to vote. Out of an estimated total population of 160,000 at the time, only 1,300 persons were entitled to vote. Reeves, therefore, now turned his attention from the apex to the base of the constitution and in 1884 he persuaded the House of Assembly to lower the qualifications for the franchise.

The qualification on freehold was reduced from £12. 16s. 4d. to £5. The qualification on occupation, formerly £32. 1s. and applicable only to town dwellers, was reduced to £15 and made applicable to persons living in any part of the island. The qualification for ratepayers was reduced from £3. 4s. to £2 for people living in Bridgetown and £1 for those living in any other part of the island. One of the most important clauses of the Franchise Act of 1884 was that which enfranchised employees who earned an income or salary of £50 per annum. [30]

Viewed through modern eyes, the provisions of the new Franchise Act may not appear to be epoch-making. They have been regarded by some, however, as a significant advance for Barbados when they are compared with the English Franchise Reform Acts of 1832, 1867 and 1884. Yet it is strange to relate that, though the franchise was "low enough" to enable many black and coloured people to register as voters, few seem to have taken advantage of that opportunity. The number of registered voters was only 1,604 in 1905-6, 2,004 in 1914-15 and 1,820 in 1918-19. Contested elections were frowned upon by the oligarchs and as a rule they occurred in only one or two of the island's twelve constituencies. [31]

The truth appears to be that the provisions of the new Franchise Act, though appearing to be liberal in the context of similar legislation in the U.K. at the time, had no meaningful impact on the electorate of Barbados. The Franchise Act of 1884 meant little to an island where property was not widely distributed. There were few free villages and no substantial peasantry, as in other territories of the West Indies, and the estate still largely dominated the social and economic life of the island. It was not until the early part of the twentieth century, as we shall see later, with the influx of Panama money, that the reduced franchise qualifications on freehold, on occupation and for ratepayers had any real meaning for the people of Barbados.

Hennessy's régime as a Governor may have seemed a failure. Yet there is little doubt that his strictures did a great deal to forward the work of progress and reform in Barbados after he had departed from the scene. Wherever he went in the Colonial Empire, he seemed to be the harbinger of disturbances, yet the Colonial Office was extremely patient with him. Perhaps they were convinced that, in spite of "his faults of temperament", in most of his controversies he was "fundamentally in the right". His courage was regarded as "indomitable" and his ability to "come up from severe punishment" and renew the battle was regarded as "inexhaustible".[32]

Perhaps it may be said, without being fanciful, that the British Government, appreciating his special qualities, developed a habit of giving "any particularly sticky or static colony a dose of this warm-hearted, vigorous and cantankerous Governor".[33] But without the wisdom of Sir Conrad Reeves, it is doubtful whether the challenge of John Pope Hennessy could have brought the island of Barbados safely through the crisis of the Confederation controversy.

Questions and Exercises to Consider

1. What do you understand by the words "a bicameral legislature"?
2. What is the meaning of Governor Rawson's statement that pestilence or emigration was apparently the only alternative to starvation?
3. What is meant by Crown Colony Government? What is representative government?
4. Write a short note on the meaning of Confederation. What were the signs that pointed to closer union between Barbados and the Windward Islands? Why did the Governor's Six Points give rise to suspicion?
5. Divide the class into two groups, those supporting the Governor and those supporting the House of Assembly. What are the arguments that each side would use?
6. Why did the Confederation plan end in riots? What do people mean when they say today "Federation going on down there"?
7. Compare the Confederation plan of 1876 with the Federal experiment of 1958-62.

8. What was the compromise that brought peace between the Colonial Office and Barbados? What did each side concede?
9. Why did Jamaica give way to the Colonial Office in 1865 and how is it that Barbados successfully maintained its position in 1876?
10. Draw a table with dates showing the gradual widening of the franchise in Barbados from the earliest years to 1951. Why did this happen so slowly?

CHAPTER THIRTEEN

The Encircling Gloom

A Melancholy Situation

The quarrels of 1876 were composed by the settlements of 1881 and 1884. The institutions of Barbados were made more representative than they had been before and the House of Assembly was set on the road leading to responsible government. The legislative machinery of the island could now deal more effectively with the social reforms to which John Pope Hennessy had called attention. The small shop-keepers, the labourers and the great masses of the people, in the words of the Governor, could now expect to receive a fairer share of the island's wealth and prosperity. More attention could be paid to the task of educating the young rather than accepting the grim alternative of "providing for them as criminals in after years". Everything seemed to point to the hope that Hennessy's call would be heeded, while there was time, and appropriate measures taken to relieve "the terrible picture of the moral and material condition of the people".[1]

Unfortunately, the year when the controversy with the Colonial Office was settled saw the economy of Barbados entering into a period of depression and instability. The cause of the condition, into which the island now slid and floundered, was completely beyond the control of the Barbadians. The primary reason for this condition was the sharp decline in the sugar industry and this decline was due to the increased competition from sugar beet which was manufactured by France, Germany and Austria, Holland, Belgium and Russia. In the earlier years of this new industry, which started from the time of Napoleon, there was no serious threat to West Indian sugar. It was found more expensive to manufacture sugar from beet in Europe than from sugar cane in the West Indies. Yet the governments of the European countries mentioned above had three reasons for encouraging the manufacture of beet-sugar. First, it helped to make these countries self-sufficient particularly in time of war when their sugar supplied from overseas could be threatened by

Cane and Beet Sugar Imports into U.K.

	Sugar Cane Imports	Beet Sugar Imports
1863	95%	5%
1873	74%	26%
1878	63%	37%
1888	47%	53%
1893	28%	72%

enemy action. Secondly, the increasing population needed employment in any industries that could be established. Thirdly, the planters of Europe welcomed the new crop of beet-root because it could be added to the list of crops which they planted in rotation to benefit the soil.

For these reasons the governments of the European countries concerned decide to grant subsidies to encourage the new industry. In addition, they imposed high tariffs on West Indian sugar, which was imported, in order to protect the product of their own territories. As the nineteenth century advanced, West Indian sugar was faced with a growing peril. First, the methods of refining beet-sugar were steadily improved, and secondly, the subsidies for the new industry in Europe were increased by their respective governments. In these circumstances, European producers made handsome profits in their home markets and then sold their surplus sugar to England. The West Indian planters was prevented by high tariffs from competing in Europe with the sugar beet producers on that continent. Nor could he compete in England with the European producers who sold their dumped sugar at a price below the cost of producing it in the West Indies.

The situation facing Barbados was grave enough, but it was made more serious by two factors. The rain fell at irregular intervals and the planter wrestled unsuccessfully with the unpredictability of the weather. The canes were attacked by a fungoid disease and to none did the latter prove more deadly than the Bourbon variety on which Barbadian cane almost entirely depended. As a result, exports began to decline from 1884 and two years later had dropped to half their value. The severity of the depression was reflected in the fall in the selling price of estate land. This declined from £65 per acre in 1884 to £63 in 1886. By 1887 sugar plantations were sold at £26 per acre and in 1896 this had dropped to £20 per acre.[2]

Bewildered by the melancholy state of the island, the planters resorted to the measures of desperation. They used less manure and chemical fertilisers and reduced the size of their labour force. But these were economy measures which only resulted in the inefficiency of the industry. Between the years 1887 and 1890 there was a remarkable improvement in the weather and the planters, stimulated by the welcome change, produced bumper crops. The size of these crops helped to relieve the situation a bit and the economy measures that had been employed were abandoned.

But this did not remove the basic cause of the economic malaise afflicting the island. Indeed, matters were soon made worse when a strange disease began to attack the roots and stems of the sugar canes. The Bourbon cane, which was rapidly becoming less and less resistant to pests and diseases, now showed that it was more vulnerable to the strange malady than any other variety. A sharp decline in the industry began in 1891 and it soon became clear that, unless other varieties of canes could be discovered, the island would be faced with irretrievable ruin.

As season followed season, the fates continued to deal with Barbados in unkindly fashion. The severe drought of 1894 brought the island to the nadir of its depression. The canes, already weakened by the almost unprecedented lack of moisture, were now attacked by such pests as moths, weevils and "shot-borers" and the fungoid disease, accelerated by these untoward conditions, made "rapid and fatal progress" among the island's canes. Poor harvests and falling prices drove the planters to bankruptcy. Those who survived the economic blizzard found it impossible to maintain the high standards of cultivation of which they had been proud in the past. They could not afford to employ an adequate labour force and they could not pay for the manures and chemical fertilisers that were needed for efficient sugar cultivation. So low had their reputation sunk that they were unable to raise the credits that were necessary for the profitable operation of their plantations. It was at this stage, in 1896, that the value of a sugar estate in Barbados fell as low as £20 per acre.[3]

Nor did this complete the catalogue of disasters that came upon the island. For on September 10th, 1898, Barbados was visited by a hurricane that killed eighty persons, blew down the wooden houses of 18,000 poor people and increased the death rate among the labouring population by increasing the incidence of typhoid and dysentery. This hurricane has been compared, without justification, with those of 1780 and 1831, the worst storms in the history of Barbados. The hurricane of 1780 killed more than 2,000 slaves and an unspecified number of free persons and destroyed most of the island.[4] The catastrophe of 1831, usually referred to as the Great Hurricane, killed 1,591 persons and inflicted damage estimated at the minimum figure of £1,602,800. In 1780 the rate of recovery was slow owing to the damage done to the equipment of the sugar factories. The recovery in 1831 was much faster mainly because Barbados enjoyed a favourable trade with British and American markets. But in 1898 Barbadian sugar, debarred from entry into the European market, was being steadily excluded from the British market. The combination of two evils, a natural calamity and an unfavourable economic climate, made the hurricane of 1898 a particularly disastrous one.

The Arduous Years

In the meantime, Barbados had not abandoned the unequal struggle that threatened its very existence. As far back as 1859, J. W. Parris, the owner of Highland plantation, reported a startling discovery. He had sown sugar cane seedlings on his land and these seedlings were from the Bourbon and Transparent as well as from native varieties of canes. This discovery, though reported in the Press, was almost completely ignored until 1883 when John R. Bovell was appointed Superintendent of the Dodds Reformatory and Industrial School. He had no faith in the traditional method of producing a new shoot by planting a small piece of cane in the land and his curiosity had been aroused by the report that the seed of the sugar cane was fertile.

Accordingly, he instructed his overseers to look out for any unfamiliar grass-like plants. In due course, one of them, a black man named J. B. Pilgrim, discovered some plantlets that he could not identify. Under Bovell's direction, the new seedlings were taken up and replanted in a field by themselves. The seedlings developed into sugar canes and the discovery by Parris was confirmed. Bovell joined with J. B. Harrison, Island Professor of Chemistry, and working together they proved conclusively that the seed of sugar cane would germinate under certain conditions.

Bovell and Harrison then turned their attention to a number

of studies that dealt with such subjects as the effect of manure on the cultivation of sugar cane, the comparative value of varieties that already existed, the raising of new varieties from seed and the incidence of cane diseases in Barbados.

It was Bovell's experiments on manures that produced dramatic and almost immediate results. The planters, faced with the steadily declining price of sugar, readily availed themselves of the practical guidance offered by Bovell and Harrison. They applied the fertilisers recommended by the two scientists. The amount of artificial manure they used in 1887 was doubled in 1888. The increased use of these manures led to the record crop of 1890 and helped in some measure to offset the low price of sugar.

But the grave problem that beset the Barbadian planter still remained to be tackled. The Bourbon cane, long the principal source of sugar supply in Barbados and the outside world, had now finally collapsed. With disaster facing the industry, Bovell intensified his studies on new varieties of cane. Some of the seedlings he had nurtured at Dodds were from the Bourbon cane and these he immediately abandoned. He turned to other varieties in his experiments and eventually selected the White Transparent for special research and investigation. This variety was finally adopted as the answer to the island's problem because it resisted more effectively the fungus disease that had destroyed the Bourbon cane.

The success of these experiments was acclaimed not only in Barbados but in other territories of the West Indies. And some years later Sir Daniel Morris, head of the Imperial Department of Agriculture, publicly submitted that, if the West Indian sugar industry was to be saved from ruin, attention must be given to the value of seedling canes, as demonstrated by the experiments of Bovell and Harrison.

In spite of the perils that beset her, Barbados was able to make some progress in respect of the social reforms to which Hennessy had called attention. Measures were enacted to provide for poor relief and improved facilities for education and to establish friendly societies and district savings banks. Laws were passed to facilitate the registration of births and deaths and to enable the Government to compile vital statistics. But in the encircling gloom of the depression the prevailing mood among the planters was for the exercise of the strictest economy and the cessation of all measures of progress and reform.

It is remarkable that in these circumstances Barbados was persuaded to improve and extend her public water supply system. Since 1859 water had been conveyed by pipe to Bridgetown. But until the closing stages of the nineteenth century the rest of the island still depended on ponds, swamps, private wells and cisterns for their supply of water. It was widely believed that epidemics of typhoid, dysentery and other bowel complaints were due to insufficient and impure water. And it was undoubtedly the feeling that the increased death rate in the island was due to the impurity of its water resources that "hastened the water question to its final culmination".[5] Yet it is open to question whether the planter-dominated Assembly, without the powerful advocacy of the Attorney General, W. H. (later Sir Herbert) Greaves, would have been persuaded to vote the substantial sums that were needed to 'nationalise' the water supply and extend the system of mains and 'stand pipes' from Bridgetown to the rural areas of the island.

The Norman Commission

There still remained the abiding problem that frustrated and angered the planters of Barbados. Whatever was done to remedy the diseases of the sugar cane and to increase the size of the island's crop, there was no hope for the industry unless it could find a favourable market.

For some years the British Government was singularly insensitive to the grave perils that confronted the West Indian sugar industry. The Colonial Office, under Sir Michael Hicks Beach, bluntly declared in 1878 that the interests of the consumer in England were stronger than those of the producer. Nothing could be done about the European bounties for the simple reason that they enabled the English consumer to get his sugar "more cheaply than he would without them".[6]

This forthright attitude was bad enough but the situation became even worse when seven years later the Government of the great Liberal, William Gladstone, rejected a proposed treaty with the United States which would have brought substantial benefit and relief to the West Indies. Under the proposed arrangement, American duties on sugar and other products would have been drastically reduced, if not abolished, and in return for this the duties on many consumer goods imported from the United States into the West Indies would have been similarly curtailed or abolished. It was a reciprocity agreement that was fervently desired in the West Indies and great was their anger when the British Government declined in 1885 to translate it into reality.[7]

In 1891, however, the British Government was forced to agree to a reduction of the tariffs on American consumer goods imported into the West Indies. A few years later West Indian sugar found a profitable market in America and it was this stroke of fortune that saved the West Indies from almost certain ruin in the 1890's. But this market proved to be full of hazards and vagaries and could not be expected to bring durable prosperity to the industry. It was in these circumstances that the British West Indies looked once again to the British Government and this time it found a more sympathetic Colonial Office under the direction of Joseph Chamberlain.

The new Colonial Secretary declared in 1897 that Her Majesty's Government had "no intention of allowing the West Indian sugar industry to be ruined". The same year a Royal Commission was appointed under the chairmanship of Sir Henry Norman and it at once set out to the West Indies where it found a situation that was "usually deplorable and sometimes desperate". In due course the Commission reported that they had reason to fear "that a very serious condition of things is rapidly approaching in Your Majesty's West Indian possessions and that the crisis will be reached in a very few years".[8]

The Commission made their recommendations with quite commendable despatch and it is no fault of theirs that five years were to pass before any action was taken on their submissions. The suggestions they proposed may be considered under three main heads.

They proposed that a Department of Economic Botany should be established and sea communications improved. Special emphasis was laid on the latter in view of the important trade in fruit that Jamaica was rapidly developing with New York. In regard to sugar, it was emphasised that the welfare of the general mass of the population and not only the interests of the sugar producers should be of paramount importance. Yet it was obviously faced with the dilemma that, unless the sugar industry in the British West Indies could be rehabilitated, the pace of social reform could scarcely be maintained.

On the vitally important issue of the European bounties, the Commission was clearly divided. While they agreed that the

178

abolition of the bounties was an object to be aimed at, they could not agree that, if their objective failed, Britain should pay bounties on West Indian sugar and that protective duties should be imposed on subsidized foreign sugar. For those colonies which were no longer sugar growers and for others which, while producing sugar, had unoccupied lands waiting to be taken up by settlers, the Commission strongly recommended land settlement in terms of peasant ownership.[9]

The recommendations of the Commission indicated that the Mother Country would have to make considerable financial sacrifices on behalf of her West Indian possessions. While declaring that retrenchment in public expenditure was inevitable in all the colonies, they recommended that substantial sums would have to be voted as grants or loans to help them over the exigent problems that faced them.

The report of the Commission was a thoughtful and positive document, though it is possible to argue that they did not foresee all the difficulties that lay in the way of the implementation of their proposals. It was a more arduous and expensive task to establish large-scale land settlements than they seemed to think at the time. It was not easy to reconcile the requirements of social reform and the necessity for administrative economy. And it was evident that the British Government would have to spend much more money to help their hard-pressed colonies than was suggested at the time.[10] Yet the report of the Commission gave a clear lead that was all the more necessary after the neglect and indifference of recent years.

Difficult and Intractable

In the case of Barbados, the Norman Commission considered that they had to deal with a more difficult and at the time intractable situation. The economic plight of the island was more acute than in the other colonies and seemed to call for special measures to ensure its survival.

An island whose sugar products represented 97% of its total exports placed the Commission in obvious difficulties. The Barbadians had done what they could to improve the growing and manufacture of their sugar and the Commissioners were left with little scope for recommendations in this area. Wages were already so low that no proposals could be made for their reduction with a view to effecting economy in the industry. It was

179

recommended, instead, that peasant agriculture should be encouraged, opportunities for emigration should be sought, the cost of public administration reduced, central sugar factories constructed and financial assistance given by the British Government until the sugar industry could be re-established in more favourable conditions.[11] Yet the Commissioners were forced to draw attention to the special difficulties that would follow any attempt to restore the island's fortunes.

For Trinidad and Jamaica particularly, the Commissioners had recommended land settlement with emphasis and firmness. In Barbados their enthusiasm was inhibited by the fact that there were no unoccupied lands in the densely populated but highly cultivated island. Yet they were not to be so easily discouraged. They recommended that, as sugar lands fell out of cultivation in Barbados, they should either be sold in small lots or leased at low rents to small cultivators. They observed that such a policy would probably be adopted at once by the Court of Chancery in the case of sugar plantations that could not be carried on except at a loss. They urged that the Government should facilitate the break up of estates in this manner by purchasing and re-selling them in small lots.[12] The obvious objective the Commissioners had in mind was the establishment of a sturdy and independent peasantry.

The Commissioners, however, were quick to recognise the problem that would arise from the implementation of the policy they recommended. They pointed out that those who had been in the habit of earning a livelihood on sugar estates could not be provided for in the manner they prescribed. The cultivation and manufacture of sugar employed more persons per acre than any other form of cultivation could support. A considerable number of labourers would be displaced on each estate which ceased to grow sugar and no adequate provision could be made elsewhere for such labourers. Moreover, the cultivation of ground provisions on the projected small lots, while contributing significantly to the island's food supply, would not provide "a source of public revenue of any considerable importance".[13]

Emigration was also proposed as "a natural and at first sight promising, suggestion". It was conceded that many black Barbadians had emigrated in the recent past "in search of subsistence" and not a few of these had proved "excellent colonists in their new homes". Experiments had been made to supply Barbadian labour to sugar planters in other Colonies. But such forms of emigration had not been satisfactory. In any case, if the sugar industry failed in Barbados, it would also fail in the other Colonies and then there would be an end to the demand for labourers on sugar estates. The Commissioners then concluded that the only form of assisted emigration that might be successful was "that of moving whole families" and settling them in territories like British Guiana, Trinidad and Dominica where there were large tracts of unoccupied land. In this way, the objective could be achieved of establishing land settlements on the basis of a proprietary peasantry. But such action, the Commissioners warned, could not produce rapid results and would have to be carried out on a large scale, involving the expenditure of substantial sums of money, if a significant portion of the island's surplus population was to be absorbed in such newly established the settlements.[14]

One of the pressing needs of Barbados, as the Commissioners saw it, was to reduce the cost of government and administration. It was conceded that the scale of expenditure was justifiable when the sugar industry was flourishing, but it could not be justified in the present critical situation. Here again the inevitable dilemma arose. Retrenchment would not compensate for the loss of revenue that could be sustained by a reduction in the sugar industry. It would not relieve the suffering of the distressed thousands and might even lead to its increase.[15]

After surveying the whole situation, the Commissioners were forced to the conclusion that the maintenance of the sugar industry "in some form and to some considerable extent" provided "the only hope" of supporting any large proportion of the island's population. They recommended, therefore, that owners of estates who desired to combine, should be given financial assistance for the establishment of central factories. They made no apology for their proposals to re-habilitate the industry. There were special circumstances in Barbados that supported them in their policy. The labour supply in the island was "more abundant and effective" than in any of the other British West Indies Colonies and the Barbadian soil was especially well suited for "growing sugar canes with exceptionally rich juice". Above all, if no help was given to sugar industry, they could be certain of great distress among the labouring population, considerable expenditure to relieve that distress and a prolonged period of difficulty to find employment for those displaced by a dying enterprise.[16]

The Norman Commission, having completed its investigations, departed for England and for some time little was done to dispel the encircling gloom that continued to brood over the island.

Questions and Exercises to Consider

1. What was meant by subsidies or bounties to sugar beet?
2. What discoveries were made by Bovell and Harrison? What was the importance of these? Find out what scientific developments have since taken place in sugar cane cultivation.
3. What is there now to commemorate the name of John R. Bovell?
4. Imagine you are a planter and write an angry letter to a newspaper criticising Britain for not providing a favourable market for West Indian sugar.
5. Does Joseph Chamberlain deserve the gratitude of the West Indies? Why is the swing bridge named after him?
6. What were the recommendations of the Norman Commission? In what way were they important for Barbados and the rest of the West Indies?
7. How much of the Norman Commission's recommendations were actually implemented in Barbados? Examine in detail the difficulties which stood in the way of implementation.
8. Explain the following:
   (a) subsistence;
   (b) proprietory peasantry;
   (c) retrenchment;
   (d) unfavourable economic climate;
   (e) fungus disease;
   (f) nationalise;
   (g) reciprocity agreement;
   (h) subsidise.

CHAPTER FOURTEEN

Prosperity and Adversity

The Turning Tide

At first it seemed that the dawn of the twentieth century was no more promising than the closing stages of its unlamented predecessor. For the calamities of the former period seemed to follow the people of Barbados into the new era when there was an epidemic of smallpox in 1902 and one of yellow fever in 1908.

The Barbadians had suffered from frequent outbreaks of smallpox in the past but this disease had been brought under control by vaccination. Unfortunately, the practice of vaccination had not been maintained and both the Government and the people had grown indifferent to, and forgetful of, the ravages that could be wrought by this dreaded scourge. The epidemic started in February 1902 and lasted until April the following year, causing the death of 118 persons. Nor was this the only loss caused by the epidemic. For the island was quarantined by the neighbouring territories and both the Government and the private sector sustained a considerable loss of revenue owing to the reduction of the transit trade it enjoyed with those territories.

The yellow fever epidemic of 1908 brought a similar trail of evils to the island; deaths and quarantine followed by losses of transit trade and government revenue. There had been no yellow fever in the island for more than a quarter of a century and this, too, had bred a spirit of complacency. There had been other epidemics of the disease in the past, notably in 1852 when it claimed Rawle of Codrington College as one of its victims, nearly causing his death.[1] Once again Barbados neglected to take the necessary precautions and its people had to suffer accordingly.

In 1902 the British Government began to take action on the recommendations of the Norman Commission. A substantial sum of money was granted by Britain to help the West Indian sugar industry out of its difficulties and Barbados' share of this was £80,000. This at once became the subject of local controversy, with opinions differing as to how this money should be spent. In British Guiana the decision was taken to distribute

183

its quota of £69,000 to individual planters who could then determine whether to pay their debts or buy new equipment. Barbados was persuaded by Sir Herbert Greaves to adopt a different policy. Its share of the British grant was used to establish the Sugar Industry Agricultural Bank and the passing of the years has confirmed that this was a wise and far-sighted decision.

The year 1903 was marked by a significant event, the removal of the bounties on sugar beet by the Brussels Convention. This, too, was a recommendation of the Norman Commission and Chamberlain had spared no effort to bring it to fruition. It is not surprising that, when the opportunity arose, the Barbadians named the swing bridge that leads into the Bridgetown after the great Colonial Secretary.

It is ironic, however, that in the meantime Barbadian sugar had found a profitable market in the United States. Barbados had benefited from the misfortunes of Cuba and Puerto Rico when the latter were unable to deliver their usual supplies of sugar to the outside world. Cuba, caught between "the millstones of Spanish taxation and American tariff policy", [2] rose in revolt in 1895 under the standard of José Martí and the insurgents, adopting a scorched earth policy, deliberately destroyed crops and holdings throughout the country. The sinking of the battleship, Maine, brought the United States into the conflict and the Spanish-American War followed. This disturbed period removed Cuban and Puerto Rican sugar from its accustomed market and led to higher prices. In these circumstances, Barbados was able to benefit for two reasons. The experiments of Bovell and Harrison were now producing better and bigger crops from the new canes and these crops were sold at the higher prices that were now being paid in the American market. Thus it was that during the period from 1898 to 1901 the value of the island's sugar exports showed a slow but steady increase. [3]

The advantages that Barbados obtained from the repercussions of the Spanish American War were only temporary. Cuban and Puerto Rican sugar soon recovered and the industries in those two islands made a leap forward. Barbadian sugar was soon ousted from the American market with the result that the island's export to the United States dropped from £554,825 in its peak year (1901) to £292,137 and then to £51,502 in subsequent years. It was at this stage that Barbados began to benefit from the removal of the European bounties. The planters increased their exports to Britain as well as to Canada and, though these markets were not as profitable as the American, they brought a welcome relief to the island's sugar industry.[4] Chamberlain's efforts and the decision of the Brussels Conference had not been entirely in vain.

Panama Money

In view of the uncertainties of the sugar market in various parts of the world, Barbados began to learn an important lesson. She could not depend entirely on one crop (monoculture) and expect anything like stability in her economy. Accordingly, she turned to look for other sources of revenue to minimise the effect of trade disturbances on her efforts to achieve a measure of economic independence.

One of the chief expedients to which Barbados now turned was emigration. Barbadians had emigrated from the island from the earliest years of their history. In the past, during the years before emancipation, the emigrants had been mainly whites who settled in other parts of the world and never returned to their native country. Immediately after emancipation, labour conditions in the island were unsettled, with workers going from one plantation to another and there was a trickle of black and coloured emigrants to other sugar colonies like Trinidad and British Guiana. This was followed, during the second half of the nineteenth century, with a greater number of black and coloured people emigrating to other territories in the Caribbean.[5] Now there was a greater wave of such emigrants. These, like their predecessors, regarded their emigration as purely temporary and sent back large sums of money to their relatives to help them eke out a livelihood in the periods of hardship and privation which frequently occurred.

Barbadians emigrated to many parts of the world in their search to improve their fortunes and those of their families. They went wherever opportunity seemed to beckon. They sailed on ships plying the waters of the Caribbean, earning whatever wages they could as seamen. They set forth to whatever places the shipping routes that touched on Barbados took them. They offered their services as domestics in the cities of the United States they were able to reach. They sold their agricultural skills in the labour markets not only of Cuba, Haiti and Central America but in Jamaica, Trinidad and British Guiana.

185

Without doubt the greatest source of income came from those Barbadians who went out to help build the Panama Canal. It is estimated that by 1909 some 20,000 men had emigrated to Panama in search of work.[6] According to the annual reports of the Barbados Post Office, the emigrants sent back to their relatives at home £7,508 in 1906 and these remittances increased to £46,160 in 1907 and £66,272 in 1909, dropping slightly to £62,102 in 1910. At the same time large sums of money were also coming to the island from America, Brazil and various territories of the Caribbean. It is estimated that large sums were also sent back in cash and bank drafts, while those who eventually returned from Panama brought home some £20,000 in savings.

Panama was the main source of this new income and the wealth thus accrued was called "Panama Money". The money that the emigrants sent to their hard-pressed relatives at home was used for various purposes; to educate their children, to raise their standard of living generally and above all to purchase land on which they provided as much as they could for their own livelihood.

We noted in an earlier chapter that after the abolition of slavery the newly emancipated classes had little opportunity to satisfy their land hunger. The planters, generally speaking, were unwilling to release land for sale to them for the simple reason that their virtual monopoly of arable acreage in the island assured them of a reservoir of labour from which they could draw to satisfy the labour needs of their plantations.

In the new century the situation was almost completely different. During the gloomy nineties of the last century, over one hundred and fifty estates were sold, mainly to clear debts. Many planters sold their estates because they were faced with ruin at a time when sugar was being sold at a price below the cost of production. This trend was to continue during the first two decades of the new century, for from 1900 to 1919, 158 estates were sold in the Court of Chancery.

These circumstances gave the returned emigrants and their relatives the opportunity they had not had before, with planters now willing to part with their estates and the price of land having fallen to £20 per acre. In the year 1900, there were 437 estates in the island; the number fell to 329 in 1912 and 305 in 1919. The major portion of more than sixty estates was converted into free villages, with the inhabitants of the latter being dependent less on the plantation system and more on their own resources. These villages arose in such parishes as St. Michael, Christ Church and St. James, St. George, St. Philip, St. Andrew and St. Lucy.[7]

It is significant that in 1840 there were 934 smallholdings, under ten acres, in existence. Ninety years later, the number of such smallholdings had risen to 18,000. The number of free villages had risen to one hundred and those already in existence were extended.[8] All this made an important change in the social and economic character of the society and it was made possible by the remittances that were sent to Barbados from Brazil, America and other parts of the Caribbean, but now principally from Panama where Barbadians went in their thousands to work in the Canal Zone.

Boom and Crash

Emigration was not the only means the people of Barbados seized to increase their revenue. The sale of fancy molasses, to the development of which Barbados had turned her attention since 1902, was increased in various parts of the world and particularly in Canada with whom a profitable business was established. This proved to be a lucrative source of revenue and compensated to a considerable extent for the loss of the sugar market in the United States. The value of molasses exports rose from £136,548 in 1903 to £232,920 four years later.

Still looking around for other sources of revenue, Barbados found it in the Sea Island cotton industry which she now set out to revive. She thus began to diversify her agriculture in order to strengthen her economy. Cotton proved to be a suitable crop for the drier parts of the island which were not particularly suited to the production of sugar. As a result, the planters began to cultivate cotton with the active encouragement of the Government, who recognised the wisdom of such an agricultural policy. It became a substantial industry for more than a decade until World War I attracted the attention of the planters back to sugar which was then selling at very high prices. When the wartime sugar boom was over, however, the planters were to regret that they had reverted to their former policy of monoculture.

The planters made other attempts to diversify the island's economy by experimenting with substitutes for sugar, but they were not successful in these efforts. Attention was soon to be given, however, to an important industry which was to provide one of the most lucrative sources of revenue for the island. This was the tourist trade which attracted visitors from Britain and from North and South America. Some of the tourists visited Barbados during the winter months, staying at the island's hotels which were soon to enter into a period of boom. Others, notably South Americans, came from Brazil on the Lamport and Holt ships which were accustomed to stop at the island for essential supplies like coal and water. These visitors stayed for a longer time, renting 'bay houses' by the seaside, chiefly in the district known as Worthing. Barbados began to learn the expertise of catering to visitors who were attracted to the island by its natural amenities, the sea, the sun and the beaches, to rest and relax from the busy pre-occupations of the outside world. Hotels like the 'Crane' and the 'Marine' were soon to proliferate and the bay houses on the sea coast became up-to-date apartments.

Though no records were kept at this time, it is estimated that the tourist trade became increasingly valuable. Indeed, the Colonial Secretary of Barbados reported that the island owned much "of its increasing prosperity to the visitors who stayed in the Island".[9]

A period of unprecedented prosperity began for Barbados with the beginning of World War I in 1914. The war in Europe destroyed most of the sugar beet fields that had once placed the West Indian sugar industry in grave jeopardy. Not enough attention was paid at first to the growth of ground provisions which had already suffered from the effect produced on the island's peasantry by the drought of 1912. The result was that the prices of imported foodstuffs, soaring because of their scarcity in the island, imposed a great deal of hardship on those least able to bear it, the labouring population. Before long the Government was forced to intervene, enforcing by statute the amount of ground provisions to be grown, the area to be planted and the control of reaping and selling.[10]

For the planters, the wartime boom represented the zenith of their prosperity, comparable only to the era during which sugar was king. It was one of those rare periods in Barbadian history when, according to an official report, the island enjoyed the combination of a large crop and almost unprecedented high prices. Estates were cleared of debts and the planters showed wisdom in applying their profits largely to improve machinery and to promote the general betterment of their estates. By now, however, they should have learnt from their own history that

The War Memorial, Bridgetown

sugar was an unpredictable crop that no-one could plan indefinitely on account of its vagaries and vicissitudes. Thus it was that sugar continued to boom, seeming to promise indefinite prosperity, until the inevitable crash came. Sugar estates which had sold a decade or two ago at £20 per acre rose to the figure of £146 per acre towards the end of 1920. The crash that occurred the following year, however, brought a sudden and complete change of fortune. Sugar that was sold in London at 146/- per cwt dropped within a year first to 25/- and then to 18/- per cwt. The usual round of catastrophe returned, with sugar as well as ground provisions suffering from the drought of 1920-21.[11] Adversity had once again come upon the island to replace the prosperity it had enjoyed for less than a decade.

Questions and Exercises to Consider

1. What is meant by "monoculture"? In what way can it be applied to Barbados?
2. What do you understand by the phrase "diversifying the agriculture" of Barbados? How far was the island successful in following this policy.?
3. Why did Barbadians emigrate in large numbers during this period? What can you deduce from the fact that the emigrants were black and coloured? What advantages did this emigration bring to the island?
4. Why did the number of smallholdings and the number of villages increase during the century after emancipation? What is meant when we speak of the 'social significance' of these changes?
5. Imagine you are a visitor to the island during the early part of the twentieth century. Write a letter to a friend saying what made your visit enjoyable.
6. How was Barbados affected by World War I? Explain why it brought prosperity to some and hardship and suffering to others.
7. Look at the War Memorial in Bridgetown and see the names of the dead in World War I. If possible invite a veteran to come and talk to the class about his experiences during that War.
8. Why did the social condition of the mass of the people improve so slowly between emancipation and the end of the nineteenth century?

CHAPTER FIFTEEN

The Democratic Movement

The Most Liberal of Men

Not the least of the influences that made their impact on the public life of Barbados in the early part of the twentieth century was that which produced C. P. (later Sir Charles) Clarke, described in his time as the most liberal of men in the politics of the island.[1] A white Barbadian who completed his education in England, Clarke came under the spell of W. E. Gladstone and watched him as the moving spirit in the campaign to equip Britain with the services and institutions that were vital for the modern state. He was fascinated with his political philosophy and absorbed the principles of Liberalism as defined by the great man himself. He attached himself to the secretariat of Gladstone's Party and served as honorary secretary of the Hammersmith Liberal Association. He even entertained the hope that he would one day sit in the House of Commons but his limited financial resources eventually forced him to leave England.[2]

Clarke returned to Barbados in 1888 at a time when the passions of men were still aflame with the great controversy of 1876. But he knew the imperfections of the island's system of government and did not regard its constitution as sacrosanct. He was resolved to make the Executive Committee system work well until such time as a more responsible form of government was introduced. He stressed that the island's institutions should be used to further the progress and welfare of all classes of the community and not in the interest of one section only. For this he was not popular with men of his own class. But Clarke realised that it was necessary for a statesman to stand outside of his own class and plan for society as a whole and this was the driving force that impelled him forward in the entire course of his political career.

Among his diverse interests were education and finance. His speeches on education reflected his Liberal spirit and may still be read with interest and profit by the present generation. In the realm of public finance perhaps lay his special talent. After his appointment as Attorney General in 1913, he gladly accepted the task of introducing the Estimates of Revenue and Expenditure in the House of Assembly and his speeches on such occasions were regarded as models of close reasoning, being once described as not unworthy of his mentor, William Gladstone. [3]

Perhaps his greatest achievement was the measure he piloted through the House in 1921 introducing Income Tax into Barbados. He had always considered it wrong that the island should depend on indirect taxation to obtain the major portion of its revenue. He maintained that under such a system the bulk of the island's expenses were met by exactions from the masses of the people, who were taxed on the necessities of life, and submitted that Income Tax was the fairest form of taxation because it fell on those who were best able to bear the burden of such an impost. The measure was fiercely opposed, but he had the moral support of the Governor, Sir Leslie Probyn, and the growing weight of popular opinion on his side and in the end he won a notable victory. [4]

Clarke's aim was to adapt the island's constitution to meet the requirements of a modern democracy and to interest the people as a whole in the work of parliamentary government. Like Hennessy before him, he recognised the need for carrying public questions beyond the House of Assembly to the larger tribunal composed of all classes and sections of the community. His speeches were directed not so much to the members of the House of Assembly but to the public at large, appealing to their sense of fair play and their rational faculties. In this way he solicited their support for the measures he sought to pilot through the House. In all that he did, he tried to introduce the philosophy and methods of Liberalism and thus it may be said that his work was of no little importance in preparing the way for the age of transition that lay ahead of the island.

Clarke lived and worked in an age when the plantocracy "sat in the seats of the mighty" and controlled the Legislature, when the powers of privilege were "entrenched" and sought to hold "at bay all the forces of liberalism and democracy". That is why in his day he was regarded as an advanced Liberal. Certainly, his views often saved the reputation of the House in the early years of the century and especially on the occasion when he succeeded in persuading a "recalcitrant" Assembly of "the justice and expediency" of Income Tax. [5]

The Flood-gates

Yet it would be misleading to damn the decade after World War I as an era of "political darkness" in the island. There can be no doubt that Conservatism was retreating all along the line. T. W. B. O'Neale, one of the more enlightened Conservatives of the day, was constrained to say at the time that the flood-gates were open and that nothing could be done to stem the onrush of the waters. Not the least of the causes of the change that affected the island was the democratic ideas that were released after the war. Yet the economic condition of the island must not be overlooked.

After the collapse of 1921, Barbados made a rapid recovery in her economic and financial situation. Good rainfall brought a bumper crop in 1923 and the price of sugar rose to 25/- per cwt. The picture of low prices and drought, leading to disease, was now completely changed. Barbados had been unable to find outlets for those of her people who had returned home during the depression of 1921. But now, two years later, New York was able to absorb two thousand of the island's surplus population, with the resulting remittances from abroad to help hard-pressed relatives at home.

Of the £462,107 which the planters owed the Sugar Industry Agricultural Bank, £417,008 had been paid off in two years. The sum collected by way of income tax was £18,244 in 1921 and rose to £31,869 in 1922 and to £121,374 in 1923. So great was the excess of revenue over expenditure that the Government was able to create a reserve fund of £100,000 to be used only in the event of a disastrous hurricane. Not surprisingly, it was reported that the year 1923 "was indeed one of exceptional prosperity".[6] And when the price of sugar began to decline in 1925, Barbados kept it as her constant aim to increase her production of sugar to offset the effect of falling prices.

With the pressure of the democratic movement and the improvement in its material condition, it was perhaps inevitable that the island should make progress in providing its people with some of the services that were necessary in a modern state. The Department of Science and Agriculture was set up in 1925 and this was followed a year later by the establishment of the Central Road Board. The Legislature became more seriously interested in matters of public health and this led to such measures as the Dental Registration Act of 1923 and the Registration of Deaths Act in 1924. The malaria epidemic of 1927 caused the appointment of Dr. J. T. C. Johnson to enquire into the public health services of the island and the valuable report he submitted led to a number of changes and innovations. Not the least important of these was the creation of the posts of Chief Medical Officer and Sanitation Officer.

In the field of education, Barbados had two outstanding achievements to her credit, the foundation of the Codrington High School in 1917 and the St. Michael's Girls' School in 1928. A form of social security was introduced when pensions were provided for civil servants and teachers in 1925 and similar benefits were accorded dependants in the following year by the Widows and Orphans Pension Act. The rights of employees were given appropriate recognition by the Weekly Half Holiday Act in 1926, this being the first public acknowledgement of the just claim of the worker to legislative consideration and statutory protection.[7]

The Legislature took an important step when it passed the Reformatory and Industrial Acts in 1925, seeking to provide treatment along modern lines for juvenile delinquents. The Bursaries Apprenticeship Act was passed in 1928 for the purpose of providing industrial training for the young. Nor does this complete the volume of legislation, seeking to provide social services and amenities and to remedy some of the ills afflicting the society. For in 1923 attention was given to the need of social and cultural facilities for women when the Girls' Industrial Union Act received the sanction of the Legislature. And in an effort to stimulate two of its most beneficent activities, the Horticultural Society Act and the Stockbreeders Association Act were placed in the statute book of the island.

The list mentioned above clearly indicates that the legislative achievement of the decade after the war was by no means a negligible one. Indeed it has been claimed, with some exaggeration, that this period was a "watershed" between the "old centuries of privilege" and the "New Jerusalem of equal opportunity for all".[8] But the significant thing during this decade was not so much the volume of legislation passed by those in authority but the fermentation of new ideas that were abroad in the island after the end of the war. The established conservatism of three centuries was challenged by a group of men who wrought a vital change in the political climate of Barbados. The old ideas of class privilege now appeared to be seriously questioned. The voice of the *Standard* newspaper and to some extent the *Agricultural Reporter* was strangely muted and no-one then would defend the old values and shibboleths so stubbornly championed in the past.[9]

At the beginning of the decade any attempt at political organisation would have been regarded as akin to sedition. Any efforts in the past to translate ideas of political combination into effective action were doomed to futility and frustration. But now the times were completely changed, owing to the influence of the democratic movement. The most diverse elements in the community—the Tory democrat, the middle class Liberal, the small business-man and the mass of the labouring population—seemed to be brought together in one cohesive body of political opinion.

The function of industry was regarded as one of service, with rights and duties to the whole community, and the different partners within it had rights and duties towards each other. In the words of R. H. Tawney, who was quoted to explain the meaning of the democratic movement:

> The first principle is that industry should be subordinated to the community in such a way as to render the best service technically possible, that those who render that service faithfully should be honourably paid, and that those who render no service should not be paid at all; the second is that its direction and government should be in the hands of persons who are responsible to those who are directed and governed, because it is the condition of economic freedom that men should not be ruled by an authority which they cannot control.[10]

The "Herald"

More than any other man, the catalyst in the changes that were taking place in Barbados was Clennell Wilsden Wickham. He had served in Egypt and Palestine with the British West Indies Regiment and he returned to Barbados in 1919, resolved to help the island to change in the midst of a changing world. He had enlisted with the B.W.I. Regiment to fight in freedom's cause and he was now prepared to do battle against the forces of tyranny and oppression at home.

Wickham almost immediately began to write for the *Herald*, a newspaper recently started by Clement Inniss. Indeed, 1919 was a year of significant events in the Caribbean. Hubert Critchlow launched the British Guiana Labour Union, having thus formed an organisation that was to be the first of its kind in the South Caribbean. Arthur Cipriani returned from the war, having also served with the B.W.I. Regiment, and revived the Trinidad Workingmen's Association. A white man who had won the admiration of men like Wickham during his war service, he quickly established a following among thousands of black and coloured people in Trinidad. And now the year 1919 saw the first appearance of a newspaper which, mainly under Wickham's influence, was to have a profound effect on the political outlook of the people of Barbados.

Boy and man, it has been said, Wickham knew life as a breezy vital thing and it was in the same spirit that he blew into the office of the *Herald* and began the task of urging the younger generation to think. It was due to him that Dr. C. D. O'Neal was induced to stay in Barbados and start the Democratic League. He became a foundation member of the League and gave it "a voice and a fighting faith". He devoted the best of his writing in the *Herald* to promoting the cause of the new organisation and to him must be given the credit for "the great political awakening" of the late 1920's. It is therefore not surprising that he has been described as "the greatest interpreter of the needs and aspirations of the average man" which Barbados had known for many years.[11]

Saturday after Saturday, Wickham wrote his exhortations to the people of Barbados. If they made up their minds, he urged, they could make the tight little island "an infinitely cleaner and sweeter place" than it was then. There was hard work to be done, people would still plough the fields, the poor would still be always with them, but they would make it impossible for any man to start earning his living before he was able to "read his Bible". "Is that too ambitious a programme", he once exclaimed, "Good Heavens! I stand aghast at my own moderation".[12]

Then he would appeal to the oligarchs of the day:

If the serious-minded people are wise, [he wrote] they will get in touch with the hopes and aspirations of the common people like myself, and find out why we are dissatisfied and what we want. It would be a very dangerous thing if it should become generally accepted that the legitimate aspirations of the working classes are always to be opposed by those higher up. I fail to see why there should be such a hullabaloo because plain John Citizen demands a share in the government.[13]

When C. A. Brathwaite was brought forward as the first candidate of the Democratic League for election to the House of Assembly, Wickham gave him the support of the *Herald,* freely and unreservedly. And it was undoubtedly due to this support that Brathwaite won a convincing victory on election day. After that significant triumph, Wickham wrote that the common people were waking up to their interests. The "reverberations" of Brathwaite's election had already produced an effect in the country districts. The League's stocks had gone up and they were assured for the future of "a plentiful supply of ammunition" for the fight. The people could not be fooled all the time. Let "the serious-minded" have a care; the island was going to progress.

Before concluding his article in celebration of Brathwaite's electoral victory, Wickham wrote:

I must salute the new spirit which is upon the waters. It is the most happy augury for the future welfare of the Island. It means that in the days to come no man will be allowed to walk into the Lobby of the House of Assembly and hang up his hat. He must be carried on the shoulders of the people. So that before a man can be elected, he will have to satisfy the voter — the man in the street — that he represents no narrow sectional interest.[14]

Wickham was no doctrinaire socialist but he was moved to protest against the rigid lines that were drawn everywhere in Barbadian society. His aim was to destroy the barriers that protected the privileges of a narrow and selfish minority and it was this minority that he had mortally offended. Eventually, the long expected blow descended on his head. A libel case was brought against the *Herald* in 1930 and the punitive damages awarded forced the newspaper to cease publication.

Wickham considered that it was of the utmost importance that every section of the community should be able to make its voice heard. Otherwise, there was no guarantee of freedom, no chance of orderly development in the community. He invited those on whose activities the *Herald* had been a check during the past eleven years to remember that there were worse things in a community than to have a newspaper that was prepared to stand up and fight. "An inarticulate majority", he warned in the last issue of the *Herald,* "brooding over unredressed wrongs and unventilated grievances is a serious menace".[15] That warning was to go unheeded for seven years when the explosion he predicted occurred in the island.

The Democratic League

Among those who returned to serve Barbados after the war was Charles Duncan O'Neal. He had read medicine at the University of Edinburgh and remained in the United Kingdom for some years after completing his medical training. He came under the influence of Keir Hardie, the hero of the British labour movement, and joined the British Labour Party. He learnt his Socialism from the Fabian Society, then led by Bernard Shaw and Sidney and Beatrice Webb. He practised his profession in Newcastle and took an active part in politics.

O'Neal had now returned to start his life's work in Barbados. It was not the first time he had re-visited the island since his sojourn in Britain. On the first occasion he had been driven to pessimism and despair by the prevailing indifference to advanced political thought, as he saw it. He went to Trinidad and settled there for some years. Then he returned to Barbados and one day strolled into the office of the *Herald*. His mood of frustration had not changed. "People here are doing nothing," he said to Wickham. "Nobody tackles real questions. All the politics is not worth a damn". He took to reading back numbers of the *Herald* and talked to a number of people. A few days later, he returned to the newspaper office and took back his word. He had been out of touch, he admitted. Some people had been waking up, but effort had to be concentrated. Thereupon he made the suggestion that led to the birth of the Democratic League.[16]

The League was launched in O'Neal's house in the Ivy, St. Michael, in October 1924. There was laid down the programme which was to guide the new organisation for more than a decade. It was to be the programme of progressive thought in the island for many years to come. Among the measures that were proclaimed on that day, as the aims of the League, were franchise reform, old age pensions, compulsory education, free opportunities for all by the provision of scholarships, trade union organisation, workmen's compensation, health services, unemployment insurance and the reform of industry and commerce by co-operative methods. O'Neal saw the Democratic League as an agency that would ventilate the grievances of the people, enunciate programmes for social improvement among the labouring population and effect the changes that were necessary in Barbados through a disciplined party, committed to a comprehensive plan of action.

In view of the failure to secure representation for the workers in a number of disputes, O'Neal then formed the Workingmen's Association. The object of the Association was to promote the cause of organised labour and generally to improve the living and working conditions of the less privileged section of the community. It was to be more than a mere trade union.[17] It was to provide its members with opportunities for education, credit facilities, formation of co-operatives and training in leadership and collective bargaining. While the Workingmen's Association was to aim at these objectives, the Democratic League was to be the political arm of the popular movement.

Other successes followed Brathwaite's victory at the polls in December 1924. During the period from 1924 to 1932 there were hard-fought campaigns that brought new members of the League into the House. These were D. Lee Sargent, C. L. Elder, H. W. Reece and his son, W. W. Reece, and E. R. L. Ward. But O'Neal himself was defeated on several occasions and did not win a seat until 1932, when his health was broken and his powers had begun to fade. By then his hope of winning power and moulding the island to his heart's desire had also begun to fade like the dream that had once inspired him with "the vision of Blake".[18]

One of the main reasons for O'Neal's failure was undoubtedly the destruction of the *Herald* in 1930. There were, of course, other reasons. The constitution of the island at the time was based on a restricted franchise. There was no working class vote as such and, if the League was to succeed, it had to win the support of the middle class. The latter were much more likely to support a programme of amelioration than one of revolution.[19] Too much time was spent on sterile debates between Liberals and Conservatives at a time when the two could have been linked together in a practical programme of similar aims and objectives. It was too easy for the oligarchs to persuade the timid middle section of the community that the League was a revolutionary organisation and that its leader was bent on spreading the spirit of "sedition" and sowing the "seeds of disaffection". O'Neal was the "doctrinaire Socialist, impudent and impulsive". He had sat at the feet of the "authentic prophets of Socialism" and found it hard to understand some of his colleagues who were his "inferiors in real political knowledge" and who counselled a more cautious approach in the business of converting people to the policies and programmes of the new party.[20]

In the circumstances, it is not surprising that O'Neal did not win the support of the middle class and never realised his dream of capturing power in the island through a strong and united political party. Yet the value of his work lay in his efforts to teach the people of Barbados the importance of political organisation, the value of trade union functions and the salutary benefits of the co-operative movement.

Questions and Exercises to Consider

1. Look up and learn the use of the following:-

   Politics   Liberal
   Franchise   Conservative
   Oligarchy   Democrat
   Socialism   Shibboleth

2. Find out who the Webbs were and what was the Fabian Society.

3. Make a list of the Statements written by Wickham. From these decide what he was trying to do. Do they reflect a particular attitude or political viewpoint?

4. From the programme of reform he advocated would you deduce that O'Neal was a revolutionary?

5. What is meant by "amelioration" as used in this chapter? Would you say that O'Neal should have advocated amelioration rather than revolution?

6. What is meant by "a restricted franchise"? What part did the middle class play in O'Neal's failure to win a greater measure of success?

7. Write a speech in which O'Neal makes a plea for change and expounds his programme of reform.

8. Arrange a debate on the question that Income Tax is the fairest form of taxation.

9. What is meant by the phrase "a period of political darkness"? Do you agree or disagree that the decade after World War I was such a period in Barbados?

CHAPTER SIXTEEN

The Masses Stir

West Indian Malaise

The world depression of 1929 caused a serious deterioration in the economic condition of the West Indies. During the previous thirty years there had been some improvement in the agricultural fortunes of this area. The wisdom of the Norman Commission seemed to be made manifest. The near collapse of the sugar industry was replaced by the comparative prosperity of alternative crops. Bananas, important as a peasant crop, particularly in Jamaica, were exported in increasing quantities. But this was struck an almost fatal blow by a rapid spread of leaf-spot disease. Cocoa, also valuable as a peasant crop and grown chiefly in Trinidad and Grenada, had long been a major agricultural export. But the world production of raw cocoa had expanded so rapidly that supply now exceeded demand, with a resulting fall in the prices that had hitherto brought prosperity to these two islands.

Also unfavourable was the outlook for such products as the coconuts and citrus fruit of Jamaica, the grape-fruit of Trinidad, the rice of British Guiana, the limes of Dominica and the arrowroot of St. Vincent. These crops faced a number of problems arising from such hazards as hurricane or diseases, competition from the Dutch East Indies, Burma and India, contraction or disappearance of markets and the use of synthetic substitutes. On all sides the export agriculture of the West Indies presented a discouraging spectacle. In the face of unremunerative prices, producers tried to reduce their cost of production and almost invariably such economy led to a reduction in the number of persons they employed. [1]

Curiously enough the one industry that seemed less discouraging was sugar. In spite of its many vicissitudes, the sugar industry had experienced a great expansion since 1929 when it reached its nadir. That critical situation was met by the appointment of Lord Olivier's Sugar Commission, whose recommendations were mainly responsible for the revival of the industry. The increase in sugar production was due to two factors: the costs of production were reduced both in the field and the factory, and preferential assistance was given in substantial measure both by Britain and Canada.

All was not plain sailing, however, for the sugar industry. Preferential assistance and technical efficiency had enabled the West Indies to increase their exports to Britain. But this was accompanied by a fall in the world price of sugar. Moreover, the progress of the West Indies as exporters was made at the expense of foreign sugar-producing countries. This was soon to produce repercussions and eventually a scheme was introduced under the International Sugar Agreement in 1937, restricting the further expansion of the sugar industry in the West Indies. This restriction led to what was becoming a familiar West Indian problem, a reduction of the number of persons employed in the industry.

The ranks of the unemployed were further increased by the virtual closing of the emigration outlets. Following the general depression of 1929, countries that had previously admitted West Indian immigrants now imposed rigid restrictions on further immigration. Caribbean countries, which formerly offered West Indians employment opportunities, also followed the example of the outside world. And Cuba went further by seeking to repatriate those West Indians whose services were no longer needed in her labour market.

In addition, the returning emigrants brought back to the West Indies new ideas and new aspirations. They looked for higher standards of living at a time when the argicultural outlook of the area could not promise to maintain even existing levels. Confined within their own territories, restive under the impact of ideas to which they had been exposed abroad, particularly responsive to the doctrines they had learnt from men like Marcus Garvey and increasingly sensitive to the implications of white capital and coloured labour, these returning West Indians were wide open to the elements that make up the psychology of discontent.

Added to all this was the steady growth in the population of the area. Within a period of forty years, from 1896 to 1936, the populations of Jamaica and Trinidad and Tobago had almost doubled and the rate of increase in other territories was also a source of concern. The over-all rate of increase in the British West Indies was estimated at between 1½ per cent and 2 per cent per annum. And it was pointed out with some degree of anxiety

202

that a population increasing at the rate of 2 per cent per annum would double itself in 35 years. [2]

The Barbadian Situation

In Barbados, conditions were no better than in any other territory of the West Indies. The Olivier Commission noted with satisfaction the "enormous advance" that had been made in the production of sugar in Barbados since 1896, the year when the Norman Commission was appointed. They observed that the experiments started by Bovell and Harrison had produced remarkable results. During the past thirty years the yield of sugar had been trebled owing to the improvements brought about by new seedlings, better manuring, better cultivation and better extraction. The Olivier Commission paid tribute to the continuous attention that had been given in Barbados to the sugar industry and to the capable committees which had been appointed from time to time to deal with the industry. It commented on the "very recognisable results" that had been achieved both in factory work and in cultivation and declared that Barbados had been distinguished among West Indian colonies for having produced the new seedling canes. [3]

The problem that faced Barbados was the same as that facing the other territories of the West Indies, the steady decline in the price of sugar since 1925. In view of the prospects of sugar the island once again tried to find some relief for its difficulties by turning to alternative crops. Cotton was cultivated again but progress in this was hampered by the ravages of pests. Barbadians returning from overseas had the opportunity to buy small farms when sugar plantations on marginal lands were sold off. These peasant farmers, while cultivating some sugar, grew ground provisions and developed an export trade with British Guiana. This trade was useful in helping to promote in some degree the island's self-sufficiency. [4]

Yet the Olivier Commission concluded that alternative crops provided few opportunities for relieving the Barbadian economic plight. It was gravely concerned over the sugar situation, especially as it affected Barbados, and it submitted two recommendations that were to have far-reaching consequences. These were that the price of West Indian sugar should be maintained by an increase in the imperial preference and that a West Indian Cane Breeding Station be established in Barbados. [5]

The price of sugar in the free world market continued to fall to such an extent that in 1935 it was less than half what it had been in 1928, the year before the Olivier Commission was appointed. Disaster was averted by the increased preference paid on sugar imported into the United Kingdom from the British territories and Barbados benefited accordingly. To this increase another special preference was added from which Barbados benefited by her extraordinary efforts in sugar production. With this help from Britain, the Barbadians were able to sell their sugar at twice the price that was being paid in the free world market. [6]

Nevertheless, the planters still believed that the prospect for sugar was a gloomy one. Would the international sugar situation continue to decline? What was the future of the syrup industry? Would the sugar crop be short in 1936 owing to lack of rainfall? Would Britain suddenly reverse its policy and deprive the West Indies of a protected sugar market in the United Kingdom, as she had done in 1846?

At it turned out, the gloomy forebodings of the planters were not realised. The rains came later in December and January and the sugar crop recovered remarkably. More syrup was sold than in any previous year and at a good price. As a result, the general financial position was better than had seemed possible a short time ago. [7]

Barbados had clearly tried to make the most of her limited resources. But there was one problem she could not solve by her own unaided efforts. The census of 1921 revealed that there were 156,312 persons in the island. By August 1937 the population had risen to 189,350. It had long excited the wonder of many, how an island of 166 square miles could support so dense a population by agriculture alone. And since the annual increase in the population was 2,000 it was obvious that Barbados before long would be unable to support the total number of persons living in the island.

In the past, as we have seen in an earlier chapter, emigration provided the opportunities that saved many black Barbadians from unemployment, poverty and distress. These had left the island and found employment as policemen, mechanics and engineers in many of the territories of the Caribbean. They had worked in the construction of the Panama Canal, as domestic servants in the United States and as labourers in the canefields of Cuba. But now all these outlets were closed. Artisans and labourers could no longer find work in the countries that once welcomed them. The better educated, who had attended the island's secondary schools, could no longer find opportunities for advancement in other parts of the world. Trinidad and British Guiana virtually barred emigration from Barbados. The doors of Panama, Brazil and America were now closed and Cuba was repatriating those Barbadians who had immigrated into that country to work for the wages they could not obtain in their own island. Clearly, the outlook for Barbados, which was bursting at its seams, was black indeed.[8]

The General Upheaval

Overpopulation was the root cause of many of the economic ills in Barbados[9] and the West Indies. But there are other factors that have to be added. The principal products of these territories were threatened with a disastrous fall in prices. Moreover, they were faced with a deadly struggle against "a growing threat of disease in almost every crop". Sugar-cane was menaced with mosaic disease, bananas with Panama disease and leaf-sport, cocoa with witch-broom and limes with redroot and wither-tip; and each of these diseases caused "widespread havoc". Nor were coffee, citrus and coconuts without their problems and Jamaica's valuable product, pimento, was "almost wiped out by rust".[10]

Rarely did the West Indies appear to be faced with such a combination of adverse factors. Falling prices, plant diseases, unemployment and under-employment, poverty, hardship and privation—this combination of circumstances imposed a heavy trial on a society that was ill-designed and ill-equipped to sustain it. To make matters worse, while the cost of living kept rising, the level of wages remained lamentably low. According to the figures placed before the British Parliament in 1938, the daily wages were 28 cents in St. Vincent, 28-36 cents in Antigua, 30 cents in St. Lucia and Barbados, 30-48 cents in Grenada, 35 cents in Trinidad, 32-36 cents in St. Kitts and 48-60 cents in Jamaica.[11]

In such a situation, the growth of discontent and unrest were inevitable and before long there was an explosion that spread to almost every territory in the British West Indies.

The first outbreak occurred in St. Kitts early in 1935 when there was a general strike of agricultural labourers in that colony. This was followed a month later by a hunger march in Trinidad, preceded by a strike in the island's oil fields. Later in the same year, there were strikes in British Guiana, a coal strike in St. Lucia and disorder in St. Vincent. After a calm year, widespread unrest occurred in 1937. There were strikes in Trinidad and within a month riots broke out in Barbados, followed by strikes in British Guiana, St. Lucia and Jamaica. The climax of all this was reached in 1938 with a general strike in Jamaica and work stoppages in British Guiana. By the time this general upheaval was suppressed 46 persons had been killed, 429 injured and thousands arrested. [12]

We have already referred to the economic conditions that led to widespread discontent and unrest. But there were other causes of the general malaise effecting the West Indies. The Italo-Abyssinian War had served to emphasise the doctrines of Marcus Garvey and further embittered the relations between white capital and coloured labour. There was no constitutional machinery to redress the grievances of the labouring population. There were no unions to settle differences between employers and workers through the methods of collective bargaining. There were no political organisations to represent effectively the aspirations of the masses. [13]

In view of all the prevailing circumstances, it is not surprising that the Moyne Commission was moved to report as follows:

Serious discontent was often widespread in West Indian Colonies during the nineteenth century, as is indicated by the occasional uprisings that occurred, leading sometimes to considerable loss of life. But the discontent that underlies the disturbances of recent years is a phenomenon of a different character, representing no longer a mere blind protest against a worsening of conditions, but a positive demand for the creation of new conditions that will render possible a better and less restricted life. It is the co-existence of this new demand for better conditions with the unfavourable economic trend that is the crux of the West Indian problem of the present day. [14]

The Barbados Disturbances

Barbados could not fail to be infected by the spirit of unrest that spread from one territory to another in the British West Indies.

On the evening of July 26th, 1937, meetings were held and attended by crowds in the Lower Green and Golden Square to protest against the deportation of their "shepherd", Clement Payne. After the meetings, the crowds became uncontrollable.

They roamed about the city of Bridgetown, smashing electric street lamps and the windscreens of motor cars. Law and order were eventually restored by the police but the official enquiry later deemed it worthy of note that not a single arrest was made in spite of "the considerable disorder and damage to property".[15]

The following day, large crowds assembled in Golden Square which, as on the previous night, had been the centre of the disturbances. From the Square they sallied forth into Probyn Street and Bay Street. There with sticks and stones they did what damage they could to passing vehicles. The shop windows of garages were smashed and motor cars pushed into the sea. They then proceeded to the Pier Head where they seized formidable pieces of wallaba wood. Armed with these weapons, they crossed the Chamberlain Bridge and Trafalgar Square and invaded Broad Street. In the city's main business centre, they attacked motor cars and pedestrians and smashed the shop windows of some of the leading shops. Under this assault, the police were even less successful than the night before. They were forced to retire before the fury of the mob and withdraw to their headquarters at the Central Police Station. Bridgetown was now virtually controlled by the rioters. To restore order, the Riot Act was read and the police were armed to deal with the situation. Before the disorders were quelled, fourteen persons were killed and forty-seven wounded.[16] Hundreds were arrested in due course and many of these were subsequently imprisoned. Some of the terms of imprisonment imposed were as long as five and ten years, though these were later reduced by the Secretary of State for the Colonies.

The disturbances were not confined to the City of Bridgetown. It is astonishing how rapidly the spirit of disorder spread from the metropolitan area to the rural districts of the island. Motor cars were stoned, shops were broken into and potato fields were raided. The curious belief seemed to prevail that the reading of the Riot Act meant that lawless acts could be committed with impunity. But it seems certain that the raiding of the potato fields and the attacks on shops in the country districts were mainly due to "hunger or the fear of hunger" on the part of people who had never heard of Clement Payne. The Deane Report also considered it noteworthy that the number of persons who suffered at the hands of the lawless was insignificant and that "the attacks were made against the property of persons of every colour without discrimination".[17]

Undoubtedly, the immediate cause of the disturbance arose from the activities of Clement Payne. A Trinidadian, who had spent some years of his early life in Barbados, he held some seventeen meetings in Bridgetown, preaching the gospel of trade unionism. In due course the authorities took steps against him for two reasons. He was getting too good a hearing on the message he had for the people and it was feared by the oligarchs that the language he used in his campaign was likely to cause disorder by those who were suffering from unemployment, hardship and privation. It was his deportation on the night of July 26th that led to the disturbances that marred the peace and harmony that had long characterised the island of Barbados.

The Deane Commission did not take the view that the outbreak of violence was "a mere flash in the pan, a spark of revolt" that would have been completely smothered by stronger police measures at the time. Indeed, after surveying the whole field, they came to the conclusion that there was a large accumulation of explosive matter in the island and that "the Payne incident only acted as a detonator". They expressed the firm view that the real cause of the disturbance was not political agitation but the harsh realities of the economic situation facing the people.[18]

Among the highlights of the official enquiry was the evidence collected of the wages paid to clerks, shop assistants, druggists, artisans and other classes of workers. The evidence revealed a shocking state of affairs. The wages paid to manual and clerical workers and the remuneration of those in positions of responsibility revealed what was rightly described as a "striking disparity". And it was a startling revelation to many to learn that the wages paid to apprentices for four or five years in the two foundries in Bridgetown were even less than those paid to agricultural labourers, the most depressed class of workers in the island. It is small wonder that the Commission was driven to the conclusion that there could be "no justification short of bankruptcy of trade and industry for the maintenance of so low a standard of wages".[19]

The Riot Song

The events of this period of unrest were commemorated in an authentic folk song which has been rescued from the almost forgotten past by Cammie Reid and Alfred Pragnell. Folk memory has perpetuated the grim realities of that time, as it did the joy of emancipation one hundred years before. The music and the poetry of the people have recorded the names of those who, as the lieutenants of Clement Payne, played no small part in the task of agitating the cause of reform. There was "Menzies" Chase who, according to popular legend, was beaten so unmercifully in Glendairy Gaol that he was unable to perform the trotting drill around the prison yard. Mortie Skeete endured no less from the lash of the detectives' sticks and the butts of the policemen's guns. "Brain" Alleyne was the intellectual of the little proletarian group whose oratory, usually ending in the serio-comic note, "tonight is a funny day", aroused the deep-seated fears of the reigning oligarchy. And Ulric Grant, whose peroration usually dwelt on the theme that "there was no justice in Coleridge Street", where the law courts were sited, brought down on his head the inappeasable wrath of the mighty. These were the little known heroes whose martyrdom was narrated and handed down by oral tradition. Even the obscure Belle, who was not cast in the same mould, was included in the "Riot Song" as a pathetic figure who could not endure the agony of the hour.

Now listen friends to muh late compose
De twenty-seventh of July I couldn't show muh nose.
Listen friends to what was composed
De twenty-seventh of July I couldn't show muh nose.
Civilian wid rocks, policemen wid guns
Doan doubt me friends it wasn't no fun
For everytime dat yuh hear a round (ie. of bullets)
Somebody dead and somebody wound.

I know you all wouldn't know muh features
I give you a joke about some o' the creatures.
Menzies de first dat I know well
Doan doubt we friends he smell real hell
De parade ground he couldn't run around
Dey had to put Menzies to walk up and down.
He get in de box in a serious way
Saying "tonight is a funny day".

But really my intention was not to rhyme
But de blows on Mortie Skeete really changed muh mind.
From de time he was under arrest
He get blows backward, front and chest

Policemen wid guns and detectives wid sticks
Friends yuh couldn't imagine how many kicks
And everytime that yuh hear my son
Mortie get a lash or butt wid de gun.

But Belle he's a man he really didn't stand
He only went fuh three weeks under remand
He was so frightened he couldn't even eat
All he used to do was eat off de meat
When de warder ask him cool if he done
Instead of answering he like he wud run
But after all he did get out fine
Because he aint spend no unfair long time.
Instead of answering he like he wud run,
But after all he did get out fine
Because he aint spend no unfair long time

Now lemme tell yuh bout Brain and Grant
Two men dey say had great intelligence
Brain mount de box wid a great surprise
Saying "Barbados must be decolonise".
Grant sit down and wait till he done
He said "Friends this here aint no fun"
But when dey done dey had it to say
"Yes tonight is a funny day".[20]

Out of the Ferment

Out of the ferment produced by the disturbances was born the
Barbados Progressive League. The situation was now to change
as swiftly in Barbados as in other territories of the West Indies.
The first enduring labour organisations emerged from the
disorders that had spread through the British West Indies.
Leaders arose who were capable of giving effective expression to
the demands of labour and these men pressed not only for
increase in wages but for a programme of political reform. Chief
among those who succeeded in making labour a formidable
political force were Alexander Bustamante and Norman Manley
of Jamaica, Robert Bradshaw of St.Kitts, Vere Bird of Antigua
and Grantley Adams of Barbados.[21]

The first steps towards the formation of the Barbados
Progressive League were taken early in 1938, with C. A.
Brathwaite as President among the "temporary appointments".

Before long the new organisation, which was originally called the Barbados Labour Party, changed its name to the Barbados Progressive League, though it was later to revert to its original name. By April 1938, a committee consisting of Adams, Dr. H. G. Cummins and W. A. Crawford set to work to revise and expand the aims and objects of the League.[22] In October the organisation was formally launched, and within less than a year Adams was elected President, with the object of making "the real leader" the "titular leader as well".[23]

The first statement of the League's policy was made late in 1939 in a memorandum that was presented to the Royal Commission under the Chairmanship of Lord Moyne. It declared that its policy was democratic and socialist. It considered that the resources of the country should be used for the benefit of all "in equitable proportions". It insisted that the amenities provided by modern science and civilisation should be placed at the disposal of all alike. Perhaps its fundamental recommendation was that the wealth produced in Barbados would not be "equitably divided" until the resources of wealth were owned and controlled by the Government on behalf of the community.[24]

It seems clear that the policy of the new organisation was largely influenced by the resolutions which were passed by the British Guiana and West Indies Labour Congress in November 1938. Adams represented the Barbados Progressive League at that Congress and took an active part in its discussions. A draft bill embodying a constitution for "the creation and Government of a Federated West Indies" was presented by him and agreed to by the Congress. The latter called on the Moyne Commission to recommend self-government with adult franchise for all the West Indian colonies. It accepted the principle of nationalising the sugar industry and recommended legislation providing for a number of measures. These included Government purchase of large estates for distribution among peasants on easy terms of sale, the prohibition of the ownership by a single individual, firm or company, directly or indirectly, of a sugar estate of more than fifty acres in extent, the ownership by the Government alone of all sugar factories and, the establishment of a single Government purchasing agency to be the sole exporters of sugar.[25]

Clearly the evidence submitted by the League to the Moyne Commission reflected the principles and convictions of the British Guiana and West Indies Labour Congress.[26]

Having established its position on a number of basic issues, the

211

LABOUR CONDITIONS INVESTIGATED

Mr. G. H. Adams Puts Case for Worker

ADVOCATES HIGHER WAGES AND LAND SETTLEMENT

Elementary Teachers Likened to Nicodemus

EIGHTH DAY

BRIDGETOWN, January 25.

THE eighth day's session of the Royal Commission under the Chairmanship of Lord Moyne was devoted to the investigations dealing with the conditions of the worker in relation to the economic condition of the sugar industry. Mr. G. H. Adams submitted a separate memorandum and also headed a delegation representing the Barbados Progressive League. This comprised Messrs. C. A. Braithwaite, W. H. Seale, E. Talma and Dr. H. G. Cummins.

The evidence follows:—

Lord Moyne: This morning we are hearing witnesses on two memoranda which have been handed in; the first signed by Mr. G. Herbert Adams, and the second by three signatories including Mr. Adams, on behalf of the Barbados Progressive League; so we will take the two memoranda together, if that suits the witnesses, as they raise very much the same points. Our witnesses from their right to their left are Mr. Braithwaite, Mr. Seale, Mr. Adams, Mr. Talma and Dr. Cummins. Taking Mr. Adams's memorandum first: You begin by saying that all classes of the community in Barbados do not get a fair deal in present conditions and you suggest that the remedy must be sought in adult suffrage, certain changes in the House of Assembly, a local Parliament Act, and strengthening the powers of the Governor. Well now, will you tell me what your franchise is at present? Am I right in thinking that it is £50 occupancy franchise and £50 income?

Mr. Adams: Yes, My Lord.

Lord Moyne: How long has that been in force?

Mr. Adams: I should say, sir, certainly about one hundred years.

Lord Moyne: It has not been changed in your lifetime?

Mr. Adams: No, sir.

ADULT SUFFRAGE

Lord Moyne: It is rather a big jump to go from that straight away to adult suffrage. You see in Great Britain the first Reform Bill was passed more than one hundred years ago and gradually the suffrage has been extended. Do you think you should take the full measure all in one step?

Mr. Adams: Yes, My Lord, I do; because it is an accident very often, more than anything else that prevents people from voting now, that is to say, the non-voters' intelligence and political consciousness are just as great as those of the man with the £50 qualification. A carpenter who is working gets $5.00 a week and he votes. A carpenter equally efficient and intelligent may be out of work and he does not vote.

Lord Moyne: Do you think the women of Barbados would use the vote?

Mr. Adams: Oh yes, My Lord.

Lord Moyne: I would like to know what is in your mind about a local Parliament Act. You see, our Parliament Act regulates the length of Parliaments and it lays down the relations between the two Houses and limits the powers of the Upper Chamber. You have not got a double Chamber system here?

Mr. Adams: We have, unfortunately, Sir.

Lord Moyne: You have got, I know, an Executive Council. Is it tell how is the second Chamber constituted. I looked it up in the Year Book and found that the Assembly is the Legislature. How is the second Chamber constituted? Has it equal powers with the first Chamber?

Mr. Adams: Yes, My Lord. The second Chamber is exactly in the position the House of Lords was in 1910 and it is all nominated.

Lord Moyne: And you want something to regulate the relations between the two Chambers?

Mr. Adams: Yes, My Lord.

A NEW SUGGESTION

Lord Moyne: Then I notice rather a new suggestion, new, to us in our inquiries in the islands, that the Governor's powers should be strengthened, and therefore I take it that you accept the view that Great Britain must continue to take an interest in your affairs. "Indeed", you say, "I see, that it is most reasonable to give the Colonial Office which is being asked to secure financial aid for us that we may improve our condition, the power to see that that

76

Progressive League proceeded to deal with more immediate and practical affairs. It demanded that a law be placed in the statute book of the island providing compensation for agricultural and industrial workers injured in the course of their employment. It urged the passing of a Wages Board Act and establishment of wages advisory boards. It called for immediate attention to the Factories Bill to provide for the registration and supervision of factories. A slum clearance and housing scheme was prepared for the whole island including the city and rural areas. This scheme was designed to include provision for new road building. The League also demanded the introduction of free compulsory education up to the age of fifteen years, with provision for free books, a hot mid-day meal and a daily milk ration for those in need. It urged the development of peasant agriculture and the teaching of co-operative agriculture and marketing.[27]

In 1940 the League was able to gain its first political victory when it gained five seats in the House of Assembly. The successful candidates were G. H. Adams, Dr. H. G. Cummins, H. W. Springer, A. G. Gittens and V. B. Vaughan. Even before this, a significant triumph had been won when the Trade Union Act was passed in 1939 under the pressure of progressive opinion at home and abroad. And in 1941 the Barbados Workers Union was formed with Adams as President General and Hugh Springer as Secretary. The League was now able to pursue its principal objective, which it had declared almost from the outset. For it had declared in January 1940 that it believed "first and foremost, in a living wage for all workers".[28]

Clearly, the leadership of the labour movement in Barbados, as in other parts of the Caribbean, realised that the masses of the people were deeply stirred by the widespread disorders in the area and they were resolved to give as effective expression as they could to the needs and aspirations of those whom they led.

Questions and Exercises to Consider

1. What is meant by population growth? How is population increase calculated?
2. Write a paragraph showing what you understand by the phrase "the world depression of 1929".
3. What effect did that depression have on the West Indies and particularly Barbados?
4. Write a letter to the Press, as if you were a Barbadian

planter and express your views on (a) The International Sugar Agreement of 1937 (b) emigration outlets (c) increasing population (d) rising unemployment.

5. Look up and learn the use of the following:

Psychology of discontent	Economic malaise
Economic depression	Repatriate
Economic self-sufficiency	Trade unionism
Unfavourable economic trend	Co-operative agriculture

6. Find out what you can of Marcus Garvey. What is meant by the worsening relation between white capital and coloured labour?

7. Imagine that you are a worker in the construction of the Panama Canal or a domestic in the United States. Write a letter to a relative at home saying how you are getting on and recommending what should be done with the money you are sending him/her.

8. How do you interpret the "Riot Song" and what light does it throw on the period? Can it be regarded as part of the cultural tradition of the poor?

9. Examine the extract on p. 212. Look up the *Advocate* newspaper of January 19th 1938 and subsequent issues and read all the evidence given before the Moyne Commission by Grantley Adams and others. (a) What was the condition of the workers at this time? (b) Why were the Primary Teachers compared to Nicodemus? (c) Why was Adams considered the leader of the working class in the years following the riots?

10. Make a list of prices of everyday commodities. Make lists of wages of various categories of workers. Decide how the standard of living would be affected in each case.

CHAPTER SEVENTEEN

Reforming the Constitution

Besetting Difficulties

The efforts of The Barbados Progressive League to introduce much-needed reforms and improvements in the island were beset by many difficulties. They did not have the instruments of power to translate their programme into reality. Barbados was still governed by the old representative system which was established in the British West Indies during the seventeenth and eighteenth centuries. While the other colonies had undergone changes in their forms of government, Barbados alone kept "an unbroken line of constitutional descent from the Old Representative System".[1] For more than half a century the real executive power in Barbados rested with the Governor, the Colonial Secretary and the Attorney General, with the addition of any such persons as the Governor might choose to appoint though four of these had to be members of the House of Assembly.

That was the apex of the constitution and its base gave little cause for more hope. In 1869 there was less than one voter in every hundred of the population. This situation was improved by the Franchise Act of 1884, yet the real power remained in the same hands. The old representative system in the West Indies had produced an oligarchy of white planters and merchants who successfully oppressed the Governor and the Colonial Office and maintained effective control of colonial affairs. Nowhere was this system more strongly entrenched than in Barbados.

The Progressive League realised that, unless the island's power structure could be changed, they would suffer the same fate as O'Neal and the Democratic League. In 1940, therefore, Adams introduced a measure to provide for adult franchise and to abolish the property qualifications for membership of the House. Inevitably, it was rejected in the House, but the members could not fail to take note of the temper and mood of the populace. Barbados had led the way in the West Indies by providing for old age pensions, albeit on a modest scale. It passed a Minimum Wage Act, providing for the creation of the necessary machinery for fixing a minimum wage in any occupation.[2] Not the least important event was that Death Duties, in spite of fierce opposition, became the law of the land.

The political difficulties facing the Progressive League were still a source of anxiety to its leaders. In 1942 the number of its members in the House was reduced from five to four owing to the resignation of one of its members. It was clear that the League could not increase its membership so long as the thousands who supported the movement were deprived of the right to vote. Accordingly, when the new House met in 1942 Adams again introduced his Bill to provide for adult franchise. The Government countered with a Bill to reduce the existing £50 qualification to £30 per annum. After a fierce battle, two compromises were conceded. The income qualification for voters was reduced to £20 and women for the first time were admitted to the vote and to membership of the House of Assembly on the same terms as men. But the League failed, in spite of vigorous efforts, to reduce the qualifications for membership of the House. Moreover, the Legislative Council, in an attempt to halt the trend of events, successfully introduced an amendment making it obligatory for all election Candidates to deposit £30 which would go to the Public Treasury if any candidate failed to win a certain proportion of the votes cast.[3]

Triumphs and Setbacks

In spite of the setbacks mentioned here, the new session, which started in 1942, was a liberal one. A look at the measures that were passed during its lifetime will confirm this view.

There were several factors that were responsible for the liberality of the new House. First, the Colonial Office was influenced by the recommendations of the Moyne Commission and the Orde Browne Report to press Barbados and the other territories of the British West Indies to adopt a more liberal policy of amelioration. Secondly there was the leadership of the Attorney General, E. K. Walcott, who successfully piloted a number of ameliorative measures through the House which had begun to grow aware of the wind of change that was blowing though the British Caribbean. And thirdly, there was the presence of Adams on the island's Executive Committee, to which he had been appointed at the beginning of the session, and no-one was in any doubt of the direction in which his influence was exerted. Modest yet welcome increases were made to old-age pensions. Death Duties, which had already been added to the island's resources, were now followed by increased income tax rates. This may well be regarded as a major victory for the Barbados Progressive League which had agitated, in season and out of season, for the principle that revenue for social and economic reforms should be raised by direct taxation and not by indirect taxation on the necessities of life.[5]

One of its notable triumphs was the passing of the Workmen's Compensation Act, a measure which the League had advocated from the outset of its career. Then there was the important amendment to the Trade Union Act that exempted individuals from liability when acting in furtherance of a trade dispute. The facilities of the Peasants Loan Bank were extended to provide for improved cultivation of crops, the irrigation of holdings and the purchase of livestock. This amendment was also designed to help the smallholder pay the balance of purchase money due on his land on the condition that it did not exceed forty per cent. In addition, the number of Peasant Instructors was increased from three to twelve, a Co-operative Officer was appointed and several agricultural stations and stud centres were established. All of this indicated a new policy by the Government for which the progressive movement could claim a great deal of credit.

Of no little significance, too, was the passing of such measures as the Wages Board Act, giving legal sanction to agreements reached by representatives of employers and workers, and the Labour Department Act, providing a central advisory body over labour matters. The accommodation at Harrison College was substantially increased and financial provision was made for a new and larger Combermere School. Perhaps most significant of all in this area was the appointment of a Director of Education who took over the control and direction of education from a statutory board of well-meaning but inexpert amateurs.

Yet the Barbados Progressive League was by no means satisfied with the political complexion of the House of Assembly. There were soon to be a number of significant changes. As a result of the £20 franchise, which became law in 1943, the composition of the House was greatly changed after the General Election of 1944. The League increased its membership from four to eight, the new members being M. E. Cox, J. B. Springer, L. E. Smith and B. L. Barrow. Equally significant was the victory won by the newly formed West Indian National Congress Party, led by

W. A. Crawford. Eight party members won seats in the Assembly and it is worthy of note that their programme of reform was much the same as that of the Progressive League.

Futile and ineffective

There was no question that a remarkable change was taking place in the political life of Barbados. The campaign for the political education of the masses went on apace. Professing the same ideology, but afflicted by personality differences, the Progressive League (which had now reverted to its original name as the Barbados Labour Party) and the Congress Party appeared to work for the same cause, that of Labour and socialism.

As was confidently expected, much important legislation was passed during the 1944-46 session. The reform and expansion of the island's educational system was regarded as a matter of the highest priority and, accordingly, a consolidating act was passed laying the foundation for the plans submitted by the first Director of Education. The value of teacher training was emphasised by the construction of Erdiston Training College, instructors for adult classes were provided and the salaries of secondary and elementary teachers were increased.

In addition, a cost of living bonus of twenty-five per cent was granted to Government pensioners in the lower categories and old age pensions were again increased. Official enquiries were made on the method of payment for sugar cane cutting and on the organisation of the Police Force. A Shop Closing Act was passed to reduce the number of working hours to reasonable limits. Measures of penal reform were adopted, extending the system of probation for adults and ensuring that extra-mural work could be assigned in certain cases instead of a term of imprisonment. Not the least important decision taken during the session was to conduct a census of the population after a lapse of twenty-five years. That census was taken early in 1946.

But all was not well in the relations between the two progressive groups, the Labour Party and the Congress Party. Early in the new session Hugh Springer was appointed a member of the Executive Committee, an appointment that increased the number of Labour representatives on that body from one to two. In view of the reputation that Springer had established as a parliamentarian and as General Secretary of the Barbados Workers Union, his appointment was welcomed.

218

There was much satisfaction with the role the Governor, Sir Grattan Bushe, had so far played in the public life of the island. He was generally given the credit for the appointment of Adams on the Executive in 1942, for the initiative he took in the passing of the £20 franchise in 1943 and the addition of Hugh Springer to the inner councils of Government in 1944. Since there were now sixteen Labour members in the House, however, it is difficult to understand why at least one representative from the Congress Party was not appointed on the Executive Committee.

This omission was responsible for the inharmonious relations that now developed between the Legislature and the Executive of the island. It could no longer be claimed that the Governor's choice of members on the Executive Committee reflected a proper "concern for the distribution of opinion in the House". This meant that the Executive was often unrepresentative of the House and sharp differences of opinion held up important items of legislation for long periods. Proposals dealing with housing and education were among the measures that suffered. "Parliament", it was recorded, "was divided to the point of deadlock, and minor issues sparked off interminable debate characterised by vicious charges and counter-charges".[6]

It is small wonder that the *Beacon*, the official organ of the Barbados Labour Party, was moved to make the bitter comment that "for futility, for ineffectiveness, for a diminution in the dignity of self-respect of a Parliamentary Assembly it was easily the worst in living memory".[7] Clearly something had to be done to correct the inefficiency in the machinery of government and it was to this task that the Governor now turned his attention.

The Bushe Experiment

Governor Bushe had no difficulty in diagnosing the defect in the island's system of Government. The system had worked well enough during the relatively placid years that followed 1876 but was unable to meet the clamour for reform that followed the disturbances of 1937. No harmony of outlook between the Legislature and the Executive could now be taken for granted.

The root of the trouble, Bushe declared, was to be found in the Barbados constitution, which was "incapable of coping with modern conditions". There was an imperfect distribution of power and responsibility. The Governor had the whole responsibility of the government but was given no power, while the House of Assembly possessed the power but had no responsibility. Bushe added that the real power was entrusted to the Legislature and not to the Executive and, accordingly, it was impossible to determine the vital issue of responsibility.[8]

The constitutional change, known as the "Bushe Experiment", was therefore adopted and laid down that in future the Officer administering the Government would send for the person who seemed best able to command a majority in the assembly and ask him to submit names from the House for membership of the Executive Committee. The object of this new arrangement was so to change the Executive Committee as to make it an effective instrument of Government, collectively responsible for policy instead of continuing as a collection of individuals selected by and accountable to the Governor. In effect a semi-ministerial system of government was established, with members of the House assuming responsibility for dealing with the affairs of particular government departments in the Executive and in the House. Significantly the position traditionally occupied by the Attorney General was to be abandoned and the role of chief spokesman of the Executive in the House was to be assumed by the majority leader.[9]

The General Election of 1946 was fought under the Bushe Experiment and it was contested by three parties, the Barbados Labour Party, the West Indian National Congress Party and the Conservative Barbados Electors Association, who won respectively nine, seven and eight seats. To avoid a return to the polls, a coalition was formed between the Labour Party and the Congress Party. In accordance with the Bushe Experiment, Adams was invited to submit four members to the Officer administering the Government, for membership of the Executive Committee; these were Springer and himself from the Labour Party and W. A. Crawford and H. D. Blackman from the Congress Party.

Almost from the outset, however, the coalition government showed little signs of working harmoniously. They differed over the appointment of the Deputy Speaker and over the priorities of the progressive programme they wanted considered by the Legislature. It was a busy session but its achievements were not outstanding. Measures discussed ranged from pleas for more standpipes, public baths, tenantry roads, rent restrictions and the purchase of land for housing estates, and the disestablishment and disendowment of the Anglican Church, which was the programme urged by members of the Congress Party, to emigration outlets, the cost of living, subsidisation of foodstuffs, vocational training, re-organisation of the medical and public health services, enquiries into the fiscal system and amendments to the Workmen's Compensation Act, the issues deemed more important by the Government itself.

One particular question illustrated the difficulty experienced by the leaders of the Congress Party in controlling their backbenchers, When a Bill to increase the Governor's allowance from £500 to £1,000 was considered by the House, it was supported by the Congress members on the Executive but opposed by its backbenchers. This caused the defeat of the coalition Government, which might well have been expected to resign, but on this occasion the conventions of the Westminster model were not applied to the working of the Bushe Experiment.[10]

It was not long before Adams seized the opportunity to bring the coalition to an end. Early in 1947 he announced that the same four members of House were to be members on the Executive Committee. Crawford at once objected, stating that he disagreed both with the representation on the Executive and with the allocation of portfolios. Later he repeated that the Executive was not "correctly constituted" and that it did not enjoy the confidence of the Assembly. Crawford claimed that the Congress Party would have chosen J. E. T. (now Sir Theodore) Brancker instead of H. D. Blackman, as their second representative on the Executive. He blamed Adams for the crisis in the coalition and so the split between the two men continued to widen. By October 1947 Crawford no longer participated in the coalition. But the Government was saved when three of his Congress colleagues, H. D. Blackman, C. E. Talma and A. E. S. Lewis, crossed the floor of the House and two of these, Blackman and Talma, served as members on the Executive Committee.[11]

Towards Responsible Government

After the breakup of the coalition Adams had twelve members in the House. But when Springer left Barbados to take up the appointment as Registrar of the University College of the West Indies, the Barbados Labour Party failed to retain his seat. Somehow Adams managed to remain head of the Government. Early in 1948 his party won a by-election when it retained the seat vacated by J. T. C. Ramsay in St. Peter and captured by K. N. R. Husbands. And later in the year, after a strenuous campaign, the Labour Party was victorious in the 1948 General Election, winning twelve of the twenty-four seats in the House of Assembly. This victory, it may be added, was partly due to Adams' enhanced prestige, following his election in 1947 as President of the Caribbean Labour Congress and his inclusion in 1948 in the British delegation to the United Nations to speak on colonial questions.

The first problem facing Adams was how to maintain his voting strength in the House. He attempted to solve that problem by offering the speakership first to J. H. Wilkinson of the Electors Association and then to Brancker of the Congress Party. Both these men declined to accept the distinction. Accordingly, he was forced to fall back on one of his own members, K. N. R. Husbands, who thus became the first black Speaker of the House of Assembly. Adams was now confronted with the same problem as in the last session, how to run the Government with a minority of members in the House. This difficulty was settled when D. D. Garner of the Congress Party crossed the floor and joined forces with the Government.

There was another problem that had to be settled. It was plain that the Legislative Council, composed almost entirely of white men with a dominant control of the planting and commercial interests in the island, would be an obstacle when the House really got going on the question of reform. Adams made it clear that he did not accept the view that the Council and the House enjoyed equal rights on how the finances of the island should be administered. Forced to accept an amendment of a money bill by the Council, he declared in the House that this did not mean that he agreed that the Upper Chamber had the right to "trespass on a fundamental principle on which the House of Commons has fought the House of Lords for more than three hundred years".[12]

There seemed to be genuine fears that the Legislative Council would seek, whenever the opportunity presented itself, to check the reforming zeal of the House. There were basic differences between the Labour Party and the class that controlled the Council on such important issues as the ownership of oil and natural resources of Barbados, the nationalisation of public utilities, holidays with pay for workers and adult franchise. This burning issue was eventually settled by limiting the delaying powers of the Council and gradually increasing the range of opinion among its membership. This solution was indicated by the Secretary of State who wrote in a despatch that the functions of the Council should be regarded in future as those of revision and delay, "thus leaving the ultimate say in the enactment of legislation, whether of a financial nature or otherwise, to the House of Assembly as composed of the elected representatives of the people".[13]

For some time, however, the Labour Party was frustrated by lack of real power and authority. The powers of the Executive remained as under the Bushe Experiment, the franchise was still restricted and the Legislative Council continued to give "at most, reluctant co-operation".[14] Matters reached a point of crisis when the Council in 1949 rejected the Bill to give holidays with pay to workers. R. G. Mapp at once tabled a motion in the House calling for the curtailment of the powers of the Council. It was seconded by Brancker and passed the House without division. The Governor replied that the matter would be dealt with in accordance with the Despatch of the Secretary of State, part of which is quoted above. The Constitutional struggle was taken a stage further early in 1950. The House provided for adult franchise and abolished the property qualifications for membership of the Assembly.

The General Election of 1951 was fought under adult franchise. The achievements of the Labour Party were such that they could look forward to victory with some confidence. There was the agreement between the Sugar Producers Federation and the Barbados Workers Union which introduced, among other things, the principle of profit-sharing in the sugar industry. Other measures included holidays with pay, the creation of a Wages Board to regulate the wages of ship assistants and significant amendments to the Trade Union Act and the Factory Act providing important benefits for workers. Practical measures were taken, such as building roads, expanding water facilities, updating the health services, building schools, assisting fishermen with beach shelters and duty-free equipment and protecting Civil Servants from political influence through the appointment of a Public Service Commission.[15]

In the event, the Labour Party won sixteen seats, the Electors Association four, the Congress Party two and there were two successful Independent candidates. Of the Labour Party's successful candidates, perhaps the most significant was Errol Walton Barrow.

Though hampered by constitutional restrictions, the Party could claim an impressive record of reforms. And in due course, it set about implementing the proposals outlined in its election manifesto. Two of the most important steps were the abolition of the centuries old Vestry System and the introduction of the ministerial system of Government.

The Vestry System was replaced by three Councils which in turn were later abolished by the successor of the B.L.P. Government. Under the ministerial system, which came into effect in February 1st, 1954, five separate Ministries were established, each of them with a clear individuality and functioning as a separate organism. The Ministers were charged with the responsibility of formulating Government policy and entrusted with the task of propounding that policy in the Executive Committee and in the House of Assembly and moreover ensuring that it was carried out by the Administration. The five Ministers appointed were Adams, Dr. Cummins, M. E. Cox, C. E. Talma and R. G. Mapp. Alone in the British Caribbean, where other territories had attained ministerial status, the leader of the Barbados Government was allowed to enjoy the title of Premier.

Culloden Farm, official residence of the Prime Minister

Under the new constitutional arrangements, the Governor was required automatically to accept the advice of the Ministers in any function that was vested in them by law. The nominated members of the Executive Council were deprived of membership of the Executive Committee. The powers delegated to the Ministers were subject to the authority of the Cabinet which became the island's principal instrument of policy. Barbados had now, with a few minor restrictions, attained full internal self-government.

The question arises why did Barbados, which had long claimed to be in the van of constitutional progress, take so long to move from the Bushe Experiment to the ministerial system of government. The answer appears to lie in the problems that began to encompass the Labour Party soon after their great victory in 1951. There were increasingly sharp differences of opinion between Adams and the leftwing section of his party led by Errol Barrow. The situation deteriorated steadily and matters were to become even worse when, with the institution of the ministerial system, Frank Walcott, the General Secretary of the Barbados Workers Union, was omitted from the new government and no member of the Party's far left was selected as a Minister.

The result of this was twofold. The "Siamese twin relationship" between the B.L.P. and the B.W.U. was terminated and this marked the beginning of a "period of bitter hostility" between Adams and Walcott.[17] Nor did the relations between Adams and Barrow show any improvement. Indeed, the rift in the Party grew wider and deeper, with Barrow eventually announcing in March 1954 that he was renouncing all ties with the B.L.P. and no longer wanted to be connected with them politically or otherwise.[17] The same year Cameron Tudor won a seat in the House, after an overwhelming victory in a by-election in St. Lucy. He was to prove a valuable addition to the ranks of the young rebels. The following year the Democratic Labour Party was formed.

With such problems exercising the minds of the Labour Party leadership, it is not surprising that Barbados began to lag constitutionally behind other territories of the Caribbean. Trinidad, which had long been regarded as one of the most backward colonies politically, attained the ministerial system of government in 1950, with Albert Gomes as Chief Minister. And Jamaica, which had been granted adult franchise in 1944, advanced ahead of Barbados, with the elected members of its executive Council being vested with full ministerial responsibility under the leadership of W. A. (later Sir Alexander) Bustamante.

The 1956 General Election was contested, in the main, by three parties, the Barbados Labour Party, the Democratic Labour Party (now joined by W. A. Crawford) and the Electors Association under its new name, the Progressive Conservative Party. The opposition parties emphasised what they considered to be important omissions in the Government's programme and the campaign proceeded with increasing hostility and acrimony. Adams was away from the island and during his absence, the opposing candidates seemed to make "irretrievable gains". But, on his return, the "wind of popular approval" began to blow once again in favour of the B.L.P. They won fifteen seats, the D.L.P. four, the P.C.P. four and Walcott successfully emerged as an Independent candidate.[18] One of the astounding results of the election was that Barrow lost his seat in the Assembly.

In 1958 a further stage was reached in the island's constitutional advance when a cabinet system of government was inaugurated in Barbados, with G. H. (later Sir Grantley) Adams as Premier. When the latter became Prime Minister of the Federation of the West Indies later the same year, the leadership of the Barbados Government was handed over to Dr. Cummins. It was perhaps significant that M. E. Cox, who had risen from the ranks and distinguished himself as a parliamentarian, was not deemed eligible for the highest elected office in the land. There may have been several reasons why Cummins was preferred to Cox as Sir Grantley's successor. Though Cummings had not proved as efficient a Government Minister as Cox, he could claim a longer period of service in the cause of reform. His amiable disposition seemed to give him a better chance than anyone else to keep the Labour Party together. Moreover, his professional background appeared to make him more acceptable to many Barbadians at the time than a man of more plebeian origin.[19] Whatever the reasons were, there is one conclusion that seems inescapable. Though the political ascendancy of the whites had been destroyed, considerations of class still appeared to weigh heavily in the Barbadian society.

Questions and Exercises to Consider

1. What is the difference between "representative" government and "responsible" government?

2. Imagine you are a member of the House of Assembly and compose a speech on any of the following:
   (a) minimum wage;
   (b) old age pensions;
   (c) adult franchise;
   (d) the Shop Closing Act.

3. If you were Governor Bushe, what kind of speech would you make in introducing the Experiment that is named after him?

4. Why did a clash arise between the House, with its growing number of black members, and the Legislative Council, still composed almost entirely of white planters and merchants? How was this conflict settled?

5. What was the ministerial system of government? Write a paragraph comparing it with the previous system and explaining how the new one worked.

6. What is meant by the Cabinet? What do you understand by the statement that the Cabinet became the principal instrument of government in Barbados in 1958?

7. Why did Barbados take so long to move from the Bushe Experiment to the ministerial system of government? Compare this with what happened in other territories in the West Indies.

CHAPTER EIGHTEEN

Independence

The Federal Experiment

Barbados was represented at the Dominica Conference on West Indian Federation in 1932 but did not appear to share the convictions of such passionate federalists as Cipriani of Trinidad, Marryshow of Grenada and Rawle of Dominica. It was not until 1938 that the island assumed a more enthusiastic stand and adopted Federation as part and parcel of the liberal and democratic movement that was sweeping through the West Indies. It became strongly convinced that it was only by joining together in a closer union that the West Indies could most speedily and effectively fulfil their national aspirations, attain full independence as a Dominion within the British Commonwealth of Nations, and achieve a standing and authority in the international community that would be denied them as small, isolated units.

The Conference held in Montego Bay, Jamaica, in 1947, was followed by a period of long and complex negotiations until the Federation was inaugurated in 1958. Adams and his advisers, notably Sir Archibald Cuke and Dr. A. S. (later Sir Arnott) Cato, gave a great deal of their time to these negotiations. For in spite of his mounting problems and difficulties at home, the leader of the Barbados Government considered the building of the West Indian Federation one of his high priorities.

The final decision for the establishment of the Federation was taken at the London Conference in 1956. There were differences of opinion on the question of the siting of the federal capital and a commission, chaired by Sir Francis Mudie, was appointed to resolve the matter. The Mudie Commission recommended Barbados, Jamaica and Trinidad, in that order of preference, as reasonable sites for the federal capital. This recommendation was sharply criticised by some of the other territories. It was submitted by one critic from Jamaica that Barbados did not belong to the West Indies in spirit, that it was vitiated by class and colour prejudice and that "it was the world's largest naturally occurring septic tank".[1] Later in 1957 the question was re-considered by the Conference in Jamaica and the decision was taken to make Trinidad the site of the federal capital.

In March 1958, federal elections were held for the five seats allocated to Barbados in the Federal House of Representatives. Sir Grantley entered five candidates including himself, the Democratic Labour Party four, the Electors Association (now the Barbados National Party) two and there was one Independent, Frank Walcott. The five members returned were four from the B.L.P., Sir Grantley, D. H. L. Ward, G. Rocheford and V. B. Vaughan, and one of the B.N.P., Florence Daysch. Such formidable candidates as Errol Barrow, Cameron Tudor and Frank Walcott were defeated. It was an overwhelming victory for Sir Grantely, but it was also to be his last great triumph over his opponents.

West Indian feeling for federation reached its high point of fervour in Kingston, Jamaica, in September 1947. There the Caribbean Labour Congress summoned the leaders of the West Indian labour movements to determine the burning issue of the day. They proclaimed their faith in federation, drafted a federal constitution and submitted this, along with their views, to the official conference at Montego Bay. That conference accepted the principle of federation and appointed committees to consider ways and means of implementing the recommendations for a federal union.

All the auspices seemed to favour the successful establishment of a federal union. Norman Manley spoke fervently on the question, pointing out that it was impossible for any of the West Indian territories to "achieve alone the basic services which it is the whole aim of politics to create and make possible for the common man".[2] And Grantley Adams, author of the federal constitution, invited the mass of people assembled at Kingston to accept the challenge of West Indian independence. As the newly elected President of the Caribbean Labour Congress, he led a torch-light procession of 30,000 demonstrators through the streets of Jamaica's capital, proclaiming that a self-governing federation was the demand of organised labour throughout the British West Indies.[3]

The emotional fervour of 1947, however, did not last during the years that ensued before the federation was finally inaugurated. There were conferences and committees, with the inevitable resolutions and reports, until February 1956 when it was agreed to establish a federal union. Even then two more years were to pass before the agreement to federate was carried into effect and most of that period was spent in efforts to whittle down the powers of the Federal Government.

In the meantime, tensions and strains were to develop between the two largest and most important islands in the projected federation. Eric Williams, who arrived on the scene in 1956, stressed that federation was "a simple matter of common sense". He declared that nowhere in the world at that time could we find a community of the size of Trinidad and Tobago playing a significant part in world affairs. "Whether federation is more costly or less costly," he concluded, "whether federation is more efficient or less efficient, federation is inescapable if the British Caribbean territories are to cease to parade themselves to the twentieth century world as eighteenth century anachronisms".[4]

Manley, on the other hand, soon began to take a totally different stand. This change of stand was mainly due to the changed economic situation in Jamaica since 1947. The rapid growth of the bauxite industry, the increase in agricultural production and the expansion of tourism to the point where it contributed almost as much as the sugar industry to the national income — these and other developments gave rise to the feeling in Jamaica that she could best improve her economic position not so much by union with other British Caribbean territories as by her own efforts, unfettered by rigid controls from the federal centre in Trinidad.[5]

While Williams, therefore, called for a strong and independent Federation, with powers of taxation in all areas and with the final word on matters affecting planning and development in all fields, Manley emphasised that the Federal Government should be severely limited in its power to intervene in Jamaica's affairs. He insisted that the federal constitution should be so revised as to make such federal control impossible, that each unit should retain control over the development of its industries and the power to levy income tax, excise duties and consumption taxes.

Federal Fiasco

The West Indian Federation was off to a slow and painful start in 1958. Between that time and the eve of the Inter-Governmental Conference, a year later, Jamaica and Trinidad were diametrically opposed on the nature and role of the Federal Government. In these circumstances, it is not surprising that the federal experiment lasted only four years. There were many reasons for this but it must suffice here to mention only a few.

In the first place, both the People's National Party of Norman Manley and the People's National Movement of Eric Williams lost the federal elections in their respective territories, Jamaica and Trinidad and Tobago. As a result, the West Indies Federal Party, of which the P.N.P. and the P.N.M. were affiliates, won an uncertain majority in the House of Representatives. Sir Grantley's government was frequently placed in a precarious position, sometimes having to rely for survival on the Independent vote of the Barbadian, Florence Daysh, and the two "fluid" votes of Grenada. In addition, with the results of the Federal Elections in Jamaica and Trinidad and Tobago, he could not call on the parliamentary talent of those two territories to strengthen his government since the electorate had excluded much of that talent from possible consideration. In these circumstances, the Prime Minister could scarcely be expected to initiate a bold and positive policy.

Perhaps, however, the fundamental cause of the failure of the Federation lay in its colonial character. First, the Queen had the authority to legislate for the Federation by Orders-in-Council in matters pertaining to defence, external affairs and the finances of the Federation. Secondly, the Governor General enjoyed the power to act "in his own discretion" and veto the laws of the Federation. Thirdly, it was an undoubted mistake not to have established a Cabinet system of government right from the start of the federal exercise.

Such being the nature of the federal constitution, it is not surprising that within two months of its inauguration the House of Representatives was asked to take the necessary steps to attain self-government and dominion status within the Commonwealth in the shortest possible time.[6] It was in this spirit that the first Inter-Governmental Conference was held in 1959 and "firm foundations" laid for the eventual death of the Federation. Strident claims were made for the attainment of dominion status at the earliest possible moment. No-one took the opportunity to urge patience and the wisdom of "feeling our way cautiously", as Manley once suggested. No-one reminded the Conference that the Federation was to be given a period of five years before its working was reviewed. No-one suggested that this original plan should be adhered to. Plainly, they should have given their attention to less contentious questions such as Customs Union, income tax, control of industries, representation and the like and then proceed to a plan "on which they could go forward together safely". The spirit that dominated the Conference seemed to be that the federal structure must be broken up or it must be fundamentally altered with the minimum of delay.[7]

The conference gave rise to a host of problems at an early and most precarious stage of the Federation. In August 1960 Manley and Williams met in Antigua to see whether they could ease the situation by settling their own differences. They succeeded in reaching agreement by abandoning their extremist positions. Williams deferred his plan for a strong federation, allowing periods of grace for such matters as customs union, industrial control and income tax. Manley, on his side, agreed not to press for freedom of movement. The meeting was described as "a triumph of common sense" but regrettably the two leaders committed the tactical blunder of keeping their conclusions secret.[8] This secrecy aroused the suspicions of the eight other territories in the Federation and had fatal consequences.

Manley and Williams held together for a time and consistently supported each other. But in less than a year their agreement broke down. When the final conference was held at Lancaster House, London, in June 1960, Manley and Williams were at loggerheads. The Windward and Leeward Islands, which felt they were being used as pawns in the struggle between Jamaica and Trinidad, were angry over the indignity of their position. It is small wonder that by the end of the conference hardly any of the leading delegates were on speaking terms with one another.

The Prime Minister of the Federation was later criticised for not providing the kind of tactful leadership that might have saved the situation. It is true that his remarks about retroactive taxation did not relieve the difficulties facing Manley and his sense of humour at times offended the sensibilities of some West Indians. Yet it is difficult to see how anyone could have saved the federal experiment in an atmosphere that was charged first with misunderstanding, then with antagonism and finally with hatred.[9] In the circumstances, it was perhaps inevitable that Jamaica seceded from the Federation in September 1961, with Trinidad following suit in January 1962. After four years of an uncertain and inglorious existence, the Federation of the West Indies was dissolved on May 31st, 1962.

A Stunning Defeat

Meanwhile, in the absence of Sir Grantley, the political situation in Barbados was changing rapidly. Barrow, who had lost his seat in St. George in 1956, won a by-election in St. John in 1958. This victory may be said to have a double significance. First, it challenged the influence the Barbados Labour Party had long enjoyed in the island's sugar belt. Secondly, Walcott, who had grown increasingly critical of the B.L.P, now for the first time in an election threw the weight and authority of the Barbados Workers Union behind the Democratic Labour Party.

The D.L.P opposition lost no opportunity to test the leadership skills of the new Premier of the Government. In 1959 Barrow was elected Chairman of the D.L.P at its annual conference and, while Brancker continued to serve as the official Leader of the Opposition in the House, no-one could doubt that, from the moment he regained a seat in the Assembly, he was the real leader of the opposition forces. Nor was there any doubt who would lead the government if the new party was successful in the 1961 election.

The plan for victory was clear enough. The leadership question was now settled and the party acquired their headquarters. A "Shadow Cabinet" was established in the best tradition of British parliamentary institutions. A Memorandum on constitutional changes was prepared, two of its most important proposals being that the Official Opposition should be represented in the Upper Chamber and that the double member constituency should be abandoned in favour of a single member system. [10]

These and other issues the D.L.P had the opportunity to discuss with the Secretary of State, Iain Macleod, when he visited Barbados in June 1960. They were well aware of the difficulties that were afflicting Sir Grantley in the Federation. Some West Indians complained that the Federal Prime Minister expatiated unduly on the Barbadian qualities of intelligence and industry and this was regarded as an adverse reflection on the people of other West Indian territories. They complained that he had not visited all the units of the Federation. They pointed to his failing health and foretold that, if he did not resign, he would be forced out of office. One Jamaican newspaper, failing to recognise that one of the intractable problems facing the Federation was the basic differences dividing Jamaica and Trinidad, put all the blame on Sir Grantley, declaring that it was difficult to "imagine anyone making as bad a job of West Indian leadership".[11]

The D.L.P was not slow to capitalise on the difficulties facing the Prime Minister and when they held their discussions with Macleod they expressed it as their considered opinion that the Federal exercise had arrived at an impasse because the Federal Cabinet had shown a "lack of clear thinking and imaginative leadership".

The Secretary of State seems to have been favourably impressed both by the content of the D.L.P memorandum and the manner in which it had been presented. Indeed, Macleod made it clear that he agreed with their proposals for constitutional changes. The popularity of the party was already rising and after their interview with the Secretary of State, their reputation was enhanced as a thoughtful and responsible group who were "capable of constituting an alternative government".[12]

But the party was not prepared to take any chances. They set about the task of establishing constituency branches. They put their trust in organisation and hard canvassing. They attacked the Government relentlessly in the House and on the public platform. Under the dynamic leadership of Errol Barrow, they directed their critical scrutiny at every aspect of public policy and nothing seemed beyond the range of their attack.

The Government sought for ways and means to maintain their prestige. But they had to face a triple attack from Barrow and the Democratic League, Walcott and the Workers Union and Ernest Mottley of the Barbados National Party (the Electors Association had once again changed its name). To meet the attack from a combination of such formidable forces, they began to press forward with their programme of development. Included in this programme was the building of a new hospital to cope with the problem of overcrowding at the old institution. Another important item in the programme was the construction of the Deep Water Harbour, an impressive project, which had already been started and was proceeding at a rapid pace. Here they ran into trouble with Walcott who pointed out that the new Harbour must be accompanied with plans for rehabilitating the two thousand water-front workers who would lose their jobs.

The Government was faced with difficulties on all sides. The level of unemployment was very high. Seven sugar factories had recently ceased operations. Some four thousand young people were leaving the schools every year and looking for jobs. The migration scheme, which took about 1,100 persons a year to the United Kingdom, mainly under Government sponsorship, seemed to be in danger from the Commonwealth Immigration Act. And it was at this stage that an official report disclosed that in 1955 the rate of unemployment varied from nineteen per cent of the labour force in the crop season to twenty-three per cent in "hard times", i.e. out of crop.[13] The report gave added emphasis to the constant criticisms of the D.L.P that opportunities for job creation should be increased and a more dynamic plan for industrialisation formulated.

With Sir Grantley caught in the storm that was raging over the Federation, with Cummins and his deputy, Cox, vainly striving to hold together a party that was growing more and more disunited, the Government seemed doomed. Even the granting of $1.7 million to the workers displaced by the new harbour did not silence the criticisms of Walcott who continued to call public attention to the grave problem of unemployment facing the island and to the need for adequate plans for rehabilitation when the harbour was completed.

In the circumstances, the defeat of the Government in the 1961 general election was predictable. The D.L.P captured fourteen seats and the B.L.P five, with every Minister but one going down in inglorious defeat. The Barbados National Party won four seats and the one successful Independent candidate was Frank Walcott.[14]

The victory of the D.L.P marked a major break in the political consciousness of the Barbadian people. Using the broom as their symbol, they had swept the once formidable B.L.P from office. A large section of the working class, which had been the mainstay of the B.L.P, had transferred their allegiance to the D.L.P. In the words of one scholar, "the partnership between the B.L.P and the B.W.U—strained in recent years—was now at an end. The B.W.U was no longer the political ally of the B.L.P. The era of Grantley Adams had come to an abrupt end. About to begin was the administration of Errol Barrow".[15]

The New Dynamism

The Democratic Labour Party assumed office on a high wave of popularity. Yet they could not fail to note that, in spite of their impressive victory, they had polled 39,543 votes throughout the country, with the B.L.P receiving 40,096 of the total votes cast.[16] They were, therefore, resolved to widen and entrench their position in the island as a whole. And the best way to do this was to fulfil as many of their promises as they could in the shortest possible time.

The new Government, led by Errol Barrow, soon demonstrated the spirit of dynamism that was to actuate it in the days ahead. Its first decision, almost immediately after taking office, was to begin a Crash Programme of Public Works, costing $250,000, for the purpose of finding work for 1,200 of the island's unemployed. This was designed to provide immediate employment until such time as its first three years Development Plan had been given its final touches. People were set to work within the first fortnight of the new régime, repairing roads, clearing twenty-six acres of land at Seawell and engaging in the preliminary tasks involved in such projects as the afforestation of the Scotland District, the erection of dams and canalisation of the Constitution Swamp.

Nor did the new Government lose any time in honouring the commitments of the last administration in the matter of salaries revision. In addition, steps were taken to enable public employees of all grades to enjoy a measure of Christmas cheer. Twenty-five per cent of their monthly salaries were loaned to Government employees, while casual and other employees were offered an advance of a week's wage. It was also decided that as from January 1962 free education would be provided at all the Government-aided secondary schools. In the same year a pilot scheme of the school meals service they had promised in their election manifesto[17] was started and four years later it was catering to considerable areas in the island.

These measures succeeded in capturing the public imagination and the initiative shown by the Government in their preliminary programme increased public enthusiasm in its dynamism. The achievements of the Government, even before the first hundred days of its existence was completed, moved one fervent supporter to say that "the golden days of Barbadian politics had dawned".[18]

Mention should also be made of the College of Arts and Science which was set up as a university campus in October 1963. This must be attributed mainly to the vision and enthusiasm of Sir Arthur Lewis, who was actively supported by the Government of Barbados. Though the idea of erecting a campus of the U.W.I. in Barbados was largely due to Sir Arthur, the D.L.P

236

College of Arts and Science, University of the West Indies

Government could certainly claim credit for its policy of free university education.

The D.L.P also turned its attention to constitutional changes. The Legislative Council was dissolved and its place taken by a Senate of twenty-one members. Of the latter, twelve were appointed by the Governor on the advice of the Premier, seven by the Governor at his own discretion and two on the recommendation of the Leader of the Opposition. In addition, the Office of Attorney General was removed from the Civil Establishment and given Cabinet status. The new Minister without Portfolio was E. R. L. Ward, formerly Speaker of the West Indies House of Representatives, who had become a member of the D.L.P when he returned from Trinidad in 1963.[19]

By the end of their five year term, the D.L.P could point to a proud record of achievements. Substantial increases were paid to workers or their dependents maimed or killed in the course of their employment. Peaceful picketing was legalised and severance pay received by many workers who had lost their jobs through the closing of factories. Holidays with pay were increased from two to three weeks per annum for those who had worked for five continuous years.

Tourism was expanded largely through the aid and encouragement of the Government and this development not only provided much needed employment but assisted in bringing the island a substantial measure of prosperity. Much attention was given to their programme of industrialisation and the building of forty-five factories was an achievement of which they were justly proud. Equal pay for equal work was introduced. Eighty thousand people were covered by a National Insurance Scheme. The growing prosperity of the island was stimulated by activity in the construction industry, and the budget of 1966 increased the salaries of Civil Servants at the cost of $4.5 million, while unionised Government Servants received $1.5 million. Moreover, increased allowances were granted to Government and old age pensioners.

It may well be said that the D.L.P, when they assumed office, used the "firm foundations" laid down· by the B.L.P to implement their own programme. Undoubtedly, they "strengthened the social structure" of the country and expanded the "quality and the range" of the facilities offered by the welfare state. Yet·it may be maintained that their policy as a whole was conducted "within the framework of the mixed economy" established by the former government. While in opposition, the party may have indulged in the socialist rhetoric of the extreme left-wing but when they won the Government they recognised the wisdom of moderation in order to gain the support of a wide cross section of the community.[20]

This is not to deny that the D.L.P made original contributions to the welfare of the island. They adopted a bolder and more sophisticated spirit in the economic management of the country. They abandoned the policy of "balance budgeting" followed by the B.L.P in the 1950's and initiated a form of "adventurism" that seemed to be called for in the sixties. The tax system was reformed, dormant funds for economic development were released and budgetary techniques were so manipulated that the economy of the island was substantially improved.[21]

Federal Negotiations

Obviously, the Democratic Labour Party wanted to concentrate on domestic issues as they had emphasised in their election

238

campaign. Their primary aims were to strengthen their political base, win the support and co-operation of a number of powerful interests in the island, devise long-term measures for the relief of unemployment and apply a new dynamic to the working of the economy. During the campaign they declared with no little emphasis that their first obligation was to expand the economy of Barbados and to improve the living standards of her people.[22] Yet Barrow was soon influenced by gentle pressures to entertain the notion of a new federal experiment. He attended a meeting in Trinidad, convened to hold discussions with Reginald Maulding, who had succeeded Iain Macleod as Secretary of State, and the leaders of the small islands gave him a hearty welcome. They were still suffering from the departure of Jamaica, following the result of the referendum, and they had nothing but contempt for the offer of unitary statehood by Trinidad and Tobago. The Little Eight now needed each other more than ever and Barbados' participation was deemed essential.

All went well at first. The Colonial Office had been reluctant to start a new federation. The D.L.P Government was naturally preoccupied with the task of grappling with Barbadian affairs.[23] The British, American and Canadian Governments seemed ready to give financial aid to a new federation and this expectation undoubtedly made for unity among the island leaders. The meeting with Maudling proceeded in this spirit of unity and agreement was reached on many questions. It was agreed that Barbados would be the federal capital, that the setting up of the federation would be followed immediately by customs union, freedom of movement and the unification of such services as the police, the prisons and the judiciary.

Maudling then asked the Little Eight — at the end of January 1962 — to prepare a plan for the projected federation. Sir Arthur Lewis was invited to prepare papers for a second conference and he completed this task with detailed thoroughness and quite astonishing rapidity. The plan was submitted to Maudling and the Conference to consider it was held in Barbados in March 1962.[24] A Regional Council of Ministers was established and offices were set up in London and Montreal to ensure the welfare of students and migrants from the eight territories. The latter were represented collectively on the Regional Research Council, the Regional Shipping Service, UNESCO, the Caribbean Meteorological Service and the Caribbean Currency Board. They shared with the Governments of Jamaica, Trinidad and

Tobago, British Honduras and the Bahamas the cost of running the University of the West Indies. They shared with British Guiana (not yet Guyana) the cost of maintaining the Eastern Caribbean Court of Appeal. It seemed a happy augury that the Little Eight's Council of Ministers gave their attention not only to the question of federation but to matters that were of mutual benefit to a larger area of the Caribbean.[25]

The Conference of March 1962 was highly successful. It provided a good basis for a new federation. The reluctance of the British Government was apparently dissolved and federation was accepted as the right answer to the problem of the Little Eight. The Constitution which had been drafted in Barbados was accepted at a London conference in May 1962. It was described as "an excellent foundation" for the proposed federation and would have made "an excellent beginning".[26]

The first major stumbling block was the question of money. Maudling had made it clear earlier that political independence must be based on financial independence. The Ministers of the Little Eight took the point that grants-in-aid should continue for a period of five years. It took the British Government twenty-one months to make up its mind before it agreed to the financial formula recommended by the Ministers of the Little Eight.

This delay was to prove disastrous. The harmony and unity with which the Ministers had started in 1962 soon gave way to anger against the British Government and frustration, insularity and petty jealousies among themselves. In February 1964 the British Government accepted the financial formula the Ministers had submitted nearly two years ago. But just before that Dr. O'Loughlin, a British Commissioner, declared in her report that the new federation needed three times what the Ministers had asked for in 1962. At once the Ministers changed their tune. They would accept nothing less than what O'Loughlin suggested. The situation deteriorated rapidly. More anger, more frustration, more insular jealousies. The early meetings of the Council of ministers had proceeded in a friendly and harmonious spirit. The tenth and last meeting ended in almost irretrievable collapse.

Actually, the first sign of fragmentation came with the defection of Grenada. During the recent election campaign in that island, the successful party promised access to the wealth of Trinidad and the electorate opted for unitary statehood with that territory rather than federation with the Eight. That in itself was

240

"not of great moment".[27] It was what happened after this that was important.

The Council of Ministers had been conceived at first as the nucleus of a federal cabinet. But soon the Ministers began arriving with advisers and it became increasingly difficult to arrive at agreement. Long wrangles developed over matters that had already been settled. They began to review and criticise the federal structure they had agreed to in May 1962. The question of the balance between the powers of the federal centre and the units was revived. Income tax, the police and the magistrates, contrary to previous agreement, were removed from federal control and given back to the unit territories.[28]

Then Antigua raised a point that provoked a major crisis. Vere Bird announced that he wanted to keep control of his island's post office. In his reservation on the Draft Federal Scheme he insisted that the Federal Government should not be empowered to acquire control of any new services "without the unanimous consent" of all constituent units. The Secretary of State took strong objection to this reservation and Antigua, proud of her efforts to build self-sufficiency, promptly decided to have nothing further to do with any negotiations on Federation. The Secretary of State refused to budge from his position and submitted that the negotiations could proceed without Antigua. But Bramble of Montserrat decided that this would never do. He had long enjoyed a "Siamese twin" relationship with Antigua and he declared that if the latter departed from the Federal negotiations, he would leave too.

The Little Eight were now reduced to five. Strangely enough, when the ninth meeting of the Council of Ministers convened in October 1964 the situation still seemed promising. The Draft Federal Scheme was considered and note was taken of the reservations recorded by several of the territories. It was decided to give the Governments time to consider these reservations and the meeting ended in an atmosphere of optimism. But this was followed in the interim by the defection of Antigua, the imminent withdrawal of Montserrat and the rejection of the Draft Federal Scheme by St. Lucia.[29] St. Kitts, Dominica and St. Vincent still declared their intention to carry on. But at the tenth meeting of the Council of Ministers, Barbados and St. Lucia became involved in a fearful wrangle. St. Lucia challenged the bona fides of the Barbados Cabinet in relation to the federal negotiations. Barrow considered Compton's remarks offensive and walked out of the meeting, which was adjorned *sine die* on April 19th, 1965.[30] Regrettably, the Regional Council of Ministers was destined never to meet again.

In vain had Sir Arthur Lewis expressed the hope that, with the removal of Adams, Manley and Williams, the three men whose "head-on collisions" destroyed the first West Indian Federation, a younger generation of West Indian leaders would show a greater spirit of compromise.[31] For the federal negotiations from 1962 to 1965 were wrecked by the same "mutual hatred and contempt" that had driven the federal ship on the rocks in 1962.

Crisis Averted

We have already discussed in an earlier chapter why Barbados moved slowly from the Bushe Experiment in 1946 to full internal self-government in 1958. The reader is now entitled to ask why the island took so long to travel from full internal self-government to independence.

The answer to the latter question should now be obvious from the events and developments that have been discussed here. Within the British West Indies, the objective had long been the attainment of Dominion status within the British Commonwealth.

In these territories the high hopes raised for federation at the Montego Bay Conference in 1gwo were frustrated by the failure of the Federation of the West Indies in 1962. Even with this failure, four years were to pass before Barbados was decolonised.

The Democratic Labour Party stated in its 1961 Manifesto that "the road to destiny is the road to independence". It boldly added that since the island had never been a grant-aided territory there was "no reason why within or without a Federation Barbados should not attain the full stature of independence now within the British Commonwealth".[32] Yet, in view of the still uncertain climate of opinion, Barrow was persuaded by Sir Arthur Lewis and Vere Bird[33] to participate in the federal negotiations that lasted from 1962 to 1965.

In Barbados the question was not whether the island should be decolonised or not, but whether the island should proceed to independence alone or within the context of a federation. Accordingly, when the Barrow Government published its White Paper, "Federal Negotiations 1962-65", the great debate on the constitutional future of the island continued with increasing vigour. That debate proceeded throughout 1965. Those taking issue with the Government were the Barbados Labour Party, the Barbados National Party and a group of young men calling themselves the "Under Forties", all of whom submitted that the best prospects for Barbados and the Eastern Caribbean lay in a federal union. They all made the same plea to the Government that it should make another effort to agree on a federal structure with the Leeward and Windward Islands. There were other groups that took part on one side or other of the national dialogue (the "Underprivileged", the "Unemployed", the "Underfed" and the "Underemployed"). But there were many who doubted the bona fides of these last groups, regarding them merely as nuisance parties.

The opinion of the country was clearly not unanimous on the issue. Even the ruling party seemed divided in its thinking. One striking development was the resignation of the Deputy Prime Minister, W. A. Crawford, and the Minister without Portfolio, E. R. L. Ward. The latter made the charge that the Cabinet never discussed the question of Barbados going into independence alone. He considered that the Government was pledged to resume the negotiations that had been interrupted at the tenth meeting of the Regional Council of Ministers and declared that "it would be dishonourable and a breach of faith to take any action so inimical of West Indian unity".[34]

Barrow moved swiftly to avert a crisis. Ward's appointment on the Senate was revoked and Philip Greaves was appointed Minister without Portfolio in the Senate. In addition, Neville Boxill, a member of the House, was raised to Cabinet rank. By these prompt decisions, Barrow succeeded in ensuring the survival of the Government at a time when C. E. Talma, a Cabinet member, and two backbenchers, Reynold Weekes and Ellison Carmichael, were rumoured to be sympathetic to the notion of federation.

The Democratic Labour Party declared in their 1961 manifesto that they would return to the electorate in three years time.[35] But 1964 was the year of the "windfall" crisis. The Executive of the B.W.U sanctioned a scheme for funding the extra profit that had been gained by the sugar industry. But the sugar workers themselves wanted their share given to them direct. The issue between them became explosive. A campaign led mainly by the B.L.P, with Sir Grantley back as their leader, was soon launched, backing the workers' demands. The B.W.U, which had become increasingly identified with the D.L.P, was eventually forced to give way and the settlement was hailed by the B.L.P as a victory over Walcott and Barrow."[36]

In these circumstances, it was tactical wisdom for the D.L.P not to fulfil the pledge given in its manifesto about a three year session. It should be added, however, in fairness to the Government, that they gave another reason for their failure to honour their commitment. That reason was that the Boundaries Commission which they had appointed in 1962 had only recently submitted its report and that the Government needed time to prepare the way for the changes that had been recommended.[37]

D.L.P Re-elected

The White Paper explaining why the Government intended to seek separate independence for the island had been published in August 1965. It was debated in the Legislature in January the following year and both Houses then asked the Secretary of State to convene a conference to discuss independence for Barbados within the Commonwealth. The Secretary of State, Frederick Lee, agreed and the Barbados Constitutional Conference was held in Lancaster House in June 1966.

A draft Independence Constitution, prepared by the Barbados Government, was considered by the Conference. This draft had been approved by both Houses of the Barbados Legislature, though it is significant that the debates on the document were boycotted by the two Opposition parties, the Barbados Labour Party and the Barbados National Party. But representatives of all three parties attended the Conference.

There were several points of difference between the ruling Democratic Labour Party and the Opposition parties. Some of these differences were settled at Lancaster House but it was found impossible to arrive at unanimous agreement. Among the major points that remained unresolved were the following. The Opposition submitted that the Senate should be so composed that it would be impossible to amend an entrenched provision of the Constitution "without the support of at least part of the Opposition". They urged that the Constitution should provide for an independent and impartial commission "charged with the duty of supervising the registration of electors and the conduct of elections". They proposed that a permanent boundaries commission should be appointed "to keep constituency boundaries under review". None of these proposals were accepted, though it was agreed that the dissent of the Opposition parties should be recorded. In the event, however, all parties agreed that Barbados should proceed to separate independence.[38]

The election was held on November 3rd, 1966, and the date of the island's independence was fixed for November 30th in the same year. Perhaps a tactical mistake was made when Barrow declared that he did not think the D.L.P should have twenty-four seats; they would be satisfied with twenty-two or twenty-three. Cameron Tudor probably made it worse when he submitted that the people should not be fooled "by silly arguments about the two Party System".[39] Inevitably the Opposition Parties seized the opportunity to make capital of the fears these statements seemed to arouse. Louis Lynch of the B.N.P sounded the alarm that Barbados was in the "shadow of a looming dictatorship". H. B. St. John pointed out that if the D.L.P won the seats they wanted they would have the two-thirds majority needed to change the Independence Constitution and remove the provisions that were entrenched in that document to ensure the freedom of the individual and the protection of a democratic way of life. Sir Grantley Adams bluntly declared that the election was "a straight fight between democracy under the B.L.P and dictatorship under the D.L.P".[40]

There was a large turn-out of electors and, in the event, the D.L.P won fourteen seats, the B.L.P eight and the B.N.P two. The remarkable thing was that in three of the constituencies won by the D.L.P, St. George, St. Thomas and St. Andrew, the B.L.P lost by narrow margins. Equally, if not more, remarkable was the defeat of Frank Walcott. This may well be attributable to the fact that his prestige was not as high as it used to be before the "windfall" crisis.

Barrow was clearly not satisfied with the results of the election. He was proud of his record in office. His party was no longer worried about the resignation of Ward and Crawford. It was united and well organised for the election. Indeed, all the signs seemed to point to an overwelming victory for the D.L.P. He had confidently expected to win more seats than he had previously held and he could only surmise "that within the last forty-eight hours something had occurred in the country to cause an upset".[41] Some of the "pundits" declared after the event that, if the campaign had lasted a week or two longer, with the growing swing against the ruling party in the closing stages, Barrow might well have lost the election.

The political career of Errol Barrow seems to have followed a curious pattern. In 1951, he was elected with acclamation to the House of Assembly under the auspices of the Barbados Labour Party led by Sir Grantley Adams. In 1956, having resigned from the Barbados Labour Party a year before, he was severely trounced in the same constituency where he had previously won a resounding victory. In 1961 he had his revenge and captured the government at a time when Adams was pre-occupied with the impending federal fiasco. In 1966, when Adams was back in the field, Barrow succeeded in retaining office but it was a close thing. In 1971 he won an overwhelming victory (when the "Old Man" had finally retired from active politics) only to suffer an overwhelming defeat in 1976 at the hands of Sir Grantley's son, J. M. G. (Tom) Adams.

Cultural Upsurge

The story of the movement towards independence cannot be told purely in political, constitutional or economic terms. It would be incomplete unless some reference was made to the cultural upsurge that manifested itself in Barbados and other territories of the Caribbean. For there can be no doubt about the literary and artistic awakening that was taking place in the area in prose and poetry as well as in painting and sculpture.[42]

No-one will question the value of the work done by Henry Swanzy in his B.B.C. programme, "Caribbean Voices", during the years before 1955. "West Indian writers owe a great debt of gratitude to Mr. Swanzy and the Caribbean Voices programme: to this source more than any other is due the quickening of whatever literary re-birth there may be in the Caribbean".[43] This was written by the editors of *Bim,* a literary magazine that has enjoyed a continuous existence since its first publication in Barbados in December 1942. But what was said of "Caribbean Voices" could also be said of *Bim* itself as a source of the literary re-birth that occurred during this period in the West Indies.

Started by E. L. Cozier and now edited by John Wickham, *Bim's* success is due, more than anything else, to the energy, enthusiasm and inspiration of Frank Collymore. It began as a Barbadian magazine but gradually its horizons were widened to take in the whole Caribbean scene. It set out its policy in a simple and unassuming manner, in keeping with the character of Frank Collymore, its chief editor for many years. It tried to encourage creative writing and to this end it published short stories, poems, critical articles and reviews. By 1960 it had achieved a remarkable degree of success. Some twenty novels were published by West Indians, many of them receiving praise from the highest quarters. Among those who had established themselves in the literary world were George Lamming and Geoffrey Drayton of Barbados, Edgar Mittelholzer and Jan Carew of British Guiana (not yet Guyana), V. S. Naipaul and Samuel Selvon of Trinidad and John Hearne, Roger Mais, Vic Reid and Andrew Salkey of Jamaica. Among the things that won them recognition was not only the exotic landscape they depicted but the novelty of the idiom they used as their medium. It is not without significance that all of these writers found in *Bim* magazine the first medium through which they could reach a sensitive reading public. And in Frank Collymore they found a friend and councellor who took a personal interest in them, offering critical guidance and unobtrusively yet effectively promoting their work in all those parts of the world where he became known as a central figure in West Indian literature.[44]

Lamming looked on the novel as something to be shaped by the imagination of the author and steadfastly refused to pay too much attention to the normal conventions of plot and characterisation. Because of his revolt against the concept of the traditional novel he may well be regarded as the most important West Indian writer. Hearne may be considered as the complete opposite of Lamming in the sense that he adheres strictly to the craft of the story-teller and this discipline makes him, like Naipaul and Reid, a far superior craftsman to Lamming. And Selvon, the most natural of them all, portrays "the truest and most sensitive picture of West Indian life" because he shows a compassion for his people whether they are in London, Port-of-Spain or the canefields of Trinidad.[45]

Frank Collymore's influence was to spread farther and wider. It embraced Derek Walcott, Edward Brathwaite and A. J. Seymour, three of the leading poets of the area. It extended to John Wickham, John Figueroa, Mervyn Morris, Gloria Escoffery, Freddie Forde and Monica Skeete and not the least of those whom he inspired were Austin Clarke and Timothy Callendar who, like Lamming, were former pupils of his at Combermere School where he taught for fifty-three years.

In addition to the story-tellers and the poets, Frank Collymore also extended his benign patronage to painters. Artists like Golde White, Briggs Clarke, Therold Barnes, John Harrison, Aileen Hamilton and Geoffrey Holder were among those who enjoyed his friendship and inspiration. By now (1950) his interest had spread not only from Barbados to the various territories of the English speaking West Indies but to other lands in the Caribbean. He paid some attention in *Bim* to the literary movement in the French West Indies and he was fascinated by the flowering of a School of primitive painters in Haiti.

Nor was the work of Karl Broodhagen, the artist who expressed himself through the medium of sculpture, ignored in the pages of *Bim*. Tribute was paid to his efforts to find an outlet for his creative ability in the medium of portraiture. But his drawings based on two dimensions did not satisfy him. He considered they were flat and lacked the depth he was trying to attain. Inevitably, he was driven to sculpture for the third dimension he craved and in his hands the lifeless clay took shape, gained poise and balance, and assumed form and character. Early in his career, he sculpted the heads of such men as Grantley Adams and George Lamming, Dudley Moore, a former Rector of St. John, and Howard Hayden, the first Director of Education in Barbados. And among the first to acclaim his success in this field was Collymore's assistant editor, Therold Barnes.[46]

Bust of Grantley Adams, by Karl Broodhagen

There is no doubt that many of those mentioned in this review were influenced by the work of acknowledged masters in the various fields of art and literature. Lamming owed much to James Joyce and Joyce Carey and to philosophers such as Camus and Jean Paul Sartre. Hearne and others were in some way the disciples of Hemingway, Steinbeck and Faulkner. Mittelholzer was to a great degree influenced by the followers of Freud. Naipaul seemed, in some respects, to follow the pattern of Stendhal. Selvon may have been influenced by Runyon but, in this case at least, the disciple surpassed the master.[47]

Yet, when all of this is said, there is one important thing that remains. While these men absorbed the lessons they learnt from sources outside the Caribbean, they succeeded in giving their work an individual stamp. They made a distinctive approach to West Indian literature and demonstrated their gift for creative originality. In this way, their work marked a distinct trend in the movement towards independence in the West Indies.

An Era Ended

In the earlier years of the twentieth century it had seemed clear to the British West Indies that the goal of independence could be achieved only through Federation. The values prevailing at the time seemed to be generally accepted. A country aspiring to nationhood had to be able to support the responsibilities and obligations of independence. It must be able to support an army, a navy and an airforce to defend itself from external attack. It must have the resources to afford embassies and consular services to give it an effective voice in the Councils of the world. And not the least of the criteria for nationhood was the obligation to maintain a satisfactory standard of living for its people.

These values were to change when the liquidation of the British Empire began after World War II. The pace was set by India, Pakistan and Ceylon (now Sri Lanka) in the period 1947-48. Ten years later these were followed by Ghana and Malaya. Other countries in Africa and Asia were to benefit from the process of decolonisation.

The changing criteria for independence were soon to have an effect in the British Caribbean and elsewhere in the British Empire. Jamaica and Trinidad were allowed to proceed to independence alone. Other small states to be given a similar status were Cyprus and Malta. The British Empire was now being more rapidly dissolved and within a few years it was transformed into a large number of sovereign states whether or not they could afford the obligations of independence. This process was undoubtedly the result of a change in outlook of the international community and it was inevitable that Barbados would soon be influenced by the climate of opinion in the outside world. By its decision to proceed to full sovereignty on November 30th, 1966, Barbados followed the example set by Jamaica on August 6th, 1962, by Trinidad on August 31st, 1962 and by British Guiana (now Guyana) on May 26th, 1966.

Thus it may be said that the process of decolonisation had been completed and a chapter closed in the political history of Barbados. While the island remained committed to the notion of regional co-operation in such areas as aviation, shipping, higher education and meteorology, its people now faced the challenge and the responsibility of independence.

It has been frequently said that Barbados did not enter upon its era of independence with any marked exhibition of national fervour. There was the national flag and the national anthem, the usual display of fireworks and the eloquent speeches. Yet to some observers there was an absence of the excitement that accompanied the celebrations of other nations when they attained the status of independence and embarked on "a new and glorious path".[48]

There may well be several answers to the question as to why Barbados entered upon its new political career without any apparent transports of joy and exhilaration. In the first place, it did not have to engage in any bitter struggle to win its independence in 1966 and there was, therefore, no sense of a hard-won victory against formidable opponents. Secondly, Barbadians have a long memory of efforts, now by one section now by another, to overcome circumstances that threatened them with tyranny and oppression. There were the revolts by the white indentured servants in 1634 and 1649 to overthrow their masters and gain control of the island. There were the attempts of those, culminating in the Insurrection of 1816, who fought to win their freedom from the rigours of a society that enslaved the body and humiliated the spirit. In 1876 the upper and middle classes fought against the Colonial Office to preserve the constitution they prized so highly; and the masses of the people rose in revolt to support the reform measures which John Pope Hennessy advocated, while exaggerating the advantages of the

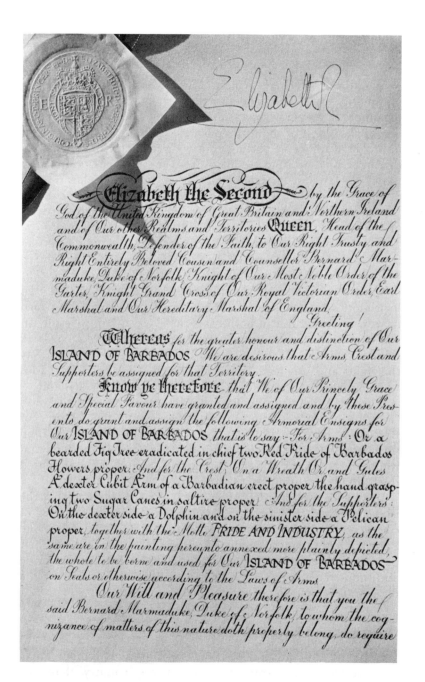

Elizabeth the Second by the Grace of God of the United Kingdom of Great Britain and Northern Ireland and of Our other Realms and Territories **Queen**, Head of the Commonwealth, Defender of the Faith, to Our Right Trusty and Right Entirely Beloved Cousin and Counsellor Bernard Marmaduke, Duke of Norfolk, Knight of Our Most Noble Order of the Garter, Knight Grand Cross of Our Royal Victorian Order, Earl Marshal and Our Hereditary Marshal of England,

Greeting!

Whereas for the greater honour and distinction of Our ISLAND OF BARBADOS We are desirous that Arms, Crest and Supporters be assigned for that Territory.

Know ye therefore that We of Our Princely Grace and Special Favour have granted and assigned and by these Presents do grant and assign the following Armorial Ensigns for Our ISLAND OF BARBADOS that is to say:—For Arms: Or a bearded Fig Tree eradicated in chief two Red Pride of Barbados Flowers proper: And for the Crest; On a Wreath Or and Gules A dexter Cubit Arm of a Barbadian erect proper the hand grasping two Sugar Canes in saltire proper. And for the Supporters: On the dexter side a Dolphin and on the sinister side a Pelican proper, together with the Motto, PRIDE AND INDUSTRY, as the same are in the painting hereunto annexed more plainly depicted, the whole to be borne and used for Our ISLAND OF BARBADOS on Seals or otherwise according to the Laws of Arms.

Our Will and Pleasure therefore is that you the said Bernard Marmaduke, Duke of Norfolk, to whom the cognizance of matters of this nature doth properly belong, do require

Copy of the Royal Warrant granting and assigning a Coat of Arms

251

confederation plan. And in 1937 there was an uprising against the system that protected the interests of the few and paid insufficient attention to the exigent needs of the many.

In addition to these protests and revolts, there were other manifestations of independence throughout the years. In 1639, the House of Assembly was established and since then Barbados, one of the oldest of the former British Colonies, has enjoyed an unbroken tradition of parliamentary government. In 1651, when threatened by too rigid a control from the Mother Country, the island declared its independence in a ringing declaration of defiance. The following year the rights and privileges claimed in that declaration of independence were confirmed by the Articles of Agreement that became known as the Charter of Barbados.

It is true that the Charter of Barbados may in some respects be compared with the Magna Carta that was signed by King John in 1215.[49] For, while the barons of England sought in that document to preserve their special privileges, so did the legislators of Barbados in 1652 aim at protecting their own narrow interests. But in both cases there was a happy result. In due course, the rights and privileges guaranteed by Magna Carta were extended to all the people of England and in the same way the rights and privileges confirmed by the Charter of Barbados were "broadened down" to include all the citizens of the island.

It is not without significance that the preamble to the island's Constitution makes appropriate reference to the Charter of Barbados. Both documents, though separated by more than three hundred years, declare their belief in "certain fundamental rights and freedoms"[50] and proclaim the spirit that has animated the Barbadians throughout their history.

In view of the record of the past, it is not surprising that the island received its formal independence almost as a matter of course, and there seems no reason to doubt, as the White Paper[51] confidently predicted, that their stability, their passionate attachment to free institutions and their sense of pride and industry will enable the people of Barbados to support the dignity and challenges of nationhood.

Questions and Exercises to Consider

1. In the 1961 general election, the Barbados Labóur Party received more votes throughout the country than the Democratic Labour Party. Yet the former were badly

beaten by the latter. Try and find out how this happened.

2. Would you have chosen Barbados as the federal capital instead of Trinidad? If so, give a list of your reasons.

3. What do you understand by the phrases "independence alone" and "independence within the context of a federation"? Write a short note explaining the difference between the two ideas.

4. How is it that the Barrow Government came so near to being toppled in the 1966 General Election after leading the island into independence? Give a list of the factors that led to such a situation.

5. Why was the Senate established in place of the Legislative Council? Find out why the members of the Senate are appointed in the way they are.

6. Has *Bim* magazine encouraged Barbadian and other West Indian writers to be themselves and to write about themselves? Would you regard this as an exercise to promote the culture of the region? Would you consider the literature it has inspired as part of the movement towards independence? Make a list of the arguments for and against these views.

7. What is meant when we say that portrait painting is based on two dimensions and sculpture on three dimensions? Write a short note commenting on the merit of the work done by (a) Golde White, (b) Briggs Clarke, and (c) Karl Broodhagen.

8. Why is the Charter of Barbados in 1652 mentioned in the preamble of the Constitution of Barbados established in 1966. Compare the main ideas set out in both of these documents.

Notes

Chapter One

1. Bullen, R. P., *B.M.H.S. Journal*, November 1966, p.17
2. Ibid.
3. Ibid, p.19
4. Barton, G. T., *Prehistory of Barbados*, p.22
5. Ibid, pp.13-14
6. Roach, C. N. C., *B.M.H.S. Journal*, Vol. VI, No. 2, February, 1939
7. Sauer, C. O., *The Early Spanish Main*, p.63
8. Barton, op. cit., p.32
9. Hughes, Rev. Griffith, *Natural History of Barbados*, p.78
10. Roach, op. cit., Vols III-VI
11. Barton, op. cit., p.22
12. Bullen, op. cit., p.17
13. Burns, Sir Alan, *History of the British West Indies*, p.42
14. Ibid, p.43
15. Ibid.
16. Berkel, *Travels in South America, 1670-1689,* quoted in Augier, F. R., and Gordon, S. C., *Sources of West Indian History*, p.2
17. Letter from Dr. Chanca, physician to Columbus's fleet on second voyage, 1494, quoted in Augier and Gordon, op. cit., p.2
18. Sauer, op. cit., p.51
19. Burns, op. cit., p.44
20. Bullen, op. cit., p.17
21. Ibid, p.18
22. Augier and Gordon, op. cit., p.2
23. Ibid.
24. Burns, op. cit., pp.44-45
25. Ibid, p.45
26. *Memoirs of Père Labat*, p.108
27. Burns, op. cit., p.45
28. Ibid.
29. Ibid.

Chapter Two

1. *Some Memoirs of the First Settlement*, p.1
2. Harlow, V. T., *History of Barbados 1625-1685*, p. 4
3. Colt, *The Voyage*, (1631)
4. Handler, J. S., *B.M.H.S. Journal*, May 1970
5. Harlow, op. cit., p. 6
6. Wiliamson, J. A., *Caribbee Islands Under the Proprietary Patents*, p. 59
7. Harlow, op. cit., p. 7
8. *Deeds of Barbados*, Vol. 1, p. 483
9. Williamson, op. cit., p. 32
10. Harlow, op. cit., p. 9
11. Ibid, p. 10
12. Williamson, op. cit., p. 54
13. Ibid, p. 61

Chapter Three

1. *Some Memoirs of the First Settlement*, p.14
2. Harlow, op. cit., pp.14-15
3. Ibid, p.18
4. Shilstone, E. M., *Advocate*, June 24, 1939
5. Ibid.
6. Ibid.
7. Harlow, op. cit., p.18
8. Ibid, p.38
9. Davis, Darnell, *Cavaliers and Roundheads in Barbados, 1650-52*, pp.56-63
10. Ibid, p.55
11. Ibid, pp.81-83
12. Foster, Nicholas, *A Briefe Relation of the late Horrid Rebellion*, pp.3, 7, 8-15
13. Harlow, op. cit., p.60
14. Ibid, p.64n
15. Ibid, p.65
16. Schomburgk, Sir Robert, *History of Barbados*, p.708 (Cass Reprint, London, 1971)
17. Harlow, op. cit., p.69
18. Ibid, pp.73-74
19. Ibid, p.79
20. Davis, op. cit., pp.179-184
21. Harlow, op. cit., p.180

Chapter Four

1. Harlow, op. cit., p.293
2. Ibid, p.298
3. Ibid, p.300
4. Ibid, p.295
5. England's slavery or Barbados Merchandise (Petition 1659)
6. Harlow, op. cit., p.306
7. White, Father Andrew, *Narrative of a Voyage to Maryland,* p.24
8. Ligon, Richard, *True and Exact History of the Island of Barbados,* pp.46-47 (Cass Reprint, London, 1976)
9. Ibid, p.44
10. Ibid, pp.114-115
11. John Scott's Description of Barbados
12. Harlow, op. cit., p.23
13. Parry and Sherlock, op. cit., p.64
14. Ligon, op.cit., p.86
15. Ibid, p.22
16. Ibid, pp.54-55
17. Information from Jack Clarke, Manager of Kendal
18. For more details on tribal origins see Patterson, O., *Sociology of Slavery,* pp.112-26, 132-3, 134-44
19. Davidson, Basil, *Black Mother,* pp.33-34
20. *Great Newes from Barbados,* pp.10-11 (London 1676)
21. Chandler, op. cit., p.120
22. Ibid, p.119
23. Ibid, p.127
24. Ibid, p.134
25. Harlow, op. cit., pp.44, 309-10

Chapter Five

1. Newton, A. P., *The European Nations in the West Indies 1493-1688,* pp.1-10
2. Ibid, p.138
3. Schomburgk, op. cit., p.284
4. Ibid, p.190
5. Ibid, pp.360-1
6. Clarke, C. P., *B.M.H.S. Journal,* November 1968, p.175
7. Ibid, p.176
8. Ibid.

9. Schomburgk, op. cit., p.192
10. *Life of Michel De Ruyter,* p.267
11. Schomburgk, op. cit., p.193
12. Ibid.
13. Clarke, op. cit., pp.177, 179
14. Ibid, p.179
15. Schomburgk, op. cit., p.195
16. Clarke, op. cit., p.179
17. Connell, N., *B.M.H.S. Journal,* Vol. XVIII
18. Spurdle, F. G., *Early West Indian Government,* p.57
19. *Act for the Supply of a further Strength of Labourers to the finishing of the forts and fortifications,* April 19th, 1681
20. Spurdle, op. cit., p.98
21. Ibid, p.101
22. Ibid, p.102
23. *Act for the speedy fortification of the marine parts of this Island,* August 3rd, 1650

Chapter Six

1. Starkey, O. P., *Economic Geography of Barbados,* p.73
2. Ibid, p.76
3. William Hillary, M.D., (1759), quoted by Starkey, op. cit., pp. 82, 98
4. Oldmixon, J., *The British Empire in America, Vol. II,* pp.33-34
5. Starkey, op. cit., p.79
6. Lyttleton, *The Groans of the Plantations,* pp.9, 14, 15
7. Hall, Acts, Nos. 4, 26, 95. Also pp.252-69
8. Williamson, op. cit., p.213
9. Ibid, p.103
10. Ibid, p.215
11. Harlow, op. cit., p.157
12. Ibid, pp.158-159
13. Ragatz, L. J., *Fall of the Planter Class in the British Caribbean, 1763-1833,* p.4n
14. Gardner, W., *A History of Jamaica,* p.160
15. Starkey, op. cit., pp.83-4
16. Oldmixon, op. cit., pp.105, 127, 128
17. Waterman, Thomas T., "Some Early Buildings of Barbados", *B.M.H.S. Journal,* Vol. III, Nos 1 and 2, pp.140-148

18. Ibid.
19. Ibid.
20. Ibid.
21. Watson, Karl S., *The Civilised Island, Barbados. A Social History, 1750-1816*, p.6
22. Ibid, p.4
23. Ibid, p.39
24. Ibid, p.32
25. Pitman, F. W., *Journal of Negro History*, October 1926, pp.624-25
26. Klingberg, F. J., *Codrington Chronicle*, p.49
27. Ibid, pp.48, 50
28. Edwards, B., *The History, Civil and Commercial, of the British Colony in the West Indies, Vol. II*, pp.211, 244
29. John Smalridge to George Smalridge
30. Watson, op. cit., p. 28
31. Ibid, pp.26-27
32. Ibid, pp.35-36
33. Goveia, Elsa V., *The West Indian Slave Laws of the Eighteenth Century*, p.35
34. Watson, op. cit., pp.36, 40, 41

Chapter Seven

1. *Minutes of Barbados House of Assembly*, March 15th, 1744
2. Hoyos, F. A., *Builders of Barbados*, pp.7-13
3. Handler, J. S., *The Unappropriated People*, p.156
4. Hoyos, op. cit., pp.1-6
5. Klingberg, op. cit., p.4
6. Ibid, p.93
7. Goveia, Elsa V., *Slave Society in the British Leeward Islands at the end of the Eighteenth Century*, pp.283-4
8. Watson, R., *Defence of the Wesleyan Methodist Missions in the West Indies*, p.112
9. Goveia, op. cit., pp.302, 303
10. Handler, op. cit., p.29
11. Ibid, p.154
12. Coupland, Sir Reginald, *British Anti-Slavery Movement*, pp.42, 57, 61
13. *I. W. I. Committee Circular*, January 19th, 1906, pp.32, 33
14. Poyer, John, *History of Barbados*, pp.334-35
15. Ibid, p.101

16. Starkey, op. cit., pp.105-6
17. Schomburgk, op. cit., p.370
18. Ragatz, op. cit., p.387
19. Schomburgk, op. cit., p.394
20. Williams, E. E., *Capitalism and Slavery*, p.203
21. Watson, op. cit., pp.1-2
22. Hoyos, op. cit., pp.22-29
23. *Report of Select Committee of House of Assembly,* pp.33-34
24. Ibid, p.26
25. Watson, op. cit., p.1
26. *Report of Select Committee,* op. cit., p. 30
27. 'Beckles of Barbados', *B.M.H.S. Journal,* November 1944, pp.3-19

Chapter Eight

1. Watson, K. S., *Red Legs of Barbados,* p.42
2. Coleridge, H. N., *Six Months in the West Indies,* p.99
3. Davy, John, *The West Indies Before and Since Slave Emancipation,* pp.55-56
4. Watson, op. cit., pp.42-43
5. Watson, *The Civilised Island,* Chapter III
6. Schomburgk, op. cit., p.405
7. Ibid.
8. *Globe,* February 25th, 1819
9. 'Records of the. House of Assembly', *B.M.H.S. Journal,* August 1950, pp.181-2
10. Ragatz, L. J., *Guide for the Study of British Caribbean History,* pp.243, 498
11. *Returns of Free Coloured People,* May 1802
12. Handler, op. cit., p.23
13. Handler, *B.M.H.S. Journal,* May 1970
14. Hall, Richard, *Acts from 1643 to 1762,* pp.129-30
15. *Minutes of Barbados House of Assembly,* March 15th, 1744
16. Hall, op. cit., pp.323-325
17. Ibid, pp.252-69
18. Handler, op. cit., pp.69-70
19. *Minutes of Barbados Council,* October 15th, 1799
20. *Act Allowing the Testimony of Free Negroes and Free Coloured People,* February 5th, 1817
21. Thome, J. A., and Kimball, J. H., *Emancipation in the West Indies,* p.74

22. *Will of Amaryllis Collymore,* January 5th, 1829
23. Handler, op. cit., p.132
24. *Will of Rachael Pringle Polgreen,* July 21st, 1791
25. Pinckard, George, *Notes on the West Indies,* Vol. I, pp.244-45
26. Handler, op. cit., p.138

Chapter Nine

1. Ragatz, op. cit., pp.409-10
2. Ibid, p.410
3. Ibid, pp.411-12
4. Klingberg, F. J., *Anti-Slavery Movement,* pp.338 ff
5. Ragatz, op. cit., p.414
6. *Report of Committee of Barbados Council* (1824)
7. Schomburgk, op. cit., pp.357, 358, 359, 418
8. Burn, W. L., *Emancipation and Apprenticeship in the British West Indies,* p.65
9. Sturge, J., and Harvey, T., *The West Indies in 1837,* p.153 (Cass Reprint, London, 1968)
10. Schomburgk, op. cit., p.418
11. Ragatz, op. cit., p.418
12. Williams, op. cit., p.198
13. Ibid, pp.199-200
14. Ibid, p.200
15. Ibid, p.199
16. Ibid, p.201
17. Findlay, G. G., and Holdsworth, W. W., *Wesleyan Missionary Society,* Vol. II, p.198
18. Schomburgk, op. cit., p.416
19. *Speeches of Henry Lord Brougham,* Vol. II, pp.55, 56, 59
20. Findlay and Holdsworth, op. cit., p.198
21. Ibid, p.195
22. Ibid.
23. Ibid, p.196
24. Ibid, p.198
25. Caldecott, A., *Church in the West Indies,* p.89
26. Ragatz, op. cit., p.432
27. Caldecott, op. cit., p.236
28. Ibid.
29. *Barbados Diocesan History,* p.36
30. Coleridge, W. H., *Charges and Addresses,* pp.30,42

31. *Barbados Diocesan History,* p.37
32. Coleridge, op. cit., p.188
33. Starkey, op. cit., p.112
34. Davy, op. cit., pp.63, 74
35. Ibid.
36. Schomburgk, op. cit., p.427
37. Caldecott, op. cit., p.96
38. Ibid.
39. *Barbados Diocesan History,* p.38
40. Marshall, T. G., *The Folk Song in Barbadian Society,* p.1
41. Courtesey of T. G. Marshall

Chapter Ten

1. Ragatz, op. cit., p.456
2. Ibid, p.457
3. Schomburgk, op. cit., p.461
4. Ragatz, op. cit., p.454
5. Burn, op cit., p.366
6. Hall, Douglas, *Five of the Leewards,* pp.19-23
7. Sewell, W. G., *Ordeal of Free Labour,* p.152
8. Burn, op. cit., p.341
9. Schomburgk, op. cit., p.477
10. Ibid, p.483
11. Marshall, W. K., *Termination of Apprenticeship,* p.20
12. Schomburgh, op. cit., pp.484-85
13. Hamilton, B., *Barbados and the Confederation Question,* pp.4-6
14. *Liberal,* September 22nd, 1858
15. Marshall, W. I., *Establishment of a Peasantry in Barbados, 1840-1920,* p.85
16. Ibid, p.86
17. Greenfield, M., *English Rustics in Black Skins,* pp.77-8
18. Marshall, W. K., *B.M.H.S. Lecture,* December 13th, 1974
19. Sturge and Harvey, op. cit., p.154
20. Thome and Kimball, op. cit., p.74
21. Cohen, D. W., and Greene, J. P., *Neither Slave nor Free,* p.252
22. Vaughan, H. A., The Middle Class Advocate, July 23rd, 1939
23. Starkey, op. cit., p.121
24. Davy, op. cit., pp.145-54

25. *Agricultural Reporter,* April 1853
26. Ibid.
27. Davy, op. cit., pp.109-110
28. Ibid, p.112

Chapter Eleven

1. Greenhalgh, H. N., *Barbados Diocesan History,* p. 68
2. Ibid, p. 69
3. Ibid.
4. Ibid.
5. Ibid.
6. Ibid, pp. 69-70
7. Ibid, p. 70
8. Mather and Blagg, *Bishop Rawle; a memoir,* p. 57
9. Ibid, p. 58
10. Ibid, p. 59
11. Ibid, pp. 59-60
12. Ibid, p. 69, *Letter from Rawle to a Friend,* August 24th, 1847
13. Ibid, pp. 65-66, *Letter from Rawle,* June 22nd, 1847
14. Ibid, pp. 66-67, *Letter from Rawle,* June 25th, 1847
15. Ibid, p. 69, *Letter from Rawle,* August 24th, 1847
16. Ibid, p. 56, *Clarke to Governor of Barbados,* March 19th, 1847
17. Gordon, S. C., *Century of West Indian Education,* pp. 15-17
18. Ibid, pp. 14-15
19. Mather and Blagg, op. cit., p. 69, *Letter from Rawle,* August 24th, 1847
20. Ibid, pp. 47-50, *Letter from Rawle,* April 23rd, 1847
21. Gordon, op. cit., p. 59
22. Ibid, p. 64
23. Ibid, pp. 62-63
24. Ibid, p. 230
25. Mather and Blagg, op. cit., p. 93
26. Ibid, pp. 102-106
27. Ibid, p. 97
28. *Hamilton, Lt.-Governor, to the Colonial Office,* 1850
29. Gordon, op. cit., pp. 96-97
30. Ibid, p. 100
31. *Mitchinson Report,* 1875

32. Clarke, C. P., *Constitutional Crisis of 1876 in Barbados,* p. 21
33. *Barbados Diocesan History,* p. 48

Chapter Twelve

1. Wrong, H., *Government of the West Indies,* pp. 71-73
2. Ibid, p. 77
3. Clarke, op. cit., pp. 138-140
4. Starkey, op. cit., p. 119
5. *Colonial Reports: Barbados (1897),* p. 17
6. *Report of West India Royal Commission (1897),* p. 207
7. Rawson, Governor R. W., *Report of Population of Barbados, 1851-71,* p. 2
8. Ibid, pp. 1, 8
9. Ibid, pp. 1, 2
10. Ibid, pp. 1, 2, 3, 8
11. Hamilton, Bruce, *Barbados and the Confederation Question, 1871-1885,* p. 3
12. *Financial Report for 1874,* p. 39
13. Caldecott, op. cit., pp. 137, 142, 144
14. Hamilton, op. cit., pp. 48-49
15. Ibid, p. 49
16. Clarke, op. cit., p. 15
17. Ibid, p. 26
18. Ibid, p. 30
19. Pope-Hennessy, James, *Verandah,* p. 169
20. Clarke, op. cit., p. 27
21. Ibid, p. 28
22. Ibid, p. 39
23. Ibid.
24. Ibid, pp. 45-6
25. Ibid, p. 26
26. Hamilton, op. cit., pp. 71, 72
27. Ibid, pp. 72, 73, 75
28. Clarke, op. cit., p. 136
29. Hoyos, op. cit., p. 73
30. Wrong, op. cit., p. 87
31. Ibid, p. 88
32. Hamilton, op. cit., p. 46
33. Ibid.

Chapter Thirteen

1. Clarke, op. cit., p. 27
2. *Report of the West India Royal Commission (1897),* Appendix III, p. 199
3. Starkey, op. cit., pp. 124, 125
4. Schomburgk, op. cit., pp. 47-50
5. *Colonial Reports: Barbados (1894),* p. 11
6. Burn, W. L., *The British West Indies,* p. 152
7. Ibid, p. 153
8. Ibid, pp. 154, 155
9. *West India Royal Commission Report,* passim
10. Ibid, p. 31
11. Ibid.
12. Ibid.
13. Ibid.
14. Ibid, pp. 31, 32
15. Ibid.
16. Ibid, pp. 32, 33

Chapter Fourteen

1. Mather and Blagg, op. cit., p. 141
2. Pa'rry, J., and Sherlock, P. M., *Short History of West Indies,* pp. 234-5
3. Starkey, op. cit., p. 127
4. Ibid, p. 129
5. See p. 000 above
6. Vaughan, H. A., *Advocate,* July 30th, 1938
7. Marshall, W. K., *B.M.H.S. Lecture,* December 13th, 1974
8. Ibid.
9. *Colonial Reports: Barbados (1911-12),* p. 20
10. *Colonial Reports: Barbados (1917-18),* p. 10
11. Starkey, op. cit., pp. 132, 133

Chapter Fifteen

1. Wickham, C. W., *Herald,* December 18th, 1926
2. Hoyos, F. A., *Our Common Heritage,* pp. 104-108
3. *Advocate Editorial,* December 18th, 1926
4. Ibid.

5. Ward, E. R. L., *Advocate,* September 29th, 1945
6. *Colonial Reports: Barbados (1923-24),* p. 5
7. *Advocate,* September 29th, 1945
8. Ibid.
9. Ibid.
10. Ibid.
11. Vaughan, H. A., *Advocate,* October 1st, 1938
12. *Herald,* December 6th, 1924
13. Ibid.
14. Ibid.
15. *Herald,* May 30th, 1930
16. Wickham, *Weekly Advocate,* November 28th, 1936
17. Hunte, Keith, *New World Quarterly,* Vol. III, No. 2, p. 85
18. *Advocate,* September 29th, 1945
19. Hunte, op. cit., p. 84
20. Wickham, *Weekly Advocate,* op. cit.

Chapter Sixteen

1. *Moyne Commission Report,* p. 22
2. Ibid, p. 12
3. *Olivier Commission Report,* p. 3
4. Starkey, op. cit., p. 135
5. *Olivier Report,* pp. 123-4
6. Starkey, op. cit., p. 136
7. *Barbados Official Gazette,* Supplement, February 27th, 1936, pp. 6, 16
8. *Deane Commission Report,* pp. 241-2
9. Ibid, p. 241
10. Orde Browne, G. St. J., *Labour Conditions in the West Indies,* pp. 12-13
11. Williams, E., *From Columbus to Castro,* p. 444
12. Lewis, W. A., *Labour in the West Indies,* p. 11
13. Ibid, p. 12
14. *Moyne Report,* p. 8
15. *Deane Report,* p. 239
16. Ibid, pp. 239-240
17. Ibid, p. 240
18. Ibid, p. 241
19. Ibid, pp. 244-245
20. Courtesy of T. G. Marshall
21. Parry and Sherlock, op. cit., pp. 283-4

22. *Barbados Labour Party Minute Book, 1938-39*
23. *Letter from Talma to Adams,* May 26th, 1939
24. *B.P.L. Policy and Programme,* November 1944
25. Lewis, op. cit., p. 43
26. West Indies Royal Commission, *Proceedings of Investigations in Barbados,* pp. 77-88
27. *B.P.L. Policy and Programme,* November 1944
28. Ibid.

Chapter Seventeen

1. Ayearst, M., *The British West Indies,* p. 88
2. Orde Browne, op. cit., pp. 60, 61
3. *B.P.L. Policy and Programme,* 1944
4. Ibid.
5. Ibid.
6. Cheltenham, R. L., *Constitutional and Political Development in Barbados, 1946-66,* p. 4
7. *Beacon,* November 2nd, 1946
8. *Official Gazette,* Vol. 81, 1946, pp. 948-949
9. Ibid.
10. Cheltenham, op. cit.; p. 42
11. Ibid, pp. 45-47
12. *Legislative Debates, 1946-48,* Vol. 60, Part 1, p. 473
13. *Secretary of State's Despatch,* April 29th, 1948
14. Cheltenham, op. cit., p. 67
15. Ibid, p. 81
16. Ibid, p. 106
17. *Official Gazette,* Vol. XC, 1955, p. 785
18. Cheltenham, op. cit., p. 136
19. Ibid, pp. 157-160

Chapter Eighteen

1. Cargill, Morris, *Advocate,* January 23rd, 1957
2. *Conference on Closer Association of B.W.I. Colonies,* Part II, pp. 57-62
3. Hoyos, F. A., *Grantley Adams and the Social Revolution,* pp. 125-126
4. Williams, *Federation, Two Public Lectures,* pp. 11-12
5. Springer, H. W., *Reflections of the Failure of the first W.I. Federation,* pp. 18-19

6. Ibid, p. 13
7. Mordecai, J., *The West Indies: Federal Negotiations,* pp. 173-4
8. Lewis, Sir Arthur, *Agony of the Eight,* pp. 5-6
9. Lewis, *Epilogue* in Mordecai, op. cit., pp. 456, 457, 462
10. *Democratic Labour Party,* 1955-65
11. *Daily Gleaner,* October 6th, 1959
12. Cheltenham, op. cit., pp. 175-176
13. Cumper, G. E., *Report on Employment in Barbados,* p. 13
14. *Supervisor of Elections Report,* 1961
15. Cheltenham, op. cit., p. 189
16. *Supervisor of Elections Report,* 1961
17. *D.L.P Manifesto, 1961,* p. 7
18. *Daily News,* December 21st, 1961
19. *Democratic Labour Party, 1955-65,* p. 21
20. Cheltenham, op. cit., p. 258
21. Ibid.
22. *Federal Negotiations, 1962-65,* p. 4
23. Lewis, *Agony of the Eight,* pp. 19, 21
24. Ibid, p. 22
25. *Federal Negotiations, 1962-65,* pp. 1-2
26. Lewis, op. cit., p. 23
27. Ibid, p. 24
28. Ibid, p. 28
29. *Federal Negotiations, 1962-65,* pp. 20, 21, 23
30. Ibid, p. 26
31. Mordecai, op. cit., p. 457
32. *D.L.P Manifesto, 1961,* p. 16
33. Cheltenham, op. cit., p. 197
34. *Advocate,* October 3rd, 1965
35. *D.L.P Manifesto, 1961,* p. 1
36. Cheltenham, op. cit., p. 247
37. Ibid.
38. *Report of the Barbados Constitutional Conference 1966,* pp. 4-5
39. *Advocate,* October 15th and 19th, 1966
40. Cheltenham, op. cit., p. 253
41. *Advocate,* November 8th, 1966
42. Hoyos, F. A., *Barbados, Our Island Home,* p. 194
43. *Bim,* No. 16, June 1952
44. Baugh, Edward, *New World Quarterly,* Vol. III, Nos 1 & 2, pp. 129-133

45. Walcott, Derek, *Sunday Guardian,* April 24th, 1960
46. Barnes, Therold, *Bim,* Vol. II, No. 8, pp. 25-30
47. Walcott, op. cit.
48. Vaughan, H. A., *Bajan magazine,* December 1976
49. Ibid.
50. *Report of the Barbados Constitutional Conference 1966,* p. 11
51. *Laid before the Legislative by Order of the Cabinet,* August 1965

Appendix

Governors of Barbados

John Powell	1627
Charles Wolverston	1628
Sir William Tufton, Bart.	1629
Henry Hawley	1630
Sir Henry Huncks	1640
Philip Bell	1641
Francis Lord Willoughby	1650
Sir George Ayscue	1652
Daniel Searle	1652
Thomas Modyford	1660
Francis Lord Willoughby	1663
Henry Willoughby ⎫ Henry Hawley ⎬ Joint Governors Samuel Barwick ⎭	1666
William Lord Willoughby	1667
Sir Jonathan Atkins	1674
Sir Richard Dutton	1680
James Kendal	1690
Francis Russell	1695
Hon. Ralph Grey	1698
Sir Bevil Granville	1703
Mitford Crowe	1707
Robert Lowther	1711
Henry Worsley	1722
Scroop Viscount Howe	1733
Hon. Robert Byng	1739
Sir Thomas Robinson, Bart	1742
Hon. Henry Grenville	1747
Charles Pinfold	1756
William Spry	1768
Hon. Edward Hay	1773
James Cunninghame	1780
David Parry	1784

George Poyntz Ricketts	1794
Francis Humberstone Mackenzie, Lord Seaforth	1801
Sir George Beckwith, K.B.	1810
Sir James Leith, K.B.	1815
Stapleton, Lord Combermere, G.C.B.	1817
Sir Henry Warde, K.C.B.	1821
Sir James Lyon, K.C.B.	1829
Sir Lionel Smith, K.C.B.	1833
Sir Evan McGregor, Bart., K.C.B., K.H.	1836
Sir Charles Edward Grey	1841
Sir William Reid, K.C.B.	1846
Sir William Colebrooke	1848
Sir Francis Hincks, K.C.M.G., C.B.	1856
Sir James Walker, K.C.M.G., C.B.	1862
Sir Rawson W. Rawson, K.C.M.G., C.B.	1866
Sir John Pope Hennessy, K.C.M.G.	1875
Sir George Strahan, K.C.M.G.	1876
Sir William Robinson, K.C.M.G.	1880
Sir Charles Less, K.C.M.G.	1885
Sir Walter Sendall, K.C.M.G.	1889
Sir James Hay, K.C.M.G.	1892
Sir Frederick Hodgson, K.C.M.G.	1900
Sir Gilbert Carter, K.C.M.G.	1904
Sir Leslie Probyn, K.C.M.G.	1911
Sir Charles O'Brien, K.C.M.G.	1918
Sir William Robertson, K.C.M.G.	1925
Harry S. Newlands, C.M.G.	1933
Sir Mark A. Young, G.C.M.G.	1933
Sir John Waddington, K.C.M.G.	1938
Sir H. Grattan Bushe, K.C.M.G.	1941
Sir Hilary Blood, K.C.M.G.	1947
Sir Alfred Savage, K.C.M.G.	1949
Sir Robert Arundell, K.C.M.G.	1953
Sir John Montague Stow, K.C.M.G.	1959

Governor Generals of Barbados

Sir John Montague Stow, G.C.M.G., K.C.V.O.	1966
Spr Winston Arleigh Scott, G.C.M.G., G.C.V.O.	1967
Sir Deighton Harcourt Lisle Ward, G.C.M.G. G.C.V.O.	1976

Bibliography

Primary Sources

Abstract of the Most Remarkable Proceedings and Occurrences of the S.P.G. in Foreign Parts from February 15, 1711/12 to February 20, 1712/13. Printed with John Moore (with Annual Sermon). (London, 1713).

Acts & Statutes of Barbados, made and Exacted since the Reducement of the same unto the authority of the Commonwealth of England (London, 1654).

Acts of Barbados, ed. J. Jennings (London, 1673).

Acts of Barbados, 1648-1718, ed. J. Baskett (London, 1732).

Acts of the Assembly passed in the Island of Barbados from 1648-1718, (London, 1732).

Barbadian Diary of General Robert Haynes, 1787-1836, eds. E.R. and L. Haynes (Sussex, England: Azania Press, 1934).

Barbados Labour Party Minute Book 1938-39.

Barbados Museum and Historical Society, *Guide to the Barbados Museum,* 4th edition, 1973.

Barbados Progressive League, *Policy & Programme,* November 1944.

Brougham, Henry Lord, Speeches of, 4 Vols. (Adam and Charles Black, Edinburgh, 1838.)

Chandler, Michael J. *A Guide to Records in Barbados* (Blackwell, Oxford, 1965).

Coleridge, Rt. Rev. W. H. *Charges & Addresses to the Clergy of the Diocese of Barbados and the Leeward Island* (printed for J. G. and F. Rivington, London, 1835).

Donnan, Elizabeth. *Documents Illustrative of the History of the Slave Trade to America,* 2 Vols. (Carnegie Institution, Washington, D.C., 1931).

Hall, Richard. *Acts passed in the Island of Barbados. From 1643 to 1762 inclusive* (London, 1764).

Handler, Jerome S. *A Guide to Source Materials for the Study of Barbados History, 1627-1834* (Southern Illinois University Press, 1971).

Minute Books of the Society of West India Planters and
  Merchants.
Minutes of the Barbados Council (Lucas MSS).
Minutes of the Barbados House of Assembly.
Minutes of W.I. Planters and Merchants (W.I. Committee,
  London).
Official Gazette, House of Assembly debates.
Official Gazette, Legislative Council debates.
Ragatz, L. J. *A Check-List of House of Commons Sessional
  Papers Relating to the British West Indies and to the West
  Indian Slave Trade and Slavery, 1763-1824* (London, n.d.).
Ragatz, L. J. *A Guide for the Study of British Caribbean
  History* (Washington, D.C., 1932).
Washington, George, The Diaries of, 1784-99, ed. John
  Fitzpatrick (Boston, 1925).
Will of Amaryllis Collymore, January 5, 1829 (Barbados
  Department of Archives).
Will of Rachel Pringle Polgreen, July 21, 1791 (Barbados
  Department of Archives).
W.I. Royal Commission (1945), *Proceedings of Investigations
  in Barbados* Reproduced from the *Barbados Advocate*
  newspaper.

Journal Articles

Barton, Guy, The Diary of Sir Henry Colt 1631. An extract
  from a manuscript in the Cambridge University Library,
  reprinted (with notes by Guy Barton), from the *Barbados
  Agricultural Reporter,* August 24 and 25, 1909; *Barbados
  Museum and Historical Journal,* November 1953.
Baughan, Edward, Frank Collymore and the miracle of Bim,
  New World Quarterly, Vol III, Nos. 1 and 2.
Beckles of Barbados, *BMHS Journal,* November 1944.
Bim Magazine, December 1942 to present date.
Boromé, Joseph (ed.), William Bell and his second visit to
  Barbados, 1829-30, *BMHS Journal,* 1962-63.
Bullen, Professor Ripley P., Barbados and the Archaeology of
  the Caribbean, *BMHS Journal,* November 1966.
Chandler, Alfred D., The Expansion of Barbados, *BMHS
  Journal,* May-November, 1946.
Clarke, C. P., Imperial Forces in Barbados, *Barbados
  Museum and Historical Society Journal,* November 1968.

272

Connell, Neville, Some Nelson Statues, *Barbados Museum and Historical Society Journal,* November 1950 and February 1951.

Dunn, Richard S., The Barbados Census of 1680: Profile of the Richest Colony in English America, *BMHS Journal,* November 1969.

Handler, Jerome S., Amerindian Slave Population of Barbados in the Seventeenth and early Eighteenth Centuries, *BMHS Journal,* May 1970.

Hunte, Keith D., Duncan O'Neale: Apostle of Freedom, *New World Quarterly,* Vol. III, No. 2.

Marshall, W. K., Notes on the Development of the Peasantry since 1838, *Social and Economic Studies,* Vol. 17. No. 3. Termination of the Apprenticeship in Barbados and The Windward Islands, *Journal of Caribbean History,* Vol. 2, May 1971.

Marshall, W. K. with Trevor Marshall and Bentley Gibbs, The Establishment of a Peasantry in Barbados 1840-1920, U.W.I. Cave Hill, n.d.

Newman, John, The Enigma Joshua Steele, *BMHS Journal,* November 1951.

Pitman, F. W., Slavery in the British West India Plantations, *Journal of Negro History,* October 1926.

Records of the House of Assembly, *BMHS Journal,* August 1950.

Roach, C. N. C., Old Barbados, *BMHS Journal,* Vols III-VI.

Vaughan, H. A., Those Truths We Hold So Dear, *The Bajan and South Caribbean,* December 1976.

Waterman, Thomas T., Some Early Buildings of Barbados, *BMHS Journal,* Vol. XIII, May—November 1946.

Official Reports

Beckles, W. A. Rev. J. P. Compiler, The Barbados Disturbances (1937), Reproduction of the Evidence & the Report of the (Deane) Commission,(Advocate Co. Ltd., Barbados 1937).

Cumper, G. E. Report on Employment in Barbados (1956).

Colonial Reports: Barbados 1894, 1897, 1911-12, 1917-18, 1923-24.

Financial Report for 1874. Brandford Griffith.

Mitchinson Education Report, 1875.

Orde Brown, G. St J. Report on Labour Conditions in the West Indies, British Guiana, British Honduras, The Bahamas and Bermuda, Cmd. 6070. (May 1939).

Paul, George P. Report on Ankylostomiasis Infection Survey of Barbados, (New York, 1917).

Rawson, Governor R. W. Report Upon the Population of Barbados 1851-71. (Bridgetown 1872).

Report by the Conference on British Caribbean Federation, Cmd. 9733. 1956).

Report of a Select Committee of the House of Assembly appointed to enquire into the Origin, Causes and Progress of the late insurrection, (1819).

Report of a Committee of the Council of Barbados, Appointed to Inquire into the Actual Condition of the Slaves in this Island, with a view to Refute Certain Calumnies Respecting Their Treatment . . . . (London 1824).

Report of the Barbados Constitutional Conference, 1966.

Report of the Commission on Poor Relief, 1875-77 (Bridgetown 1878).

Report of Supervisor of Elections, 1961.

Report of West India Royal Commission (Norman), (London 1897).

Report of West Indian Sugar Commission (Olivier), Cmd 3517 (London 1930).

Report of West India Royal Commission (Moyne), Cmd 6607, (1945).

Returns of Censuses 1679, 1715, 1871, 1881, 1891, 1911, 1921, 1946, 1960.

White Paper: Federal Negotiations, 1962-65, and Constitutional Proposals for Barbados (Bridgetown, 1965).

Secondary Sources

A. *Contemporary*

Barbot, J. *A Brief Description and Historical Account of the Caribbee Islands in North America and their present State* (1732).

Bayley, F. W. N. *Four Years Residence in the West Indies* (London, 1830).

Berkel. *Travels in South America, 1670-1689.*

Clarke, Sir Charles Pitcher. *The Constitutional Crisis of 1876* (Barbados Herald Press, Barbados, 1896).

Coleridge, H. N. *Six Months in the West Indies* (London, 1806).

Colt, Sir Henry. *The Voyage of Sr. Henrye Colte Knight to ye Island of ye Antilles in ye Ship called ye Alexander* (1631).

Davies, John. *The History of the Caribby Islands, Rendered into English* (1666).

Davy, John M.D., F.R.S. etc. *The West Indies Before and Since Slave Emancipation, comprising the Windward & Leeward Islands' Military Command* (London, 1854, Cass Reprint, 1971).

De Ruytor. *Life of Michel* (Amsterdam, 1698).

Foster, Captain Nicholas. *A Briefe Relation of the Late Horrid Rebellion. . . .wrottem at sea by Nicholas Foster* (London, 1650).

Great Newes from Barbados. A True and Faithful Account of the Grand Conspiracy of the Negroes against the English, and The Happy Discovery of The Same (London, 1676).

Hakluyt, R. *Principal Navigations, Voyages, Traffiques & Discoveries of the English Nation (1599)* Everyman's Edition, Vol. III.

Hall, Richard A. *A General Account of the First Settlement and the Trade and Constitution of the Island of Barbados, written in 1755.* With a foreword by E. M. Shilstone, (Barbados, 1924).

Halliday, Sir Andrew. *The West Indies* (London, 1837).

Herrera, Antonio De. *The General History of The Vast Continent and Islands of America, commonly called The West Indies (1601)* Historiographer To His Catholic Majesty, translated into English by Captain John Stevens (2nd edition 1740), Vol. I.

Hillary, William, M.D. *Observations of the changes of the Air and the Concomitant Epidemical Diseases in the Island of Barbados* (London, 1759).

Hughes, Rev. Griffith. *The Natural History of Barbados* (1750).

Labat, Pere J. M., *Memoirs of,* Translated and abridged by John Deane (1931).
Nouveau Voyage Aux Iles de L'Amérique, 1722.

Ligon, Richard. *A true and exact History of the Island of Barbados* Humphrey Mosely (London, 1657, Cass Reprint, 1976).

Lyttleton, Edward. *The Groans of the Plantations* (London, 1688).

Mather, G. and C. J. Blagg. *Bishop Rawle. A Memoir* (London, 1890).

McKinnon, Daniel. *A Tour Through the British West Indies in the Years 1802 and 1803* (London, 1805).

Oldmixon, John. *The British Empire in America* Vol. II. (London, 1741).

Orderson, J. W. *Creoleana: Or, Social and Domestic Scenes and Incidents in Barbados in Days of Yore* (London, 1842).

Pinckard, George. *Notes on the West Indies* (London, 1806).

Poyer, John. *A History of Barbados from the First Discovery of the Island in the Year 1605 (?), Till the Accession of Lord Seaforth, 1801* (Mawman, London, 1808).

Rivers, M. and Foyle, O. *England's Slavery or Barbados Merchandize: Represented in a Petition to the High and Honourable Court of Parliament* (London, 1659).

Sewell, W. G. *Ordeal of Free Labour in The British West Indies* (Sampson Low, Son & Company, Ludgate Hill, London, 1862).

Some Memoirs of The First Settlement of Barbados . . . Extracted From Ancient Records (Anon.) (Barbados, 1741).

Sturge, Joseph and Thomas Harvey. *The West Indies in 1837* (London, 1838, Cass Reprint, 1968).

Thome, J. A. and J. H. Kimball. *Emancipation in the West Indies* (New York, 1838).

Watson, Richard. *A Defence of The Wesleyan Methodist Missionaries in the West Indies* (London, 1817).

White, Father Andrew, S. J. *Narrative of a Voyage to Maryland* Maryland Historical Society's Fund Publication No. 7 (Baltimore, 1874).

Modern

Augier, F. R. and S. C. Gordon. *Sources of West Indian History* (Longman, 1962).

Ayearst, Morley. *The British West Indies: The Search for Self-Government* (George Allen and Unwin, London, 1962).

Barton, Guy. *Prehistory of Barbados* (Advocate Company Limited, Barbados, 1953).

Bell, W. (ed). *The Democratic Revolution in the West Indies* (Cambridge, Mass., 1967).

276

Burn, W. L. *Emancipation and Apprenticeship* (Jonathan Cape, London, 1937).

The British West Indies (Hutchinson House, London, 1951).

Burns, Sir Alan. *History of The British West Indies* (George Allen and Unwin, London, 1964).

Burrows, Montague. *Worthies of All Souls* (London, 1874).

Caldecott, A. *The Church in The West Indies* (S.P.C.K., London, 1898).

Campbell, P. F. *An Outline of Barbados History* (Barbados, 1973).

Cheltenham, R. L. *Constitutional and Political Developments in Barbados: 1946-66* Unpublished doctoral thesis. (Manchester, October 1970).

Cohen, D. W. and J. P. Greene (ed.). *Neither Slave nor Free* (Johns Hopkins University Press, Baltimore and London, 1972).

Connell, Neville. *A Short History of Barbados* n.d.

Coupland, Sir Reginald. *The British Anti-Slavery Movement* (Frank Cass, 1964).

Curtin, Philip D. *The Atlantic Slave Trade—A Census* (University of Wisconsin Press, 1969).

Davidson, Basil. *Black Mother* (Victor Gollancz, 1961).

Davis, N. Darnell. *The Cavaliers and Roundheads of Barbados 1650-52, with some account of the early history of Barbados* (Argosy Press, Georgetown, British Guiana, 1883).

Democratic Labour Party 1955-65: Ten Years of Service (Advocate Commercial Press, 1965).

Edwards, Bryan. *The History, Civil and Commercial of The British Colony in The West Indies* 5 Vols. (5th ed. London, 1819).

Fermor, Patrick Leigh. *The Traveller's Tree* (John Murray, London, 1950).

Findlay, G. G. and W. W. Holdsworth. *The History of The Wesleyan Methodist Missionary Society,* Vol. II. (Epworth Press, London, 1921).

Gardner, William. *A History of Jamaica* (London, 1873).

Gordon, S. C. *A Century of West Indian Education* (Longman, London, 1963).

Goveia, Elsa. *Slave Society in The British Leeward Islands at the End of the Eighteenth Century* (Yale University Press, 1969).

Goveia, Elsa. *West Indian Slave Laws of the Eighteenth Century* (Caribbean Universities Press, 1970).

Greenfield, S. M. *English Rustics in Black Skin* (1966).

Hall, Douglas. *Five of the Leewards 1834-70* (Caribbean Universities Press, 1971).

Hamilton, Bruce. *Barbados and the Confederation Crisis 1871-85* (Crown Agents, London, 1956).

Handler, Jerome S. *The Unappropriated People: Freed Men in the Slave Society of Barbados* (Johns Hopkins University Press, 1974).

Harlow, Vincent T. *A History of Barbados 1625-85* (Oxford, 1926).

Christopher Codrington 1668-1710 (Oxford, 1928).

Hoyos, F. A. *Story of The Progressive Movement* (Beacon Printery, Barbados, 1948).

Road to Responsible Government (Letchworth Press, Barbados, 1906).

Background to Independence (Advocate Press, Barbados, 1967).

Barbados, Our Island Home 2nd ed. (Macmillan, London, 1972).

Builders of Barbados (Macmillan, London, 1972).

Grantley Adams And The Social Revolution (Macmillan, 1974).

Klingberg, Frank J. *Codrington Chronicle* (University of California Press, 1949).

The Anti-slavery Movement in England (Newhaven, 1926).

Lewis, W. A. *Agony of the Eight* (Advocate Commercial Press, n.d.)

Labour in the West Indies: The Birth of a Workers' Movement (Fabian Society and Gollancz, May, 1939).

Lynch, Louis L. *The Barbados Book* (Tonbridge, Kent, 1964).

Marshall, T. G. *The Folk Song in Barbadian Society* (1976, Unpublished Monograph).

Marshall, W. K. *Lecture at Barbados Museum and Historical Society* December 13, 1974.

McLellan, George, H. H. *Some Phases of Barbadian Life. Tropical Scenes and Studies* (Demerara, 1909).

Mordecai, John. *The West Indies: The Federal Negotiations* (George Allen and Unwin, London, 1968).

Newton, A. P. *The European Nations in the West Indies, 1493-1688* (Adam and Charles Black, London, 1966).

Operation Takeover. Manifesto of the Democratic Labour Party, 1961.

Parry, J. H. and P. M. Sherlock. *A History of the West Indies* 2nd ed. (Macmillan, London, 1966).

Patterson, Orlando. *The Sociology of Slavery. An analysis of the origins, development and structure of Negro Slave Society in Jamaica* (Granada Publishing Ltd., London, 1973).

Pitman, F. W. *The Development of the British West Indies, 1700-63* (Yale Historical Publications, IV, 1917).

Pope Hennessy, James. *Verandah. Some Episodes in the Crown Colonies 1867-1889* (George Allen and Unwin, London, 1964).

Ragatz, L. J. *Fall of the Planter Class in the British Caribbean. 1763-1833* (New York, 1963).

Reece, J. E. and C. G. Clark-Hunt (eds). *Barbados Diocesan History 1825-1925* (London, 1925).

Sauer, C. O. *The Early Spanish Main* (University of California Press, 1966).

Schomburgk, R. H. *The History of Barbados* (London, 1848).

Sinckler, Goulbourn. *The Barbados Handbook* (London, 1913).

Smith, Abbot Emerson. *Colonists in Bondage: White Servitude and Convict Labour in America 1607-1776* (Gloucester, Mass: P. Smith, 1965).

Springer, H. W. *Reflections on the Failure of the First West Indian Federation* (Harvard, July, 1962).

Starkey, Otis P. *The Economic Geography of Barbados* (Columbia University Press, 1939).

Treves, Sir Frederick. *The Cradle of the Deep* (New York, 1913).

Verrill, A. Hyatt. *The West Indies of To-day* (New York, 1931).

Watson, Karl S. *The Civilised Island Barbados. A Social History 1750-1816* Unpublished doctoral thesis (University of Florida, 1974).

Watson, Karl S. *The Redlegs of Barbados* Unpublished master's thesis, (University of Florida, 1970).

Wessel, G. A. and S. Leacock. *Barbados and George Washington* (Advocate Press, Bridgetown, 1957).

W.I. Committee Circular, January 19, 1906.

Williams, Eric. *Capitalism and Slavery* (University of North Carolina, 1944).
Federation: Two Public Lectures (Trinidad, 1956).
From Columbus to Castro: The History of the Caribbean, 1492-1969 (André Deutsch, 1970).
Williamson, J. A. *Caribbee Islands Under the Proprietary Patents* (Oxford, 1926).

Index

A Campos, Pedro, 12, 14
Abolitionist movement, 87-92, 109
Absentee landlords, 69
Adams, (Sir) Grantley, 210, 211,
  213, 216, 226, 228, 229, 233,
  235, 242, 243, 245, 246, 248;
  head of Government, 220-2;
  President of Caribbean Labour
  Congress, 222, 229; British
  delegate to U.N., 222; Premier,
  224, 226; relations with Walcott
  and Barrow, 225; Prime Minister
  of Federation, 226, 231, 233-5
Adams, J. M. G. (Tom), 246
African Institution, 90, 91, 109
African Slavery in America (Paine),
  87
African slaves in Barbados, 40-2, 45,
  63, 73, 79-80, 82, 96; planned
  uprising (1675), 41-2, 45, 102;
  further planned risings (1696 and
  1702), 45, 102; social hierarchy,
  74; skilled slaves, 74; field slaves,
  74; death rate, 75, 83, 90;
  annual importations, 76; training
  in trades, 76; work and working
  conditions, 76-7, 79; slave laws,
  80; and religion, 83-6, 117, 118;
  attacks on slavery, 86-7;
  abolitionist movement, 87-92,
  129; abolition of slave trade
  (1807), 88-90, 109; amelioration
  of conditions, 89-90, 109-13; and
  registration, 91, 95; insurrection
  (1816), 60-2, 92, 94-5, 99, 102,
  104, 113, 117, 121, 141, 250;
  demand for abolition of slavery,
  109; consolidation of laws, 112;

education, 117, 118;
  Emancipation, 119-22, 125-7,
  132
Agricultural Reporter, 137, 166,
  195
Agricultural Societies, 137
Alexander VI, Pope, 47
Alexandra Girls' School, 154
Alleyne, 'Brain', 209, 210
Alleyne, Sir John Gay, 68, 82-3
Alleyne School, 154
American Revolution, 89
Amerindians, the, 1-14; brought to
  Barbados by English, 17, 24, 102
Anne, Queen, 68
Antigua, 205, 210, 241; and
  emancipation, 127-9; becomes
  Crown Colony, 159; immigrants
  from Barbados, 160
Apprenticeship system, 126-30
Arawaks, the, 2-13; fishing, 3-4, 8;
  agriculture, 4, 8; artefacts, 4, 5,
  10; appearance and clothing, 6;
  houses, 6; villages, 6; system of
  government, 10; and the Caribs,
  9, 10, 11; right to live as free
  men, 12-13
Articles of Agreement (1652), 30-1,
  55, 252, ratified by English
  Parliament, 31
Ashanti slaves, 40, 42
Atkins, Sir Jonathan, Governor, 42,
  64
Austin, Betsy, 106
Ayscue, Sir George: commands fleet
  against Barbados, 29-31, 50, 55;
  fails to obtain surrender, 29;
  conducts negotiations, 30-1

Bananas, 201, 205

Baptists, 83

Barbados Defence Association, 164-7

Barbados Diocesan History, 142

Barbados Electors Association, 220, 222, 223, 226, 229, 234

"Barbados Fleet", Commonwealth squadron (1651), 29

Barbados Labour Party, 211, 213-26, 229, 233, 238, 243-6; electoral victory (1951), 223-5; party dissensions, 225; defeat (1961), 235

Barbados National Party, 229, 234, 243-5

Barbados Progressive League, 210-11, 213, 215-18

Barbados Society for the Education of the Poor, 143

Barbados Society for Promoting Christian Knowledge, 143

Barbados Workers Union, 213, 218, 223, 225, 233-5; and "windfall" crisis, 243-4

Barclay, Anthony, 134

Barnes, Therold, 248

Barrancoid people, 1-3

Barrow, B. L., 217

Barrow, Errol Walton, 223, 225, 226, 229, 233, 241, 244; leaves B.L.P., 225, 246; Chairman of D.L.P., 233, 234; Premier, 235, 236; and federation, 239, 242, 243; surmounts Government crisis, 243; and 1966 election, 245; victory in 1971, 246; defeated (1976), 246

Barton, G. T., 7

Bascom, John Sarsfield, 98, 99, 129, 135

Bathurst, Earl, 113; plan for amelioration of slavery, 110

Beacon, Labour Party organ, 219

Beckles, John, Sr., 95, 99

Beckles, John A., Chief Justice, 90, 95

Beet sugar: competition with cane sugar, 119, 136, 172-3; removal of bounties, 184

Belgrave, Jacob, 105

Belgrave, Jacob, Jr., 105

Bell, Captain Philip, Governor, 24, 27

Berbice, 119, 121

Bim, literary magazine, 246-8

Bird, Vere, 210, 241, 242

Blackman, H. D., 220, 221

Blower, Pieter, 38

Bourbon variety of cane sugar, 173-6

Bourne, London, merchant, 106, 134

Bovell, John R., 175-6, 184, 203

Boxill, Neville, 243

Bradshaw, Robert, 210

Brancker, J.E.T. (Sir Theodore), 221-3, 233

Brathwaite, C. A., 197, 210

Brathwaite, Edward, 247

Brazil, 187, 205; sugar production, 136; tourists in Barbados, 188

Bridges, Sir Tobias, 50

Bridgetown, 19, 83, 94, 99, 105, 106, 116, 117, 140, 141, 160, 164, 165, 203; Nelson statue, 58; fire (1666), 64; Moravian mission, 84; Royal Naval Hotel, 106; Central School (Boys' and Girls'), 117, 142, 151; Ice House Restaurant, 166; franchise qualification, 169; water supply, 177; Chamberlain Bridge, 184; disturbances (1937), 206-8

British forces in Barbados, 50-8; permanent garrison established (1780), 51; and Rodney's capture of Martinique, 51; defences, 52-3, 55; military establishment, 55-8; defence against Napoleon, 58; authority for defence and offence, 58-62; death rate, 89; and 1816 insurrection, 94

British Guiana (Guyana), 128, 181,
   183, 201, 205, 250; and slaves,
   113; immigrants from Barbados,
   130, 160, 185; free villages, 132;
   Crown Colony rule, 157; Labour
   Union, 196; strikes, 205, 206
British Guiana and West Indies
   Labour Congress, 211
British West Indies Regiment, 195,
   196
Britton's Fort, 53
Broodhagen, Karl, 248
Brougham, Henry (Lord), 117, 121,
   129
Brussels Convention (1903), 184, 185
Bulkeley, Rowland, 140, 141
Bullen, Professor R. P., 2
Bursaries Apprenticeship Act (1928),
   194
Bushe, Sir Grattan, Governor, 219;
   "Bushe Experiment", 219-20,
   223, 242
Bussa, slave leader, 92, 94
Bustamante, (Sir) Alexander, 210,
   226
Buxton, Sir Thomas Fowell, 109,
   113, 116, 117, 121, 126-7, 129
Byde Mill, rioting at (1876), 167

Cabinet system, 226
Caciques (Arawak chiefs), 10
Callendar, Timothy, 247
Camden, Earl, 111
Canada, sugar imports from
   Barbados, 185, 202
Cannibalism, 10-12
Canning, George, 110, 117
Carew, Jan, 247
Caribbean Labour Congress, 222,
   229
"Caribbean Voices", B.B.C.
   programme, 246
Caribs, the, 2, 3, 7-13; pottery, 7-8,
   10; evidence of settlement in
   Barbados, 7-8; physical
   appearance and clothing, 8;

warlike nature, 9, 10-11; and
   human sacrifice, 9; weapons, 9,
   11; culture and customs, 9; food,
   9-10; system of government, 10;
   cannibalism, 10-12; and the
   Arawaks, 10, 11; disappearance
   from Barbados, 12, 16; enslaved
   by Spaniards, 12-13
Carlisle Bay, 52-3, 64, 167; fort, 29
Carlisle, first Earl of, 17-22, 66;
   granted proprietorship of Caribee
   Islands, 18; Barbados included in
   grant, 18; supplants Courteen,
   18; "tenant-in-chief", 19;
   appointment of trustees, 22
Carlisle, second Earl of, 21-3, 27
Carmichael, Ellison, 243
Carnarvon, Lord, 159, 168
Carolina, immigrants from
   Barbados, 42, 43
Cassava, 4, 10, 17
Caterpillar plague, 63-4
Cato, Dr. A. S. (Sir Arnott), 228
Cattle, 79, 89
Cavaliers in Barbados, 25-8, 30, 66;
   Moderates, 27, 30
Central Road Board, 193
Chamberlain, Joseph, 178, 184, 185
Chambers, Richard, 14
Chapman, Peter, 132-3
Charles I, King, 27, 28, 52
Charles II, King, 27, 28, 52
Charles' Fort, 53, 57
Charter of Barbados, *see* Articles of
   Agreement
Chase, "Menzies", 209
Cholera outbreak (1854), 160
Christ Church parish, 94, 187;
   schools, 154
Church Missionary Society, 142
Church of England, 26, 27, 83, 85,
   87, 117-18, 141, 143, 151, 162;
   Book of Common Prayer in
   force, 27; churches, 69, 115-16;
   dioceses established in West
   Indies, 117-18; and

Federal negotiations (1962-5), 239-43; Little Eight, 239-41; plan drafted, 239; Conferences, 239, 240; Regional Council of Ministers, 239-42; draft Constitution, 240; financial problems, 240; British Government's delay, 240; defection of Grenada, 240; Antigua and Montserrat withdraw, 241; wrangle between Barbados and St. Lucia, 241; Council ceases to meet, 242, 243

Federation of the West Indies (1958-62), 228-33, 242; Conferences (1932-57), 228-9; choice of Trinidad for capital, 229; federal elections, 229; opposing views of Jamaica and Trinidad, 230-1, 233; inauguration, 230; Constitution, 231; Inter-Governmental Conference (1959), 231-2; Lancaster House Conference (1960), 232; Jamaica and Trinidad secede, 232; dissolution of Federation, 232

Fertilisers, 176

Figueroa, John, 247

First World War, sugar boom, 187, 188

Fleetwood, Bishop William, 84

Folk song, 122-3, 208-10

Forde, Freddie, 247

Fox, George, 86-7

France, struggle for supremacy with England, 48, 51, 55

Franchise Act (1884), 169, 215

Franchise qualifications, 169, 215, 216, 223

Francklyn, Washington, and 1816 insurrection, 92, 94

Free coloured people, 100, 102-6, 108, 132, 133; rights, 103-4; civil rights campaign, 104; progressives and conservatives, 104; full legal equality (1831), 104, 134; acquisition of plantations, 105; property and wealth, 105-6; tavern keeping, 106; prostitution, 106; liberal policy, 134-6; attitude to slaves, 134, 135; alliance against planter class, 135-6

Free villages, 132-3, 136, 169, 186-7

French Revolution, 87, 88

Garner, D. D., 222

Garvey, Marcus, 202, 206

General Elections: (1946), 220; (1951), 223; (1956), 226; (1961), 235; (1966), 245; (1971), 246; (1976), 246

Girl's Industrial Union Act (1923), 194

Gittens, A. G., 213

Gladstone, W. E., 177, 191, 192

Globe, Salmagundi newspaper, 98

Gomes, Albert, 225

Goveia, Elsa, 80

Grant, Ulric, 209, 210

Granville, Sir Bevil, Governor, 55

Greaves, Philip, 243

Greaves, W. H. (Sir Herbert), 177, 184

Green, Mary Bella, 106

Grenada, 126, 201, 205, 231, 240; elected assembly, 157, becomes Crown Colony, 159

Haiti, 92, 185

Hamden, Renn, 112

Hamilton, Aileen, 248

Hamilton, Joseph, 134

Hardie, Keir, 198

Harris, Thomas, 105

Harrison College, 141, 154, 162, 217

Harrison, J. B., 175-6, 184, 203

Harrison, John, 248

Harrison, Thomas, 141

Harrison's Free School, 152, 154

Harte, Rev. W. M., 120

Hawley, Henry, Governor, 20-2; harsh rule, 21-2; establishes House of Assembly, 22; removed from post, 23
Hayden, Howard, 248
Haynes, Robert, 94
Hearne, John, 247, 249
Herald newspaper, 195-9; ceases publication, 197, 199
Hicks Beach, Sir Michael, 177
Hilliard, Major William, 38
History of Barbados (Poyer), v
History of Barbados (Schomburgk), v
Hodgkinson, F., 129
Holder, Geoffrey, 248
Holdip, Colonel, 39˙
Holetown (St. James's town), 14, 15; fort, 29, 55
Holidays with pay, 223, 237-8
Hookworm, 97
Horticultural Society Act, 194
House of Assembly, 66-8, 82, 99, 104, 129, 148, 167, 172, 177, 192, 216, 218, 219; established (1639), 22, 23, 252; power of passing laws, 24; and threatened invasion by English Parliament (1650), 62; and the militia, 49, 60, 61; request for British garrison, 50; and fortifications, 60-1; and expeditions to neighbouring islands, 60, 61; planters' representatives, 65, 73; status, 68-9; authority and influence, 69; Salmagundi victory (1819), 99, 135; and amelioration of slavery, 112; first coloured member (1843), 135; and the Six Points, 163; and plan for Crown Colony, 164; impasse with Colonial Office, 168; lowers franchise qualification, 169; and introduction of income tax (1921), 192; Democratic League members, 197, 199; Progressive League members, 213; appointed

members, 215; first Black Speaker, 222; and Legislative Council, 222-3
Houses: Arawak, 6; Carib, 9; English settlers', 16; planters', 69-71, 138; slaves' huts, 74-5
Huncks, Henry, Governor, 22-4
Hurricanes, 64, 89, 120, 175, 193; Great Hurricane (1831), 118, 119, 142, 175; (1898), 174-5
Husbands, K. N. R., 222

Income tax, 193, 217; introduced (1921), 192
Indentured servants, 21, 32-5, 40, 42-5, 63; transported convicts, 32-3; kidnapping, 33; cruel treatment, 33-4; risings (1634 and 1649), 34, 250
Independence: White Paper (1965), 224; Constitutional Conference, Lancaster House (1966), 244; draft Constitution, 244; Opposition dissent, 244-5; independence attained (Nov. 1966), 245, 250
Indian corn, *see* Maize
Indigo, 24, 45
Inniss, Clement, 195
Insect pests, 174
International Sugar Agreement (1937), 202
Italo-Abyssinian war, 206

Jackey, slave leader, 92, 94
Jamaica, 91, 103, 112-13, 128, 159, 178, 180, 185, 201, 202, 205, 210, 230-2, 249, 250; immigrants from Barbados, 42; revolt of slaves (1831), 121; free villages, 132; Assembly, 158; Morant Bay rising (1865), 158; becomes Crown Colony, 158; strikes, 206; adult franchise, 225; ministerial system, 226
James I, King, 14, 18

reduction in crop, 119; located labour system, 130, 131, 133, 161; improved methods and machinery, 137-8; cost of production, 137; foreign tariffs, 173; fungoid disease, 173, 174; falling price of plantations, 173, 174; economy measures, 174; catalogue of disasters, 174-5; loss of British market, 175; germination of sugar cane seeds, 175; new varieties of cane, 176; American market, 178, 184-5, 187; and the Norman Commission, 178-84; British grant, 183-4; removal of bounties on sugar beet, 184; boom in First World War, 187, 188; post-war slump, 190; recovery, 193; expansion, 201; Olivier Commission, 201, 203-4; restriction by International Agreement, 202; decline in world price, 202-4; mosaic disease, 205; proposals for nationalisation, 211; profit-sharing, 223; "windfall crisis", 243-5

Sugar Industry Agricultural Bank, 184, 193

Sugar Producers Association, 223

Surinam, immigrants from Barbados, 42, 43

Swanzy, Henry, 246

Talma, C. E., 221, 224, 243

Taverns, 106

Tawney, R. H., 195

Taylor, Henry, 158

Taylor, John Dunscombe, 127

Taylor, Ronald, 1-2

Teacher training, 151-4, 218

Thorne, Joseph, 134

Thoughts on Slavery (Wesley), 134

Times, The, first coloured newspaper, 135

Tobacco, 4, 17, 22, 24, 32, 44; inferior to Virginian, 35, 70; English tariff raised, 35; ceases to be staple crop, 35, 38

Tobago, 119, 126; elected assembly, 157; becomes Crown Colony, 159

Toussaint L'Ouverture, 92

Tourist trade, 188, 230, 238

Trade Union Act (1939), 213; amended, 217, 223

Trade unions, 213
  see also Barbados Workers' Union

Transparent sugar cane variety, 175; White, 176

Transportation to Barbados, 32-3

Treaty of Paris (1763), 157

Treaty of Tordesillas, 47

"Treaty of Turkey and Roast Pork", 26

Trinidad, 91, 113, 119, 121, 128, 180, 181, 196, 201, 202, 205, 230-2, 249, 250; registration of slaves, 90; immigrants from Barbados, 130, 185; free villages, 132; Crown Colony rule, 157; Workingmen's Association, 196; unrest, 205, 206; ministerial system, 225

True and exact history of the island of Barbados, A (Ligon), v

Tudor, Cameron, 225, 229, 245

Tufton, Sir William, Governor, 21, 24

Typhoid, 175, 177

"Under Forties", 243

Unemployment, 202, 234-6

United States, 184-5; proposed trade treaty rejected, 177; reduction of tariffs on U.S. imports, 178; immigrants from Barbados, 185

University education, 236-7

Vaughan, V. B., 213, 229˙

Vestry system abolished, 224

Villeneuve, Admiral, 58

"Virginian Fleet" (1651), 29, 30

Virginian tobacco, supplants
    Barbadian, 35, 70

Wages, 130-1, 161, 179, 205, 208,
    223; minimum, 215-16
Wages Board, 223
Walcott, Derek, 247
Walcott, E. K., 216
Walcott, Frank, 225, 226, 229, 233-
    5, 244
Walrond, Edward, 26-8
Walrond, Colonel Humphrey, 26-8
Warburton, Bishop William, 87
Ward, D. H. L., 229
Ward, E. R. L., 199, 237, 243, 245
Warde, Sir Henry, Governor, 111,
    113
Warner, Sir Thomas, 21
Water availability and supply, 6, 16,
    39, 177, 223
Watson, Karl, 79
Wealth of Nations (Adam Smith),
    87
Webb, Sidney and Beatrice, 198
Weekes, Reynold, 243
Weekly Half Holiday Act (1926),
    194
Wesley, John, 87
Wesleyan Methodists, *see* Methodists
West Indian National Congress
    Party, 217-23
West Indies Federal Party, 231
Western Intelligence, newspaper, 98
White, Golde, 248
Wickham, Clennell, 195-7
Wickham, John, 246, 247
Widows and Orphans Pension Act
    (1926), 194

Wilberforce, William, 88, 91, 94,
    109, 126
Wilkinson, J. H., 222
Williams, Eric, 230-2, 242
Williams, Francis, 141
Willoughby, Francis, Lord,
    Governor, 27-30; Declaration
    against British Parliament 28-9;
    raises army; 29; declines to
    surrender to Commonwealth
    fleet, 29; negotiations with
    Ayscue, 30; strengthens island's
    defences, 52; clash with House of
    Assembly, 66-8
Willoughby, William, Lord,
    Governor, 50, 61, 68; relations
    with Assembly, 68
Willoughby's Fort, 53
"Windfall" crisis (1964), 243-5
Windward Islands: ties with
    Barbados, 162; plans for closer
    union, 162-3
Wolverston, Charles, Governor, 19,
    20
Workingmen's Association, 199
Workmans, free village, 133
Workmen's Compensation Act, 217
Worthing, "bay houses", 188

Yams, 17
Yarico's Pond, 39
Yeamans, Sir John, 51
Yellow fever, 64, 89; epidemic of
    1908, 183
Yeoman farmers, 35, 44, 45, 63, 98-
    100, 135; irruption into House of
    Assembly, 99

Books by the same author

Some Eminent Contemporaries
Two Hundred Years
The Story of the Progressive Movement
Our Common Heritage
Princess Margaret and the Memories of the Past
The Road to Responsible Government
The Rise of West Indian Democracy
Background to Independence
Barbados, Our Island Home
Builders of Barbados
Grantley Adams and the Social Revolution
Tom Adams
A Quiet Revolutionary